Praise
How to be brave
in business and wi

The best way to create a WOW experience for customers is to first create a WOW experience for employees. This book can inspire both. **Tony Hsieh, #1** *New York Times* **best-selling author of** *Delivering Happiness* **and CEO of Zappos.com, Inc**

BOLD is one of the most inspiring and insightful books on what it takes to build a pure and compelling global brand for today's generation, in this digitally disruptive age. **Angela Ahrendts, CEO Burberry**

Packed full of original ideas and inspirational stories that'll give you the confidence to do things your way. **Richard Reed, Co-founder of innocent drinks**

A company's culture and commitment to its people – both employees and customers – are too often overlooked. This book offers great examples of how important both are to long-term success. **Ray Davis, President and CEO of Umpqua Bank and author of** *Leading for Growth*

We don't belong in this book. It's too chock full of amazing stories, told by those actually involved, about how brands tick. But you'll have to decide for yourself. **Robert Stephens, Founder and Chief Inspector, The Geek Squad**

Reading this book is reassuring and reminds one of what is really important and the source of success in business! **Sonu Shivdasani, Chairman and CEO of Six Senses Resorts and Spas**

A fascinating insight into the benefits of being bold. **Peter Bakker, CEO TNT NV**

BOLD nails it. Our boldness lies in our people: 8,000 minds who are passionate and committed to revolutionizing air travel – believing the unbelievable, dreaming the impossible, and never taking no for an answer – every single day. **Tony Fernandes, CEO and Co-founder, AirAsia Bhd, Tune Group of Companies and Team Lotus Formula 1 racing**

The voices captured in *BOLD* are penetrating, deeply insightful, revealing and always refreshingly candid (if not brutally honest). You won't want to put it down, and perhaps you shouldn't, as *BOLD* will become the essential management handbook for years to come. **Joe Wheeler, Executive Director, The Service Profit Chain Institute**

Fortune favours the brave. This book can help show you the way. **Ronan Dunne, CEO, Telefonica O2 UK Ltd**

This book sets a new direction for customer experience. The brands featured are thinking big about changing the landscape of their industries by creating dramatically different customer experiences. Learn directly from the CEO's of brands as diverse as AirAsiaX to Zappos. Smith and Milligan's new book will help organizations chart a course to success for many years to come. **Bernd Schmitt, CEO of The EX Group and author of *Customer Experience Management* (2003) and *Big Think Strategy* (2007)**

Remarkable; being bold is the ticket to sustainable success. Smith and Milligan have written a masterful blueprint for success using a combination of courageous examples coupled with powerful insights. A must read. **Chip R Bell, co-author of *Take Their Breath Away***

Memory creation IS the currency of your brand. Companies who experience business prosperity are clear about the unique experience they will deliver and are bold enough to stay the course to make it their operational DNA. In this book, Smith and Milligan provide a mirror to evaluate and determine what experience your company will become known for, and a learning journey into some of the best being delivered today to customers throughout the world. **Jeanne Bliss, President CustomerBLISS, author of *Chief Customer Officer* and *I Love You More than My Dog: Five Decisions for Extreme Customer Loyalty***

If you read only one business book this year, make *BOLD* the book! Every page is dripping with amazing insight and foresight on how to win the hearts (and wallets) of high value customers. Beginning with Chapter One, you'll feel like you have scored personal coaching sessions with the most brilliant minds in the business, and they are sharing their hard-won lessons directly with YOU. Don't start this book at bedtime. You'll find it mighty hard to put down. **Jill Griffin, 'Loyalty Maker' strategist and author of *Customer Loyalty, Customer Winback* and *Taming the Search-and-Switch Customer***

Bold is very much the word of today in business. The speed of change in practically every business model requires managers to explore new ideas like never before. This is not easy and I would suggest that anyone going through this process should read about the experiences of the successful change agents documented by Shaun Smith and Andy Milligan in this excellent book. **Michael Birkin, Founder Red Peak**

A really heartening and inspiring book, Packed with examples, facts and insights, drawn from an extraordinary range of organizations, but with one thing in common – the drive to think and act in a truly distinctive and different way. A big and bold read indeed. **Rita Clifton, Chairman of Interbrand**

BOLD

BOLD

how to be brave in business and win

Shaun Smith
& Andy Milligan

KoganPage

LONDON PHILADELPHIA NEW DELHI

First published in Great Britain and the United States in 2011 by Kogan Page Limited

120 Pentonville Road	1518 Walnut Street, Suite 1100	4737/23 Ansari Road
London N1 9JN	Philadelphia PA 19102	Daryaganj
United Kingdom	USA	New Delhi 110002
www.koganpage.com		India

© Shaun Smith and Andy Milligan, 2011

The right of Shaun Smith and Andy Milligan to be identified as the authors of this work has been asserted by them in accordance with the Copyright, Designs and Patents Act 1988.

ISBN   978 0 7494 6344 1
E-ISBN   978 0 7494 6345 8

British Library Cataloguing-in-Publication Data

A CIP record for this book is available from the British Library.

Library of Congress Cataloging-in-Publication Data

Smith, Shaun.
    BOLD : how to be brave in business and win / Shaun Smith, Andy Milligan. – 1st ed.
       p. cm.
    ISBN 978-0-7494-6344-1 – ISBN 978-0-7494-6345-8   1. Success in business.
2. Creative ability in business.   3. Relationship marketing.   I. Milligan, Andy.   II. Title.
    HF5386.S694 2011
    658.4'09–dc22

                                                                2010051626

Typeset by Graphicraft Ltd, Hong Kong
Production managed by Jellyfish
Printed and bound in the UK by Ashford Colour Press

Contents

CHAPTER SIXTEEN   Bold practice survey 305

Introduction

> *Whatever you can do, or dream you can do, begin it.*
> *Boldness has genius, power and magic in it.* JOHN ANSTER*

Why *BOLD*?

The future will belong to the bold. The world of business is now so crowded that only those who have a significant and dramatically different story to tell will grab the attention of consumers. In a world of 'greenwash' and PR spin, authenticity will shine through. In the face of unprecedented levels of marketing spend and increasing consumer cynicism, simple recommendations from 'consumers like us' will carry the day. In an age when we have come to expect good levels of service and product quality as a given, only an exceptional and memorable experience will earn customer loyalty. At a time when legal loopholes and corporate caveats allow companies to wriggle out of their responsibilities, those who stand by their promises will stand out from the herd. It requires courage, conviction and imagination to be bold – but the rewards can be immense.

In the first book that we wrote together, *Uncommon Practice: People Who Deliver a Great Brand Experience*, we argued that the businesses that would enjoy sustained success would have the delivery of unique customer experiences as a key strategy and the alignment of their people, processes and products with that strategy at their heart. Every one of the brands we wrote about in that book has succeeded and is still succeeding today, almost a decade later, because of their commitment to those principles.

But the world has changed dramatically in the years since we wrote that book. The whitewater economy that we've been living through shows little signs of calming, the financial services crisis has led to massive consumer distrust of large corporates, a tsunami of social media has overwhelmed organizations and left many stranded, and the convergence of digital and mobile technology together with increasing deregulation of markets has put power in the hands of consumers as never before. If that were not enough, the impact of global warming and social inequality is undermining the very foundations on which many enterprises have been built.

Business models are changing, some are broken for good, the distribution and exchange of products, services and information have radically shifted, there are

*Note: This quote is often attributed to Goethe. The academics believe it originated with John Anster. Take your pick.

questions about the long-term viability of brands that use precious resources, and nobody is sure exactly how the communications and media landscape will look in 10 months let alone 10 years.

In the midst of all this change – uncertainty or opportunity, depending on your point of view – we have observed two distinctly conflicting approaches from organizations attempting to succeed.

The first, most obvious and, in our opinion, the most dangerous is that of companies who become internally focused on financial re-engineering and management restructuring. Balance sheet repairs, cost cutting, trigger-happy redundancy programmes: the corporate equivalent of rearranging the deck chairs on the Titanic – all the usual signs of a business with, in the words of Jack Welch, 'its ass to the customers'.

But we have also seen a different breed of organization emerging. They succeed because they have the courage, confidence or just sheer chutzpah to pursue a purpose that is beyond profit; to engage, entertain and educate their audiences, who see their customers and employees as members of a like-minded community, who create an almost cult-like following around their brand – both within and without their organization – who are not just different but dramatically different and who push to the extremes the consequences of their desired positioning and strategy. They are often based on the personality and values of the people who found and lead them – but not always; sometimes their path has been deliberately chosen by executives to differentiate them from the sameness of companies in the sectors they share. They eschew typical 'faceless' corporate behaviour and dare to put their shareholders' concerns behind those of their customers and employees, and behind their obligations to the wider public. Even during the most difficult times – such as the global financial crisis from which recovery will be long and painful for most – they are relentless in pursuit of improvement and zealous in communication, and take action in accordance with what is best for their brand, not just their bottom line. But this is not some corporate Quixotic tilting at windmills. They also happen to be incredibly commercial and, in most cases, outperforming their sectors. In short, they are bold. Not reckless. Just bold: they stand out from others because they stand up for something.

We wanted to look at companies who we believe demonstrate this boldness and share with readers the stories of what they do, how they do it and, most importantly perhaps, why they do it – their purpose.

Why have we chosen these companies?

The organizations we have chosen are bold in different ways:

- Some are bold because their purpose is 'heroic' – whether it be to fly into space or save the planet.

- Some are bold because what they do is so dramatically different to what has been done before – whether it be a logistics company that treats its employees as a key asset in a commodity market or a bank that acts like a fashion store.

- Some are bold because they have stuck to their principles regardless of the 'market norms' – whether it be an advertising agency that refuses to pitch for new business or a retailer whose sole purpose is to create 'Wow' moments for customers.

All are bold because they have an unshakeable belief in what they stand for and let their actions follow their beliefs.

We started with a long list of possible companies suggested by our own experience of living and working around the world and by those of colleagues and friends from across the globe. The criteria for inclusion were:

- They have to be organizations who have a clear brand positioning that significantly differentiates them.

- They have to be known for delivering experiences that are genuinely remarkable.

- They have to have 'fandom' – a base of customers and employees who have a genuine love for or deep affinity with the brand.

- They have to be successful and growing and this success had to be sustained or sustainable.

- They have to have earned a reputation for 'changing or challenging the rules' in their respective marketplaces.

From the long list of organizations we then chose those whom we felt would represent the broadest range: from start-ups by young entrepreneurs to long-established family businesses, from organizations who are avowedly not for profit to those who have demanding shareholders, and from niche regional players to global leaders. Our aim was to provide inspiration to people in any kind of organization and to counter the criticism – so often mistakenly levelled at organizations who put their principles first – that 'only small, entrepreneurial companies can afford to do that'. We also wanted to shine the spotlight on those organizations whose stories are less well known internationally.

We believe that being bold is an attitude of mind but is evidenced by what people do and thus how any organization acts. So anyone and, by extension, any type of company can be bold if it wants. The key is that it must want to be bold and be willing to behave accordingly, not just claiming it does bold things. As one of our interviewees put it, 'Don't tell me how funny you are; tell me a joke that makes me laugh.'

How to read this book

We have written this book so that you can read each chapter and decide what the main learning points are before reading our insights and seeing if you agree with us.

In addition, the book can be read cover to cover – and there is a narrative connection from each brand to the next – or you can just dive in to any chapter at random. Either way, we are sure you will be stimulated and inspired by the stories that the people tell in their own words.

Each chapter is structured with a short introduction explaining the company and why we included it. There then follows the edited verbatim interviews with the chief officers or principal people responsible for shaping its actions and communications. This book has been written with the iPad™ generation in mind and therefore we have provided 'e-features' throughout, links to websites and online video so that you can hear the interviewees speaking or find out more about their brand. Whilst we have done our best to test these links and select stable URLs, the internet is constantly changing, so if you do come across a link that leads to a dead-end we apologize.

For those of you reading *BOLD* on your iPads, you will find that some of the links require Flash to run which is not currently supported by Apple. For those of you reading on Kindle, Chapter 16 is best read in landscape format.

We provide a few subheadings just to help signpost the reader to key topics. Then at the end of the chapter we summarize what we believe are the main insights about being bold from that organization.

At the end of the book, we provide:

- an overall summary of the main themes and actions that consistently characterize these bold brands;
- a profile of the bold brands and the practices that we believe create boldness in business;
- a simple survey that you can use to assess how bold your own organization is and compare your profile with the brands we feature.

Finally, we have provided, as a kind of epilogue, a few key questions to ask yourself how bold you are. Because there is one learning we will share with you at the very start as it is the most obvious and important one: being bold starts with individual people having belief in something, a commitment to achieving it and a determination to see it sustained. Boldness starts with you.

We hope you enjoy the book.

Shaun Smith and Andy Milligan

GALACT1C

Chapter One
Virgin Galactic

Virgin has long been thought of as the ultimate 'challenger brand'. Its business model has been to take on large, established companies in a sector and seek to rewrite the rules, usually in favour of the customer. Being bold, brave and innovative are in the very DNA of the brand and its visionary founder, Sir Richard Branson.

This is what they say about themselves: 'We believe in making a difference. Virgin stands for value for money, quality, innovation, fun and a sense of competitive challenge. We deliver a quality service by empowering our employees and we facilitate and monitor customer feedback to continually improve the customer's experience through innovation.'

If you click here: **http://www.virgin.com/entrepreneur/got-a-big-idea/** you will find this message:

"We're always looking for the next BIG thing.
Especially if it builds on our exciting businesses or creates brand new ones.
So if you think you've an idea that fits the bill and has the potential
to become a major global business, we are open to your ideas."

This approach had led Virgin to create more than 200 branded companies worldwide, employing approximately 50,000 people in 29 countries. Virgin's businesses span music, media, mobile phones, travel, financial services, entertainment, leisure and many others. But none has captured our imagination in the way that Virgin Galactic has.

In February 2011, the very last NASA Shuttle will take off and land. Essentially NASA will cease to have a manned space programme as their future projects have been shelved. The era of the political 'space race' will finally be over. The successful flights of Virgin Galactic's VSS Eve, the launch vehicle, along with VSS Enterprise, the passenger vehicle, represent nothing less than the dawn of a new era. The possibility of ordinary people travelling into space, and the means to carry commercial payloads cost effectively through private endeavour, have made space, not the 'final frontier' in the immortal words of Captain Kirk of the USS Enterprise, but a 'new frontier' for business.

VSS Enterprise

© 2011 Virgin Galactic

Bold practices

Virgin Galactic

- Virgin Galactic aims to fly 600 people in the first year of operation – that is more people than have been in space in the last 50 years.

- The mother ship, VSS Eve, is the largest 100 per cent carbon-composite plane currently in service and is the most environmentally friendly aircraft in the world.

- The passenger vehicle, VSS Enterprise, was completely redesigned based on customer feedback about their expectations of space travel.

- The cost of a passenger flight is $200,000 compared with the cheapest Soviet-era passenger seat at $20–30 million.

- Over 300 customers have registered and the company has over $40 million in deposits before the first passenger flight has even taken off. Such is the power of the Virgin brand.

- The aircraft will operate initially from the purpose-built Spaceport America in New Mexico but can operate from any commercial airport in the world.

- The name 'Virgin Galactic' was registered before the first flight was ever made.

Sir Richard Branson – the visionary

Richard Branson is the flamboyant chairman of the Virgin Group, one of the UK's great success stories and one of the most innovative brands on the planet. Sir Richard now devotes 50 per cent of his time to Virgin Unite, his charitable organization for tackling many of the world's most difficult issues.

The environmental case

It was Stephen Hawking who first got me thinking about space travel, when he explained clearly and concisely to the BBC that mankind had no option but to get to space as quickly as possible and start doing things up there that we have been doing on planet Earth, but in a much more efficient manner.

Our population is now heading towards 9 billion people by the middle of this century – that's three times more than when I was born. With the end of the oil era approaching, and climate change progressing faster than most models have been predicting, the utilization of space is essential not only for communications but also for the logistics of survival through things such as weather satellites, agricultural monitoring, GPS and climate science. I also believe that someday we will be able to use space as a source of energy for the planet, through solar-power satellites, using the most sustainable source available – our sun.

In the unscientific view which people unfortunately sometimes take about the problems we face on this planet, aviation has often been singled out as a key component of climate change. I believe that aviation has to get much more carbon efficient than it is today, but it is important that people begin to realize that seemingly benign industries such as IT have in fact overtaken aviation in terms of their CO_2 output. The explosive growth of the internet has resulted in a world in which we have nearly a half a billion servers, each one consuming hundreds of watts. Industries like this would benefit enormously from the ability to launch low Earth orbit satellites that could literally take some of the heat out of the planet, for example by serving someday as the repository of our information technology.

The economic case

So the fact that our system will have the capability to launch small payloads and satellites at low cost is hugely important. As far as science is concerned, this system offers tremendous potential to researchers who will be able to fly experiments much more often than before, helping to answer key questions about Earth's climate and the mysteries of the universe. And for applied research, it is currently just too expensive to be able to do most of the things in space from which industries like biotechnology could really benefit. The beauty of WhiteKnightTwo (VSS Eve) and SpaceShipTwo (VSS Enterprise) is that they can help change the paradigm of our relationship to space, achieving an era where space accessibility becomes a commercial and scientific norm, rather than an exception.

The experience case

The other thing that I really admire about the system is that it has the architecture that could someday be developed into a passenger-carrying vehicle, able to take people from A to B around the planet, outside the atmosphere. That may not happen for some time, but the first generation of space tourists will be paving the way as they marvel at the beauty of our planet and experience the freedom of weightlessness and the blackness of space.

It's very important that we make a genuine commercial success of this project. If we do, I believe we'll unlock a wall of private sector money into both space launch systems and space technology. This could rival the scale of investment in the mobile phone and internet technologies after they were unlocked from their military origins and thrown open to the private sector.

Edited from NYC Unveil event; **SOURCE**: Virgin Galactic website, 23 January 2008

Hear more from Sir Richard on:
http://www.youtube.com/watch?v=t4h247PPOrY

Will Whitehorn – the president

Will has had a long career with Virgin and worked in a variety of roles including corporate affairs director before becoming president of Virgin Galactic.

The origins of Virgin Galactic go back a long way into the history of the man who formed Virgin Group, Sir Richard Branson. He was interested in space when he was a kid and I remember when I first started to work for Virgin over 23 years ago he was seriously interested in the Soviet space programme that allowed paying customers to go on missions.

Then the Soviet Union collapsed and the opportunity to do something like that went away for a long time. When the Russians did finally come back and offer people the chance to go to the international space station as paying ... I wouldn't say space tourists but space explorers, it cost $20 to $30 million. So the origins of Virgin Galactic are in Richard thinking about going into space and trying to understand why it was so expensive.

When we watched the Apollo moon landings they had a profound effect on us and people genuinely believed then that we would soon all be going into space. Stanley Kubrick's film, *2001: A Space Odyssey*, which I saw as a nine-and-a-half-year-old, gave that impression and the scientists certainly seemed to think that it was possible. However, one of the things that Stanley Kubrick didn't have access to when he made *2001: A Space Odyssey* was an economist. Had he done so, he would have been told that going into space is a very expensive proposition.

Insights often start with a question

It was 1995 and Richard and I were sitting in a bar in Marrakesh, Morocco with Buzz Aldrin the astronaut, as one does. We were talking about space access and Richard asked Buzz the question, 'Why have they never used a balloon or an aeroplane or something like that to launch a rocket rather than try and blow themselves apart on the ground?' – which is a very sensible question. And Buzz answered it, saying, 'Well, they did, actually. They experimented with balloon launches in the US navy in the late 1950s off aircraft carriers, and they also had a project called the X-15 project that was a space plane launched from a B52 bomber.'

All of that was abandoned in the 1960s because of the budgetary constraints around trying to get two people onto the moon by the end of the decade and President Kennedy's pledge to the American people that America would win the space race. As a result, NASA became an organization wholly geared to a political mission; not one geared to the industrialization of space. That conversation was really the foundation of Virgin Galactic. Sir Richard gave me a watching brief to look at the technology of space launch and to see whether or not there was a possibility of creating a project to develop a space launch system for the future.

So that is what I did until the late 1990s when a couple of things happened. One was that I got approached by a company in the Mojave Desert called the Rotary Rocket Company. It was running a project to build a carbon-composite reusable launch vehicle that could get into space and re-enter the atmosphere using a sort of helicopter device. I decided to go and look at this project and registered the company name 'Virgin Galactic', because I thought if I was going to Mojave to see this project we ought to have a name. Richard joined me there and we decided not to invest in it for a number of reasons, but it sparked our ideas further, and whilst we there, purely by chance, we met an aircraft designer called Burt Rutan.

At that time, Virgin and Steve Fossett were co-developing an aircraft entirely made of carbon composite to fly around the world on a single tank of fuel. For Virgin it was a combination technology and sponsorship project, for Steve Fossett it was about wanting to attain a world record. So Burt Rutan was commissioned to build the aircraft. I was overseeing the construction of the vehicle for Virgin Atlantic Airways and I was in the factory one day when I happened to see a spaceship. Burt Rutan had been approached by Paul Allen, the Microsoft entrepreneur, to win

Air launch   © 2011 Virgin Galactic

the Ansari X-Prize, which was a $10 million prize for the first ever private space flight of humans into space, which had to be repeated again within ten days. Burt decided that he could develop a technology to win that prize and so had partnered with Paul Allen to fund the attempt. I phoned Sir Richard and I said, 'Burt's building a spaceship! I can't believe it. This looks really exciting technology, we've got to get to grips with it; it's something we should be looking at very seriously.'

Be bold; be first

I knew two things at that stage; first, I knew that they were building it on a budget that totalled less than $30 million and they planned to get two people into space with it. Secondly, it was going to be launched from the air, so that meant it had to be flexible and you could always launch something else from the air: it needn't be that particular spaceship. So we began to look at it very seriously and everything started from that point in time. We announced the business was going to start before we had even seen SpaceShipOne fly and even before it won the X-prize because we thought if we're going to do this we've got to be very bold and be there first.

When we announced the business in 2004 we knew we had to have a business plan in order to build the space launch system. We knew how expensive it was to do the things that are done currently in space. It costs $1 billion a launch for the Shuttle and even the cheapest rocket launch to get a cosmonaut to the international space station is $50 to $60 million per person. The international space station has cost nearly $20 billion to develop as an orbiting laboratory. The average launch for a 200 kilogram-plus satellite is from $30 million up to $200 million. **So our insight was to find a technology that is so far removed from the current cost of putting people into space that it makes it commercially viable.** Then we figured the applications would almost discover themselves.

Winning over the shareholders

Richard was very keen on the business but the Virgin Group was initially, and quite rightly, reluctant because the history of space has been littered with more disaster than success. But once the prototype was successful and Burt won the X-prize, we were 'off to the races'. And indeed a very simple business plan based around rebuilding the first spaceship seemed to indicate that for an outlay of maybe $150 million, we could offer space tourism at $200,000 a ticket – and this was what we announced.

We were set a mission and a goal by Virgin Group of getting $10 million of deposits from potential customers. Obviously we could hand the deposits back if we decided not to proceed, but we needed to get $10 million of deposits in the first place before we could go ahead and start to design and construct the actual system. So we went out to talk to the people, the real people who expressed interest in becoming the first passengers; people like Philippe Starck, Victoria Principal and Trevor Beattie.

Customer-oriented design

Our customers told us the primary things they wanted from the experience. If they went into space they wanted weightlessness and that classic view of the Earthrise from the windows: all the things they'd seen in the NASA newsreels. That immediately told us something which was significant from the point of view of the team: which was that we couldn't use Burt's first design, SpaceShipOne. The reason being because you couldn't get enough people into that tiny cockpit to make it a shared experience; you wouldn't be able to experience weightlessness because there wasn't the room to float around inside the cabin, and the pressurized portholes were so small that you couldn't get the panoramic view of Earth. Our customers wanted to experience the weightlessness, to see the blackness of space, to see the curvature of the Earth. They wanted to experience the sensations of breaking the sound barrier within six seconds of launching, reaching 3,000 to 4,000 miles an hour. They wanted to experience the G-forces on their body. That said to us, 'Okay, the market says we've got to create this experience, so let's

Earthrise

© 2011 Virgin Galactic

design a business plan around it.' Research that NASA commissioned in 2002 found that there was potentially a market of up to a couple of hundred thousand people who wanted to go to space at a price point between $100,000 and $200,000. There was no precedent for building a business plan to do this, so we said, 'Let's start with this market and see if we can justify the expense over a period of ten years, carrying 50,000 people on a sliding scale, getting cheaper by the time we get to year five.' It's classic marketing, you know; if you are designing a new plasma screen television, it starts at $20,000 and ten years later it is $2,000. So we built a plan based upon that. We did lots more of our own research; we put up our website and invited people to sign up. We ended up with 85,000 registrations on the website. And in the meantime we got the deposits from the first 300 customers and we now have $40 million in deposits. That earned us the right to go ahead and build what we now know as VSS Enterprise, the passenger vehicle, and VSS Eve, the launch vehicle.

Creating an end-to-end branded experience

The Virgin brand has been very important to our success. We have to take the customers on a journey with us and they pay their own costs to get there. We simply don't have the resources at a time when we're investing hundreds of millions in

VSS Enterprise

developing this technology to do more. But what we do is include our customers at every step along the way as part of our brand: they visit the factory; they get presentations from Burt Rutan; they get the chance to go to Richard's private home at Necker Island and spend some quality time with him, Buzz Aldrin, Burt Rutan and Brian Binnie, the SpaceShipTwo pilot. Every single one of our customers is fascinated by what we're doing and they want to be intimately involved in the process. **So it is less about a ride into space and much more about an end-to-end branded experience.**

If you're a Virgin Galactic customer you know that you're helping to build something that could well revolutionize access to space. It is not very different from those very early customers who would board a Ford Trimotor airplane to fly across America; it was slower than getting the train, but they believed in the future and they wanted to help it to happen. That's the fantastic thing about this project. The customers actually know that they're helping the future to happen.

Redefining what is possible

Let me give you some idea of the scale of this project. Since Yuri Gagarin went into space in 1961, shortly followed by Alan Shepard, there have been 500 people who have gone into space in total. We will carry over 600 people in the first year of operation. By the end of year 10 in the business plan we'll have carried over 50,000 people into space.

Every time the NASA Shuttle takes off it uses the equivalent of a one-kiloton nuclear explosion of energy underneath it. This is dirty energy because it's big old solid rockets that are burning huge amounts of fuel. And if you go to Cape Canaveral, you will see the area around the Shuttle launch pad is completely dead; no life exists there. A launch produces the same environmental output as the whole population of New York does over a long weekend holiday. The Virgin Galactic system will produce the same environmental footprint as a single round-trip business-class ticket from London to New York on a Virgin A340.

Making money and saving the planet

Having said that we are very much aware of the bigger environmental picture, let me be clear: Virgin Galactic is about making money. It is a classic Virgin approach, which is to take a market that either has become a monopoly or has become very inefficient and introduce a niche product that can begin to reshape that market. Virgin Atlantic was a totally niche product when it started and it has played its part along with Virgin Blue, Ryanair, Virgin America and easyJet to reshape the aviation industry and made it become more efficient. We recently did a financial analysis which valued this business with the technology we've developed at over $900 million. And we're still a year away from launch.

But the exciting thing about this project is that it really is not about space tourism. We are right on the edge of planetary starvation at the moment, and there would be over a billion people starving right now without space technology. That's how important it has become. So when I hear somebody who says, 'Why are we focusing on space when we have all these problems on Earth?' I think this is somebody who hasn't really thought holistically about what's going on with our planet. You know, history teaches us that industry has largely been a solution to most of our problems, not the cause. The major cause of our problems is the huge population growth that we've had, and the fact that we actually devote most of our fossil fuels to producing food. And everything else – everything else – is at the margin. Now if it costs $1 billion a time to get anything into space you can't utilize that place outside our delicate atmosphere to do the things we need to do. So you can't put solar farms in space. You can't put your server farms in space (in 2010, IT contributed more than double the amount of CO_2 emissions of aviation). With Virgin Galactic these things become possible.

Virgin Galactic provides the potential of being able to carry people around the planet outside the atmosphere so that flying London to Sydney will take just two hours compared with the 23 or so hours it takes now, and transport passengers and payloads into space cost effectively with minimum harm to the environment. And that is the breakthrough that mankind needs.

Stephen Attenborough – the commercial director

After working in the City of London for a number of years, Stephen was between jobs when he heard the news that SpaceShipOne had won the Ansari X-Prize. It inspired him to become part of the fledgling business.

Like a lot of people, I have always admired Virgin. I think many people of my generation do. Will Whitehorn had told me a lot about this project because it was one that was obviously very dear to his heart. In quite typical Virgin style, they made the big announcement and then had to create a business around it. And it was exactly the right way to do it because if we hadn't told the world what we were going to do then we probably would never have been brave enough to go out and create a market and get the job done.

Being bold

We announced what the experience was going to be like on 27 September 2004, pretty much as we were signing the deal. And that was a big, bold thing to do. But if we hadn't done that we wouldn't have excited the attention of the media, we wouldn't have excited people's imagination and we wouldn't have got our first customers. And then we wouldn't have got the funding from Virgin to go off and build the thing. It's upside down but you have to do it that way.

I started shortly after the announcement was made that we were launching Virgin Galactic and I literally started with a small box of stationery but a very cool culture. I met Richard for the first time shortly after I started. What he said to me was there are two really important things with this. The first is that we have to achieve unprecedented levels of safety from day one. We'll do that by having the right technology, building the commercial vehicles in the right way and testing them for as long as they need to be tested and by bringing the experience we have from the other transportation businesses to make sure we have that ingrained culture of safety in the spaceline operation. We think that that's something that's manageable. The other thing is that we have to make this a commercial success. It's going to be the great flagship for the brand. But it needs to stand on its own two feet.

We understood that we had the potential of transforming space access in a very meaningful way. Whilst this is important commercially, I think it is important on a much bigger scale. If we're going to manage the dwindling and limited resources that we have on this planet, with the burgeoning global population, we need to make better use of space. And in order to do that, we need to be able to find a better and cheaper way of getting there.

The Virgin ethos

Although I thought it was going to be fun and it would be great to work on something that was going to give a few people a wonderful experience, the thing that really sold it to me was that we were doing something which was very important and there was probably nobody else in the world that would be willing to do it. I think one of the fundamental principles of Virgin is to go into industries where there is a cartel and break it up. It's what Virgin's history has been made of, really. And this is a particularly bold example of that but, nevertheless, it fits the bill.

I think one of the joys of being here is clearly that we're working on something important and cool and being part of a great brand. We're an incredibly 21st-century manifestation of all the great things about Virgin in the 20th century. One of the things that we've tried to do is to make sure that we have always talked about Virgin Galactic in the wider context of the Virgin group. And what we're doing is very much in support of the wider group ethos, and that goes right down to breaking cartels, but also showcasing cutting-edge technology which is going to be absolutely essential to the survival of some of our other businesses. We have built in the last two or three years the world's largest all-carbon-composite aircraft. Nothing like this has been built before. The whole body and the wing spar, and everything, are all in carbon composite. One of the reasons that we're doing this is that Virgin Atlantic wants and needs in the next five to ten years to be buying all-carbon-composite commercial aviation aircraft. We know that we have to run our energy-intensive businesses more efficiently and so **there is a real link between what we're trying to achieve here and what Virgin is about as a brand**.

Making customers part of your story

One of the things I realized when I started was that this was going to be a high-net-worth private-client-type business which would need to keep their attention for several years before we ever delivered a product. And so we needed a 'product' before we could actually deliver the real thing. So we decided it was going to be around great communication and we made that our number-one priority. Our customers, without exception, want to experience space for themselves. They've read the accounts of astronauts, they've dreamt about this; they love the idea of having that perception-changing moment when you see the planet that we live on from a completely different perspective. And so, of course, they are in it for that reason. But I think that they also love being a part of this story and they regard themselves as pioneers in a new industry. The vast majority are entrepreneurs of some description; most of them self-made and most of them work for themselves or have their own businesses. And I think they really understand the challenge of what we're doing from a business perspective and the importance of what we're doing from an industry perspective and are passionate about being part of what's enabling this to happen. What they don't want from us is golfing days and expensive corporate hospitality but what they do want is great communication and what they really want more than anything is privileged access to this brand community. They are people from different walks of life, different backgrounds and 40 different countries. But they all share this common vision and want to be part of this unique group.

Trevor Beattie – the passenger

As a young boy, Trevor was fascinated by space. He went on to found BMB, one of the leading advertising agencies in the UK but he never lost sight of his boyhood dream.

What got me involved with Virgin Galactic had its roots in July 1969 – watching Neil Armstrong walk on the moon. Most of the Virgin Galactic customers have that in common, I reckon.

I've always been fascinated and obsessed by all things aeronautic and astronomic – by aircraft, by rocketry, by space. Even though it has nothing to do with my profession, it is my obsession. And so I knew about the Ansari X-Prize and had heard of Burt Rutan. I have met two geniuses in my time. Burt is one and Prince, the musician, is the other.

Moon Walk   © 2011 Virgin Galactic

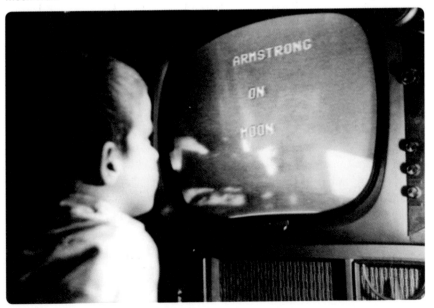

The X-Prize

The Ansari X-Prize is almost an old Victorian challenge. You know: 'We challenge you, mankind, to send a human being into sub-orbital space and return them to Earth, whence they came, and then return and repeat the same stunt two weeks later.' I love that! I thought it's a real Phileas Fogg 'around the world in 80 days' challenge for our time. It was great. And so you had blokes on the Yorkshire moors firing up what were essentially big fireworks, and people in Belgium attempting it, and all of them failing and not even getting close. And I really got the impression that people finally ganged up on Burt Rutan and said, 'Burt, look, could you win this X-Prize for us?' And Burt's body language seemed to say 'Well, I could, but I'm too busy trying to get us to Mars.' And they nag him and say, 'Well, look, just give us five minutes of your time. Do you know how to crack this problem for mankind?' And Burt says, 'Of course I do, but I'm busy.' Then Richard Branson nags him, so he finally goes 'All right, let's bloody do it, then. Here's the solution to your problem. What is it? Two words: air launch.' I love that.

So he designed SpaceShipOne, and Brian Binnie, the legendary test pilot, flew the first of the X-Prize flights and right then I knew that within two weeks they would do it all over again and would win the X-Prize.

Book me a seat

I said to Antoinette, my PA, 'Get on to Richard Branson immediately: phone him and tell him that when they win the X-Prize next week I will be there and I'll sign up as the first customer and I'll bring my chequebook with me. Within an hour Branson called back and said, 'We're not doing it in two weeks' time; we're doing it the day after tomorrow. Come to LA. Be my guest: come on out and see it.' So I said, 'Okay, I'm coming! So I literally ran out of my office, packed a bag, flew to LA. No sleep. Then it's four o'clock in the morning and I'm in the Test Pilots' Café at Mojave airfield having breakfast. And they rolled the craft out and performed the second flight and won the X-Prize! I vividly remember Burt's comment the day he won the X-Prize: 'SpaceShipOne; NASA, nil.'

And then there I am at the press conference with the world's media covering the launch of Virgin Galactic. My friends at home are watching Sky News, saying, 'Hang on a minute, that bloke on the TV looks a bit like Trevor; that's strange.'

Later I met with Richard and said, 'Sign me up. I'm going. Count me in. I'm your first customer. I'm bloody going!' And you know, I have never ever had a second thought about the safety. You have the ultimate team of Burt Rutan and Richard Branson with the skill and ability of test pilots like Brian Binnie and Mike Melvill. Burt has designed and built and flown more aeroplanes in the last 20 years than Airbus and Boeing put together. It's no wonder people are now lining up to join Galactic.

The company you keep

The irony is that NASA, through the 'right stuff', painstakingly selected people to go to space. They went there as engineers and they came back as poets and men of God. This time it's the poets and artists and crazy people who are going. Will we come back as engineers? I don't know. But it's a self-selecting bunch and this is what is really interesting about Virgin Galactic. They have no say, really, as to who goes because we are paying customers. Of course we have to pass medicals and train in the 'vomit comet' – I mean do the centrifuge training – and they will fail people who don't pass the tests. But other than that, if you have the money and the inclination you can book your seat in the same way as you would fly Virgin Atlantic. So it's a self-selecting bunch.

Then how do you handle this self-selecting bunch of very strange individuals? And this is what Virgin has done brilliantly, because the first hundred customers then became the Founders – we have become great friends, gathering at regular events in irregular places all over the world!

When people hear that I am going into space, their first reaction is, 'Isn't that the most irresponsible thing that you could do?' I believe that the first bunch of people who go are pioneers: pioneers in the old Victorian adventurer sense, and pioneers in a business sense too, because in 20 years' time, space flights won't cost $200,000 or be full of millionaire businessmen; there will be children, there will be families going up... It will change the nature of how we think about space.

So **I think that the pioneers, the founders, are bold people**. Are they irresponsible? I don't know – maybe. Sometimes they belong together, those words.

The final chapter

I've got a scrapbook I put together when I was a kid, called 'The Space Race'. It contains all the news cuttings of Apollo XIII and so on. It's the only thing I've got left from my childhood. I don't know why and how, but it's stayed with me all my life. At the end of it, in my final chapter, it says: 'What next? What will the future bring?' And I wrote this little chapter about what I thought would happen. At the very end there is this little space. It's my ambition to get a press cutting of when I go up and stick it in the back of my childhood scrapbook as the final entry and get Buzz Aldrin to sign it. And that will be a sort of completion for me: my childhood dream come true.

The Space Race

See 'Future Astronauts: Living The Dream':
http://www.youtube.com/watch?v=8fPErmu3IL0

Brian Binnie   © 2011 Virgin Galactic

Brian Binnie – the pilot

After a distinguished career in the military as a test pilot, Brian Binnie found him-self at the right place at the right time with the 'right stuff'.

My mother used to say to me at a very early age that if she was a 'wee laddie' – she was Scottish – she'd want to grow up and be an astronaut. I didn't quite under-stand what an astronaut was when I was five years old but she explained it to me and it planted the seed. And, **while I couldn't appreciate all the business about rockets and stars and space, I could appreciate that anything that got itself off the ground was going in the right direction**, and so I became enamoured with birds and planes and model airplanes. When I got older, I studied them, went to university, and decided I was going to get the kind of flying education that only the military can provide, and so I joined the navy, believing that their brand of flying was the most entertaining and challenging and exciting.

For the next 20 years I did the carrier aviation stuff: went to Navy Test Pilot School and so on. But, at the end of 20 years, I felt there was an unfulfilled chapter of my life. I left the military and saw an opportunity to move to Mojave to work for a company called Rotary Rockets. They built this funny looking helicopter thing that scared the bejesus out of us who flew it. But that's another story...

During that time I became friends with Burt Rutan, the designer of SpaceShipOne and after Rotary Rockets ran out of funds he said 'Why don't you wander down to our place and we'll figure out something for you to do?' So I did and it was shortly after this that the SpaceShipOne programme was put under contract with Paul Allen of Microsoft fame. And so we were off.

Make your own opportunities

I always had faith that as long as I prepared myself, opportunity would find me – even if I didn't necessarily know where to look. After the navy I passed up some conventional career choices and while I had the distinct sense that doors were closing around me I was poised to step into another that might open. Coming to Mojave was not an obvious choice, you know; it's a little desolate, it's in the middle of nowhere, it's somewhat run-down. You need to know it was not a terribly popular decision from the family's perspective.

Enterprise drives innovation

We grew up in a world where there was so much promise in the space arena and then it was never fulfilled; it sort of fizzled before our eyes, and only the select few that were lucky enough to get through the government space agency programmes experienced the benefit of the technology. The way that space evolved was entirely different from, say, aviation. Aviation is such a colourful and magnificent field because it was developed by entrepreneurs in competition, entrepreneurs that were trying to support a business plan, that were maybe spurred ahead by various prizes. They all had this belief that 'If a couple of bicycle mechanics could build an airplane, then, gosh, I can do a better job.' And so there was a proliferation of different designs and people out trying different things. And what we have today are capabilities that nobody had any appreciation of at the turn of the last century. It was just that they were pursuing a passion. Space has never had that opportunity; it's always been in the hands of the government. You know, as inspiring as the Apollo programme was, what followed was a big letdown. NASA never matured any of the early rocket motors; they put them on the shelf and they built something that was bigger, more complicated, more expensive and, I would suggest, more dangerous. They flew them a few times and then shelved them.

The progression from the Mercury to Gemini, to Apollo, to eventually the Space Shuttle was not one that opened doors for people; it shut them. If we'd let the government control aviation in the same way they have space, then the only airplane flying today would be something like the equivalent of the B-2 bomber. End of story.

A new model

There has been a general frustration among those of us that really believe that many opportunities have been lost along the way and it's time to start over – literally.

What better place to start than in the sub-orbital arena, where you have to worry about all the same things that the big rockets that go into orbit do: you've got gravity, you've got rockets, you've got the vacuum of space, you've got the re-entry problems, you've got the issues of reusability and reliability and affordability to deal with. If you use the aviation model as your guide, then you would build a rocket that has modest performance but is safe, sound, reliable, people can get into and get out of it, and the performance can be matured over time. And along with it you get a sense of closure on a business plan. And I think that's where we are. Sir Richard appreciates this as a stepping stone to bigger and better things, and a lot of us believe that here is a path forward and we're on it. It's an exciting place to be.

We are pulling out the stops for the first group of customers, giving them centrifuge training, physiological training. We are going to provide a zero-G experience; there are various airplanes now that can give you that weightless experience for about 20 or 30 seconds at a time. Our mothership was built with the ability to do the same thing, so that if you're flying in the mothership, perhaps watching the launch of the group of customers in front of you, then after they're released and on their way, you can go through a weightless experience yourself. So we view the training and preparation as part of the whole end-to-end experience.

© 2011 Virgin Galactic

DNA

Going into space in shorts and sandals

Because of the way the mothership is built and designed and the materials that we have used, it is almost as capable as a front-line military fighter and yet look at the huge size of it. It's got modern fanjet engines that can really give it the performance it needs when carrying a spaceship, and yet when it's not carrying a spaceship it is incredibly fuel efficient. Those four engines pack enough thrust that sans-spaceship we can take the runway at idle power, accelerate to takeoff speed and then climb away, raise the landing gear, and climb to 50,000 feet – all with the throttles still at idle!

To see the first manned flight of the VSS Enterprise, click here: http://www.youtube.com/watch?v=mDUVe3a496Y

We have taken a very different approach to going into space. One of the reasons our vehicles have evolved in the way they have is we've taken an entirely different approach where we said, truthfully, we would rather go to space in shorts and sandals than wear the traditional space or pressure suits because we're only up there for such a short period of time. I don't want to be encumbered by all of that bulky equipment. And so we put our effort into building the kind of structure that cocoons you for the entire flight. We go to space just wearing lightweight flight suits.

The common denominator is a new way of thinking about space, space travel and space business. For us it's centred around tourism initially, but we think, like many applications, there are going to be uses that we just really can't conceive of at this point. So we think, for a lot of reasons, we're on the right track here.

A new way of doing business

You know, **I think that our approach speaks to the spirit of our times; there are other ways of doing business**. I think Sir Richard sees in Burt Rutan a lot of himself. Burt is a very unconventional kind of person; he doesn't mind making waves or rocking the boat or taking the contrarian view. And I think that's been the secret to our success. He's not afraid to try things, and just as almost as importantly, he's not afraid to fail. I think Sir Richard is the same kind of guy: he does things in an unconventional way. Sometimes, along the way, this got him into trouble, but he was willing to take himself to the edge and learned a lot of life's lessons and earned its riches and rewards. I think he sees a lot of that richness in Burt Rutan and the people that Burt surrounds himself with. I think there's a natural synergy between the two gentlemen, the companies that they represent, and their outlook in terms of what needs to done to make a real difference to our world.

Bold lessons

The power of a shared vision

The outstanding feature of the Virgin Galactic story is the power of a shared vision. The impact of seeing the 1969 moon landings on Richard Branson, Brian Binnie, Trevor Beattie and others shaped the rest of their lives. That image inspired them in separate ways to follow a dream without knowing how, when or where it might be realized. They were each successful in their respective fields but that early vision remained with them until they each quickly grasped the opportunity of Virgin Galactic without a second thought.

The pioneer spirit

History has shown that many of the innovations that we have come to take for granted were a result of entrepreneurs, pioneers and early adopters willing to invest their own money, and sometimes lives, in a big idea. We will look back at the early beginnings of Virgin Galactic in much the same way as those early grainy images of the Wright brothers at Kitty Hawk and wonder how some people have the ability to see beyond problems to find solutions. The remarkable thing about Virgin Galactic technology is that it shows how with ingenuity we really can 'have our cake and eat it': economic, environmentally friendly and experiential from a customer perspective.

The end-to-end Virgin Galactic experience

It is incredible to hear the customer talking about their Virgin Galactic experience when they have yet to take off. Virgin has very cleverly made the whole experience of preparation, training and communications a branded customer experience in itself, one that has forged a close community of users who are passionate advocates for the brand.

Challenge conventional beliefs

In an age when health and safety considerations, risk management and shareholder expectations are all reasons to follow the well-trodden path of status quo, it is refreshing to see how the founders of Virgin Galactic are challenging the norms, questioning established practice and finding completely new answers to old questions. Yet the perennial balance of customer needs, shareholder returns and employee welfare are as important as ever. After all, this is first and foremost a commercial enterprise. But the starting point is a bold proposition.

For more on Virgin Galactic see:
http://www.virgingalactic.com/

Virgin Galactic shows the power of a vision to challenge conventional thinking and that is something it has in common with our next bold brand, which has transformed its industry in the UK.

Chapter Two
O2

There are many inspiring stories in this book but one of our personal favourites is the story of O2. All so often, people say that you can't be bold if you work for a large corporate. O2 proves them wrong.

O2 started life as BT Cellnet, the mobile business of British Telecommunications. As part of the deregulation in the industry, BT Cellnet was spun off as a separate entity in 2002 and rebranded as mmO2. The very name was designed to bring 'a breath of fresh air' to the industry. However, the *Financial Times* was less convinced and, in an editorial at that time titled 'BT's unwanted orphan', said the name was 'daft' and the brand practically 'worthless'. Four years later that worthless brand was sold to Telefónica for a mere £17.7 billion. By 2008 O2 had overtaken its giant parent to become the largest provider of telecom connections in the UK and the fourth best-loved brand in Great Britain.

So what did O2 do to turn around an ailing business and become a powerhouse in the UK economy? We won't steal the thunder of the executives whom we interviewed by giving away too much here, but suffice to say it was the classic approach of starting with customer insight, having a clear point of difference, aligning your people with it, tearing up the industry rule book and then seeking to dramatize your difference through bold innovations. The O2 values are 'Bold, Open, Trusted and Clear'. They sum up very well what this brand is about.

Today O2 is market leader in the UK, being number one in terms of total revenues, earnings, new customers, lowest churn, customer base – having achieved more new connections than all of their competitors combined – and customer satisfaction. In June 2010, O2 was announced by Satmetrix as having the highest NPS (net promoter score, a measure of customer advocacy) in the UK market at 24 per cent, when the industry average is a miserable 3 per cent.

For more on O2 click here:
http://www.o2.com/about_us.asp

O2   © 2011 O2

Bold practices

O2

- It bought the naming rights to the 'white elephant' Millennium Dome and, partnering with AEG, rebranded it the O2 Arena, which is now the most successful music venue in the world.
- O2 measures 'fandom': the willingness of its customers to become an advocate for the brand.
- O2 pioneered SIM-only tariffs, making it easy for customers to leave if they wish.
- Fair Deal offers existing customers deals as good as or better than those available to new customers.
- O2 products are designed to be as simple to use as possible.
- O2 took 500 people out of head office and put 2,000 people into the retail stores and call centres to reallocate costs to those areas that customers value most.

- O2 has bought JaJah, a VoIP technology that is a direct threat to O2's existing technology.
- O2 launched Apple's iPhone into the UK market.
- O2's values are 'Bold, Open, Trusted, Clear'.
- O2 believes itself to be in the 'experience business', not the 'mobile phone business'.

Ronan Dunne – the CEO

Ronan Dunne was appointed CEO of Telefónica O2 UK in January 2008, having previously been CFO.

I think that the difference between O2 and other companies who operate in this space is that we are a brand first and foremost, rather than a company that happens to have a brand. This manifests itself in the fact we have a lot of people working with O2 who are driven by the belief they can genuinely make a difference. If we think we can change the rules of the game and truly make a difference, then we focus on doing what it takes to make that difference. **The DNA of O2 is changing the rules of the industry or not playing by the rules at all.**

The brand is bigger than the business

We've always seen the brand as being bigger than our core mobile communication business. We've always felt that our mandate with our customers is absolutely predicated on being brilliant in our core offering, but it is having built that relationship with them which, we believe, has allowed us to talk to our customers about things other than plain vanilla mobile communications.

I think part of this attitude was driven by the reality of what we were not. When we started we weren't the best voice provider or text provider. In fact we were average, in a market which was becoming more and more commoditized. The challenge for us was, **if we were going to differentiate ourselves from the crowd and actually stand for something, what was it going to be**? Our hypothesis was that we could differentiate in a commoditized market by looking at the experience we delivered as opposed to the technology.

Becoming experience focused rather than technology led

If you take our industry, there are some very obvious examples of being technology focused rather than customer-experience focused. The old BT Cellnet – which was the antecedent of O2, of course – was as guilty as any. We launched WAP services and said, 'Surf the net.' BT Cellnet completely oversold the capability of WAP and fell into the trap of trying to sell our customers technology like GPRS. Who knows or cares what GPRS is? So we changed our philosophy and started to focus much more on the customer rather than the technology.

We did a lot of work on segmenting our customer base and asking them, 'What are the things in your life that mobility is starting to enable and how can we influence your experience?' Today I would describe your mobile phone as the remote control by which you live and manage your life and connect to the people and things that matter to you. I'm not sure I would have used that language five years ago, but that is the reality. **We're an enabler of great experiences** – we're not in the voice and text business. That's the key.

I think it's all driven by a belief that you can create an enduring relationship with a customer. The example that I would use is our introduction of SIM-only tariffs called 'Simplicity'. Now that in itself is not a breakthrough idea, you could argue, but the truth is there's a fundamental about a SIM-only tariff which absolutely breaks the premise that the contract mobile business was built on. The premise was: 'In order to justify giving you an expensive piece of hardware I need to lock you into a contract.' The industry had built itself a model which was based on attracting and trapping customers so that they couldn't leave, by making the barriers to exit high. The big idea and insight in Simplicity is, **if you give your customers the freedom to leave, what you actually give them is the confidence to stay**. The proof point is that the churn on our SIM-only contract base is lower than for our with-handset contract base. So customers have maximum flexibility to leave, but paradoxically, more of them choose to stay. For me, that is a perfect example of playing by a different set of rules. Our competitors thought we were crazy, they thought our customers would leave in droves. The reality was very different because we said, 'If we build a great end-to-end experience, then customers will have no reason to leave.'

We didn't just simply change the contract terms. We had prepared for a fundamental change; we'd built the customer experience, we'd built the network experience, we'd built the shopping experience, we'd built the tariffing innovation. We got to the point where we said, 'Now our deeds are matching our words.' Now what's the ultimate vote of self-confidence? It was to invite customers to tear up their contracts and stay because they wanted to, not because the terms and conditions said they had to. The industry had created a whole load of very constraining terms – weasel clauses – so no wonder our industry had a reputation which paralleled that of used car salesmen.

Simplicity   © 2011 O2

Changing the way that the industry works

Telecommunications is notorious for making the simple incredibly complex. When a new customer contacted us, the first thing that the industry would say to the customer was, 'What you need to do is...'. Well, if that's the start of any conversation, you've lost already. The conversation should be about what we can do for you, not what you need to do for us in order to be able to use our services.

We became ruthless at taking out the things that customers don't value and refocusing more of our energy and our resources on the things that customers truly value. A great example of that was our 'Fair Deal' proposition, which on the face of it looked like financial suicide. We said, 'We promise you as an existing customer that you'll get at least as good a deal as a new customer and you'll get also something extra for your loyalty.' This was completely contrary to the acquisition model where deals were only there for new customers. We had recognized early on that the acquisition model created a situation where you left a lot of your existing, loyal customers very unhappy and we also saw that the long-term value in the industry is in the retention of customers. Attracting customers only to then allow them to leave and then replace them with new ones is a crazy way to run a business.

Our philosophy was: create an enduring relationship. Well, how do you do that? You build trust. You take away the scams, the small print that people think is unfair. You make your tariffing more transparent and simpler so all the weasel is gone, so what you see is what you get. It is no coincidence that the values that we chose to launch O2 with were 'Bold, Open, Trusted and Clear'. To build a trust relationship with customers you have to be really clear in your communication. You have to be bold to change the rules of the game. You have to take risks.

By introducing Simplicity and Fair Deal, **we were essentially writing a £500 million cheque against our P&L**. History shows that, rather than lose money, we were the only operator over that period who continued to grow profitability. None of our competitors did.

It starts with belief and customer insight

The thing that got us through those early days was, in a very O2 way, we had a very, very tough and open and honest debate as a board. We finished the conversation by saying we may not be able to fully analyse this as a business case on a few PowerPoint slides, but we all believe it's the right thing to do – based on experience, based on intuition, based on the power of the brand, and also, based on the one thing that this brand has always been good at: customer insight.

We've always talked to our customers, we've always listened, and we've always taken insights on board. We were convinced all along that if you treat your customers well, if you are transparent, if you offer them consistent, honest, fair value all the time, we would have the underpinnings of a great business. The question that none of us was as clear on was: would this be a great business for the future but would our profits run away from us while we were getting there?

We looked each other in the eye as a team – finance, marketing, sales, the operation side – and said, 'Do we, or do we not, believe this?' And as a team we absolutely signed up. As a result every tough conversation we had subsequently was in the context of 'If we believe doing the right thing for the customer is ultimately the most profitable business model, have we solved this particular issue?'

If each time we had a problem we had argued it without the benefit of that context then it would have all fallen apart. That basic premise of the long-term sustainable profitability of the business being underpinned by creating a differentiating customer experience was the rock on which we built the brand.

You can say all you like about customers having a good or a bad experience, but the time they vote with their feet is at contract renewal time, so the real proof is how many people are staying. We started to see that measure turn around almost immediately and it has improved quarter over quarter for five years in a row now, which is pretty stunning.

I can't emphasize enough that every single debate about every decision in the business was framed around a genuine belief, held just as much by the finance director as by the marketing director: that doing the right thing for the customer is a sustainable profitable business model. If you don't believe that, don't even start with the rest. The truth is, when you embark on the journey you can't stop halfway and say, 'You know what, I believe in customer experience, but I'm not going to do that,' or 'We can't afford to do that,' because **it only works when it all works**.

It's about the company you keep

One of the biggest things we did was to partner with Apple to bring the iPhone into the UK market. There was no economic advantage or financial incentive for Apple to choose O2 over any other telco in the UK. What motivated them to partner with us was that O2 was the brand that had more of their type of customers in it and the brand that they felt was the one most aligned to their own experience.

Apple is a very different company from us, but in their own way they approach their market in a very similar way to us. Everyone now is trying to find an iPhone 'killer'. Apple didn't try to build a Nokia killer or a BlackBerry killer, it just decided to define the space and then let everybody else compete with them. We've tried to do the same thing in our space, which is to say we'll try and set the rules by which we think the game should be played and then others can choose to compete as they wish. As a result we've been very attractive to partners who are attracted to brands that are both innovative and very experientially driven.

Our relationship with AEG at the O2 Arena is a good example. It was a hugely bold move on O2's part to take a 'white elephant' that was the Millennium Dome and put our name above the door. But the key thing is, we didn't just put our name above the door, we entered into a partnership with a company who have a reputation for being the leading live entertainment event provider in the world. We now together have our name above the door of the world's most successful live entertainment venue by ticket sales, and we have created a priority ticket category for our customers. If we'd just been sponsoring a building, then, frankly, we would never have done it – we would have exposed ourselves to potentially a huge reputational risk. But we partnered with an experience company who had a track record.

On the face of it, as a brand we've no right to be one of the biggest distributors of live entertainment tickets in the UK. But the reality is **we are in the entertainment business because we're in the experience business**; it's perfectly natural. But if you define yourself as being in the mobile phone business there's no logic to it. So the mindset which says we're in the business of creating experiences liberates us to do an awful lot of things, like entering financial services, for example. Financial services is an industry where, with a few exceptions, the concept of a customer experience isn't in their vocabulary. So we think it's a great opportunity for us to change the rules.

Transforming companies from within

One of the things that people forget is that the old BT Cellnet and O2 are the same company. When we spun off from BT the *Financial Times* wrote an article saying we were essentially 'worthless'. Four years later we were worth £17.7 billion. So one of the most interesting things about our story is how the company reinvented itself.

We didn't have a 'night of the long knives' where the top people in BT Cellnet suddenly disappeared and a new management team came in. We changed from within, substantially the same people and the same company: the same engineering bred and led business that BT had always been. Mobile inside BT attracted a lot of the brightest thinkers and the best innovators, so when we left the mothership we probably set sail with some of BT's best people from the point of view of innovation and insight. What we recognized was that best-in-class engineering can be a real benefit to a great customer experience. It's not that the two were mutually exclusive, it was just that you don't sell engineering to your customers. So what we did was, we took the strength of a really best-in-class engineering organization and we coupled it with great customer insight.

Turning people into fans

We absolutely mandated those people to be part of the success rather than saying, 'Engineers, you've had your day – now it's the marketers' turn.' Engineers want to make customers' lives better too. They may not have the language for it sometimes, but if you can articulate the insight for them, then they become part of the solution, not part of the problem. As I said earlier, it only works when it all works. Everybody in this business passionately believed that they were part of the solution, the guys in retail, the guys in customer service, the guys in IT technology, the guys in finance.

The fact is, **if you cannot turn your employees into fans there's no way that you will turn customers into fans**. So we have a customer promise, but we also have a people promise and a philosophy that says when we become fans of our customers they will become fans of us. If people in our retail stores and customer service know that our business is about turning customers into fans and they

Fans   © 2011 O2

understand what it is that they have to do to achieve this, how much more enjoyable their jobs become.

The vast majority of our people have a good understanding of what our strategy is, what we're trying to achieve, where we're trying to get to, and they can pretty well articulate what that means for them on a daily basis. Individual engagement and that sense of a team destination are hugely powerful. We keep close to the customer by keeping close to our people, who are the day-to-day manifestation of the brand, and there's nobody better to tell you when you're not walking the talk than your own employees. They will tell me, 'Ronan, that's bullshit, that's not what's happening.'

We're better, connected

Our strap-line is, 'We're better, connected'. This attitude drives us to be bold in finding ways to connect people to the things that matter most to them. If we are to continue to be successful we need to continue thinking outside the box, not being constrained by the rules by which the game has been played in the past. I think that we just define the exam question differently from our competitors and as a result it liberates us to come up with a lot more interesting answers than others in this industry.

To hear more from Ronan click here:
http://www.youtube.com/watch?v=GXxdKiAN7CU

Tim Sefton – the strategy guy

Tim is customer director. Tim joined O2 in 2000, having previously worked for BT and British Airways. Prior to joining the UK board, Tim was senior VP strategy and development for Telefónica O2 Europe.

Our brand promise is: 'Helping customers connect'. The longer version of that is: 'Helping customers connect with people and things that matter to them in a simpler, easier and better way'. Having this at the heart of our business and not limiting our brand philosophy to 'communications' gives us a real sense of purpose.

We set out to build a brand and not run a business. And so, out of that falls customer centricity because if you want customers to be real fans of your brand, then actually you have to get real insights about what you can do for customers, which is better than they currently get. So that's our higher purpose.

Connecting to a higher purpose

Our initial driver was: how can we create a business that delivers a better customer experience than was typical? By defining ourselves not as a mobile operator but by that higher purpose led us to do a number of things which you wouldn't

The O2 Arena   © 2011 O2

otherwise have expected. The most famous example is the O2 Arena. Tactically, of course, it was a great sponsorship opportunity, but the strategic coherence which helped all the internal alignment fall into place was: if we're a company that's about enabling better customer experiences then this is an opportunity to create a showcase of what we, as a business, stand for, both for employees and for customers. So it became an icon for our brand.

See Florence Welch backstage; O2 Priority access: http://www.youtube.com/watch?v=YrDvAv-4IFI&feature=related

Creating a virtuous cycle

One of the things we talk about is a virtuous cycle whereby, if you do the right thing for customers and you do the right thing for employees, then you see that come back to you in the form of business results. What we found is that as long as we get the balance right and invest enough in our customer experience and our employee experience, then if every now and again we need to make some short-term tactical adjustments to deal with market changes, we can accommodate them within our overall strategic context without losing momentum. I think some businesses end up making too many short-term decisions and lose momentum – which, in turn, loses them the confidence and the latitude to be able to invest in the customer experience.

You need some things going on which enable you to manage through the harder times and still retain morale. For example, when we opened the O2 Arena, the first event that we held for the public was for all the O2 employees too. We took everyone off the phones, everyone out of the shops, and everyone out of corporate and, apart from literally a skeleton staff, we had the big event where the Kaiser Chiefs, Tom Jones and various other artists performed. That was a great lesson from the point of view that people looked forward to it but also, more importantly, from the stories that they told afterwards. That happened at exactly the same time as we were downsizing in parts of the organization. I think the ying and the yang of business are really important. There are tough things that you have to do in business sometimes and the temptation is to believe that you need to stop doing everything else for the sake of sensitivities. Our experience is that that is a mistake because what you're doing then is compromising the way you manage 10,000 people on the basis that 200 are leaving. It's the same with customers. You can't be held back by the 1 or 2 per cent of customers who might not be huge fans of what you're doing for one reason or another. **If you run your business purely to avoid provoking criticism from a minority then you lose the boldness required to take some risks that will benefit the majority.**

Stay the course

We talk about turning customers into fans, and one of the attributes of a fan, as we see it, is forgiveness. And forgiveness comes from longevity; experiencing consistently high levels of service over time, so that when, on occasion, you get something wrong the customers will forgive you. A good example of that is Marks & Spencer, who went through a rough period. Businesses do go in cycles but as soon as they started putting things in place which delivered a better customer experience, the customers started coming back to them. We saw that the longevity that they created as a business by satisfying customers over many years allowed forgiveness. That is why we try to keep a degree of consistency and coherence about what we do. **If you chop and change your brand every time you appoint a new marketing director because they want to bring their own agency and create their own look, then it's a case of brands being run on behalf of egos, not on behalf of customers.**

The power of narrative

I once heard someone from Nike tell the story about how Bill Bowerman as the founding father instilled the principles in the organization. Then it fell into place – what we needed for our brand was a narrative. We were always very clear that the O2 brand was set up the way it was to do things differently: to be O2 – oxygen, a breath of fresh air. Therefore **our DNA is all about being challenging, trying to think differently, bringing a fresh perspective**. That leads to the question: how should O2 implement anything it's trying to deliver? Well, obviously, it needs to be fresh and different from what's gone before. So that is it: that's the narrative that continues to drive us.

Our brand values of Bold, Open, Trusted and Clear then become the founding principles for how we behave. For example, going back to when we launched in 2002, calling a mobile phone company O2 was bold.

We also created something called a Customer Plan, which went against the grain of what was happening in the industry at that time. We decided that we needed to cut out a lot of the cost that was in corporate overheads in the organization. We had people working on projects which were not demonstrably delivering on what customers really wanted at that time. By cutting that out we created a fighting fund that we invested in the customer experience to drive loyalty and retention. And we advertised the concept. The tag line was: 'Loyalty rewarded'. It was the first time customers had seen a mobile operator talking about rewarding loyalty. That campaign was a big gamble because we didn't know what we were going to need to invest in rewarding our existing loyal customers to balance out what we already invested in new customers.

Tell the brand story

I think this is where the power of storytelling and narrative is helpful, because a lot of organizations find it difficult to get alignment between all the different players and decision makers. What we had, and still have, is a narrative of what we are about and the values we share. That allows us to make decisions based on: this is what we're all about, this is what we believe in, and we think we've got the right customer insight, so let's give it a go. A good example of this approach is the way we've launched O2 Money. Our insight was that a lot of consumers are out of control with their money. So how could we build a business that enabled people to manage their money better? We thought, 'Well, actually what people really want at the moment is to be in control.' So therefore we'll launch products which put them in control and whereas the pre-paid card industry was all fee-based, we made our products totally free.

Another example is our acquisition of a VoIP provider called JaJah. What it does is enable calls to be made cheaply over the internet. And also it enables people to call through social networks. If you look through the traditional lens of a telco, that looks like a threat because it's effectively enabling customers to call each other and bypass your technology.

But our promise is 'Helping customers connect' and if that's the way they want to connect and we don't deliver it, somebody else will. So **a move that might be interpreted by our competitors as bold, to us looks like necessity**.

Trying not to piss customers off is generally a good idea

We try to identify opportunities by looking at qualitative data and just trying to understand the insights. Quite often, **what we look for are what we call 'piss-off factors'**. We look for the things which piss customers off, the grievances they hold against the industry that we think we can do something about. We're looking for the trends that are impacting customers' lives at a macro level. For example, one of the trends that we're very aware of is that trust in big institutions is declining. Because customers by and large don't trust big institutions, this has a direct impact on how they feel about us at the macro level, and therefore we will look to see what we can do that will enable us to be more trusted than our peer group.

We also study detailed segmentation analyses which, I guess, is fairly typical for the industry. But what sets us apart, I think, is that **we are more likely to focus on trend-spotting in the world of fashion or in completely parallel universes and try and see how we could apply those insights to our business**.

We think the way that people learn will be vastly different over the next few years. I was in India recently and I saw a demonstration of a class being held by video conference with people participating from all around the world. That's so different from my experience of education, which was when one teacher stood up in front of the blackboard. And so we think that demand for connectivity is going to continue to grow exponentially. And that's what shapes a lot of our thinking here. We have to think about ourselves in the new world that we're moving into.

The O2 story

One day we were having a board meeting about transforming the business and I was a bit concerned about the way that the conversation might go because the agenda appeared to be focused more on cost cutting. So I wrote a narrative on a train journey to the office. I opened the board meeting by reading this story about the vision I have for customers in the future; the story was about people going through their day-to-day lives using O2 products and services enabled by the lower-cost, more efficient ways we were building to support it. I finished by saying to the board, this is what transformation is all about. Two days later we were going to a leadership conference and someone suggested that it would be very powerful just to share that story with all those employees. So I stood on stage at the leadership meeting with those same scribbled notes of paper.

Those notes started getting pretty dog-eared but we realized that there was power in having a story which wasn't about cost cutting, it was more about transformation from a business that was doing certain things very well into a business that could be better if we could do other things more efficiently. So Gav Thompson came up with the creative execution. Rather than telling one story, he came up with a number of different characters and conveyed the message through their individual stories. The point of the story behind the story is the importance for me of going back to right where we started in O2, having a narrative that runs through the business – and one that isn't about numbers.

O2ville   © 2011 O2

Gav Thompson – the brand guy

Gav joined O2 as head of brand strategy in 2007 after spending 13 years in a variety of senior roles in brand agencies.

We believe in the power of connecting people and we have a very simple belief, which is that a more connected world is a better world.

Simplify, simplify, simplify

As an industry we have a legacy that has been built up over the years on complicating things for customers. What we have tried to do is to simplify the business and **add value where the customers want it, and simplify where they don't**. For example, we don't think customers should have to wait for us to pick up the phone when they call us with a question, so we're very strong on ensuring that our customers have to wait as little time as possible, but we also acknowledge that there's no point picking up the phone within 20 seconds if we can't answer their query and they end up wasting 20 minutes because we couldn't give them an answer.

It sounds so simple but you just look at it through the customer's eyes and then make the system, the service and processes as efficient as possible around what the customer wants, not what we want.

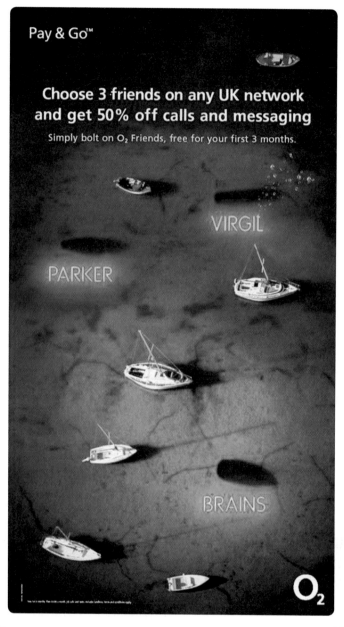

Pay & Go

Providing value to customers

The most interesting part is where we can create value for our customers. Take a simple thing like going to Twickenham to watch rugby. We invite our customers to visit us at a special O2 area where we give them a pie and a pint. So if you're an O2 customer, all you need do is text us and we'll let you into this special area, a marquee, where you'll get to meet the players and have a beer with them. It is very simple stuff: let's just give our customers a better experience watching rugby.

See how O2 provides priority access to rugby matches:
http://www.youtube.com/watch?v=Kzj-hcK8YCU

When you talk to our customers about what they like about O2, it is the incremental little touches that we're a bit better at than the other guys. One of my favourite expressions is that **if we make 10 things 10 per cent better, we become 100 per cent better**. And that's the real ethos of the company: we all want to make that 10 per cent improvement and in doing so, we become much, much better.

Be loyal to your customers

We launched our own tiered loyalty programme. We identified that our higher-spending customers felt undervalued so we decided we should give them a little bit more love than everyone else, and so now we have platinum, gold, silver and

Orbit   © 2011 O2

blue tiers, which is an idea we borrowed off the airline industry. We treat all our customers extremely well but if you're in the platinum or gold tier, you get little surprises, little extra touches, that you're not expecting; for example, you might get a call one day, inviting you to see a top act appearing at the O2 on us. That little bit of surprise and delight goes a long way.

Whenever we've developed a proposition it's always been designed bottom up. We ask: how can we make a better experience for all of our customers? And only then: what's the cherry on the cake we can deliver for our priority platinum customers? It's not how most brands do it. Most brands do something great for the top end and forget the bottom end. **The culture of O2 is incredibly democratic**; we want to give all our customers something that is a bit better than our competitors are doing. So when you visit the O2 Arena, if you are an O2 customer, any O2 customer, you don't have to queue up – you can use the VIP entrance. When you go to Twickenham to see the rugby, any of our customers can get into our private area. **What makes us different is we do put a lot of our philosophy into practice; we don't just talk about it.**

Insight first, data second

We are an insight-led business and we then use the data to either prove or disprove the insight. We don't start with data; we haven't got a lot of data crunchers in the business that study data and come up with a theory. The way it works is people like me and the marketing guys come up with a theory and then we'll use the data to either prove or disprove that. It doesn't sound like a big thing but I do think **it's significant that we are more of an instinct and insight company than a data- and process-led company**.

Most of us spend a day a month in stores; we've all adopted individual stores. So I go to my local store for a day a month and hang out with our staff but also just talk to customers with no real agenda; I'm not trying to sell them anything. Occasionally you hear a customer saying something and you think, 'Oh, I've never thought of it like that.' And so that's again the difference of O2 – rather than run a focus group, we'll go hang out in a store for a day or we'll go on the road with our sales force for a day. And that is the O2 way, it's about instinct and insight and listening; spending the day hanging out with our staff or listening to our customer care calls. A lot of us who don't necessarily work in the customer-facing part of the business spend a lot of time with customers, either actively or passively. It sounds really corny but we really do run our business with the customer at the heart of it: it's not just a marketing slogan.

Keep the customer at the heart of the business

I work in the customer directorate and our job is to wrap the business around the customer and, in doing so, work out where the weaknesses and strengths are. All of our new business ideas come out of our department whose sole job is to keep the customer at the heart of the business.

For example, we've launched a new product called 'Flow', which is a flexible travel insurance product. So rather than having to buy a fixed-rate annual policy for a family of four, we have a policy that you can dial up or dial down as your requirements change, depending whether you're in the country or out of the country, and that can be just for you or for members of your family as well. It's how travel insurance should be; it's just dead simple.

We talk to our customers in simple, clear language which demonstrate empathy and understanding of their situation. Most customers find what most mobile networks talk about confusing and complicated and they hate the hard sell of the mobile world. We've consciously moved away from all of that. We're not going to ram deals and offers down our customers' throats and confuse them with minutes and batches and bundles. We're going to talk to them about simple solutions that we think they'll understand and value. We've designed them to be the kind of things they're looking for.

Keep it simple

The reason O2 works is because it's just simple; we have a way of looking at the world, a way of treating our customers, a way of talking to our customers that's unified, which puts the customer at the heart. We believe in making it simpler, making it better and the power of connecting people. That's it.

We are more comfortable as a kind of brand that doesn't do big, bossy brand ads because we want the message to come through everything, from how our stores look and feel, how our people are when you talk to them in the contact centres, how we send you out an e-mail, how we send you a text. Success for me is every touch point we have with our customers, saying that we believe in the power of communication and connecting people.

One of my favourite sayings is: 'Don't tell me you're funny, tell me a joke.' I personally really dislike brands that just talk the talk and don't actually deliver it. So we haven't done a brand ad for two years. I won't say we are not at some point going to do another one but I think all of our ads are brand ads and all of our communications are brand communications and I'd rather there wasn't a difference. So I think the message that we're trying to convey comes from all of our touch points.

Becoming our customers' partner

As the world becomes more complicated and customers become daunted by the technology, our opportunity is to become our customers' partner on their journey of navigating the complex world of connectivity. Because of the way we see the world, because of the trust our customers have in us, because of the shared vision we have in this company, we can launch products and services that will deliver better connections and help our customers lead a better life. We like the idea of the phone being an interface between you and the connected world.

It may sound a bit silly, but **we believe that our future lies in giving our customers some love**. We believe that if we love our customers, then they'll love us back. We think customer satisfaction is a blunt measure; we talk about fans and fandom. The idea that when we become fans of our customers, they will become fans of ours is a notion that drives the business.

We've gone out to all of our people and talked about giving our customers some love. Most companies don't talk about loving their customers; they talk about giving a better service, getting a better customer satisfaction index score: but when you have a great brand experience with a Virgin Atlantic or whoever, you come away from that experience feeling like you've got some affection, an emotional connection with that brand. Now I think that's a really powerful, bold, idea. That actually the key to greater brand loyalty, the key to greater levels of diversification in our business is love. I think that's a bold thing for a mobile network to strive for.

Bold lessons

It only works when it all works

Ronan Dunne's phrase captures the essence of an experience brand: it isn't about the marketing, it isn't about the product, it isn't about the service; it is everything that you do. And it all has to work together.

Yin and yang

It seems a strange concept to apply to a modern corporate but in order to really set yourself apart from the crowd you need to manage the hard and the soft, the inside and the outside, the people and the processes. O2 is a company that is expected by its parent, Telefónica, to deliver against some very tough commercial goals. But executives also talk about 'fans' and 'love'. As Gav Thompson says, 'we believe that our future lies in giving our customers some love'. One of the things we are seeing is that the narrow, accountancy-based, scientific view of the world taught so often by the business schools is being overshadowed by some of the values that motivated the founders of many of the great brands in the past.

Create a virtuous cycle

Like many of the other bold brands, O2 shares a belief in a virtuous cycle of happy employees, happy customers and happy shareholders. But this doesn't mean focusing on your employee experience and trusting everything else will follow. We believe that the business must be driven from the customer back. Start by designing the customer experience and then align the employee experience with it. Happy employees make for happy customers but you need to design your business model the other way round. That is why it's a cycle, not a linear process.

It's about what you do, not what you say you do

'Don't tell me you're funny, tell me a joke.' So much of advertising has been about making promises; we believe that the future is going to belong to those brands that deliver their promise through every touch point. O2 doesn't do big ads that talk about 'Helping customers connect'; it creates an experience that actually helps them to do so.

Experiential marketing

O2 places much more store on viral and experiential marketing than on traditional media. The licensing of the O2 Arena was a bold move but one that has created huge amounts of awareness and goodwill for the brand. There is only one O2 Arena so, once again, it is very hard for competitors to copy.

The courage of conviction

As Ronan Dunne says, 'To build a trust relationship with customers you have to be really clear in your communication. You have to be bold to change the rules of the game. You have to take risks.' That means having the courage of your conviction. Most organizations talk about customer loyalty when what they really mean is customer retention, all too often achieved through erecting barriers to exit. True loyalty comes from the organization being loyal to its customers by giving them value they can't get anywhere else and then making it easy for them to leave. And guess what? Just as in any affectionate relationship, they don't. Simplicity and Fair Deal are two O2 propositions that liberate the customer from the restrictive practices of the industry.

Measure what matters

That takes us on to the last learning point, which is to measure what matters. In the case of O2 they measure 'fandom', which is a very high bar to jump. It essentially means those customers who are so loyal to the brand that they will stick with it through thick and thin. You don't desert your favourite team because they lose a game. You don't desert your favourite brand because they don't have the latest and coolest device.

See how O2 has changed the rules of the industry; click here:
http://www.youtube.com/watch?v=JEZTvnX1n2k

The breakthrough for O2 was when it began thinking of itself not as a phone company but as a brand that connects people with the things that matter most to them. And that is a thought that our next bold brand shares.

Chapter Three
AirAsia X

Somebody once said that if you want to make a million dollars in the airline industry, start with two million. The fact is that the industry is one of the toughest to make money in. Tony Fernandes, the CEO of AirAsia, took a slightly different route: he mortgaged his house and together with some friends and investors bought AirAsia, a moribund airline carrying RM40 million (Malaysian ringgit) or US$12.5 million of debt in 2001. In 2009, the airline earned a net profit of over RM500 million (US$ 161 million).

AirAsia quickly established itself as one of Asia's leading airlines. With its promise of 'Now everyone can fly' it has extended operations to 20 countries around Asia. Its bold vision led to the carrier ordering 200 new aircraft from Airbus in the midst of the recession. It has won numerous awards, most recently being voted best low-cost carrier in the world in both 2009 and 2010.

So how does an airline charge significantly less than its competitors and still make money? The answer, so far, has been to unbundle the price of the ticket and charge customers accordingly, a model adopted by Southwest Airlines, easyJet, Ryanair and AirAsia.

But whilst passengers might be willing to forgo food and amenities for a short flight, it is a different proposition when flying between continents. AirAsia X is the answer. It is the only long-haul carrier that offers flat-bed seats, seat-back entertainment and Asian-style service at a price 60 per cent lower than competitors. It is committed to offering X-citing low fares, X-emplary levels of safety and care and an X-traordinary service experience.

AirAsia X was started in 2007. Its purpose is to extend the brand to long-haul destinations and build brand awareness in Australia and Europe. The airline has announced plans for an IPO in the second half of 2011 to provide funding for growth independently of its parent. The IPO is also intended to ensure that the business models remain pure. As Tony Fernandes said recently, 'If you keep them together they contaminate each other.'

Hear more on AirAsia's X plans. Click here:
http://www.cnbc.com/id/15840232?video=1523010493&play=1

AAX A330   © 2011 AirAsia X

Bold practices

AirAsia

- AirAsia was the first airline in the world to eliminate fuel surcharges.
- In 2009 it offered a million free one-way tickets, with 400,000 being snapped up within 24 hours.
- AirAsia ordered 200 new Airbus aircraft in the depths of the recession.
- At the time of writing, AirAsia is the number-one ranking Facebook account in the transportation field.
- AirAsiaRedTix.com is the portal where customers can book music and entertainment and download, music, videos and news.

- AirAsia's vision:
  - to be the largest low-cost airline in Asia and serving the 3 billion people who are currently underserved with poor connectivity and high fares.
- AirAsia's mission:
  - to be the best company to work for, in which employees are treated as part of a big family;
  - to create a globally recognized ASEAN brand;
  - to attain the lowest cost so that everyone can fly with AirAsia;
  - to maintain the highest-quality product, embracing technology to reduce cost and enhance service levels.
- AirAsia X launched the first SMS booking service in the airline industry
- AirAsia X launched FlatBed premium seats that are available on all of its long-haul flights.

Azran Osman-Rani – the CEO

Azran became CEO of AirAsia X in 2007. He was formerly senior director of business development for Astro All Asian Networks, a digital satellite and radio broadcaster.

AirAsia X is an interesting story because it's about taking the low-cost airline model and applying it to long-haul operations, and doing this when everyone in the entire aviation industry said it cannot be done. The so-called experts, Southwest Airlines, easyJet, Ryanair said 'This won't work. It's against the model. We're not going to do it.' Aviation experts point to a number of reasons why they think it cannot be done and a number of people have tried and failed, from Freddie Laker in the UK in the 1970s to People's Express in the US in the 1980s, and more recently, Oasis in Hong Kong.

Is there a better way of running an airline?

So what we did is to create a business model from almost a blank sheet of paper. When we started we even looked at some of the existing AirAsia practices and said, 'No, we're not going to do that, we're going to change and do things completely differently.' We brought in a team made up of people with airline experience, and some like myself, who have zero airline experience. **We really just started to question every single thing about the airline model** and asking if there was a different way of doing it.

We believed that there are a number of fundamental assumptions driving the way airlines operate that we decided to challenge. We believe that if you give people a much lower fare, more people will travel. And the second thing we believe is that there is a way of operating at a dramatically lower cost than other airlines because they tend to be very homogeneous in their business model: everybody does things a certain way. And so we re-examined all the aspects of how you fly long haul, and launched AirAsia X in probably what has been the most challenging macro-environment in history. We are at the stage where even with the small number of planes in our fleet, we've got the world's lowest unit-cost level, significantly lower. In 2009 our unit cost was 2.8 US cents per available seat-kilometre. By contrast Singapore Airlines is about 6 cents, Cathay Pacific is about 7 cents, BA and Qantas are at about 8 cents per seat-kilometre. So at an operating cost of 2.8 cents, we are not talking about a 20 per cent or 30 per cent reduction, where the big boys can discount price and squeeze us out of the market. It is great being able to say, 'Wow, we're in a profitable position, growing very, very rapidly over the last three years in an unfavourable macro-environment.'

The customer insight

Our breakthrough insight is that the entire long-haul aviation industry has been focused on what I call the 'time-sensitive, price-insensitive' customer, whereas we've built an airline model around the 'price-sensitive, time-insensitive' customer, which was a segment that's basically been previously untapped. Let me explain. Aviation has always had its origins in serving the premium end of the market. Flying 30 years ago was about fine china, white linen, silverware: the whole glamorous experience. Over the years airlines have evolved but still continue to cater primarily to the premium market: business class passengers – that's where they make the bulk of their revenue. But to do that you have to fly when the business passenger prefers to travel. Just to give you an example, Cathay Pacific on average report their aircraft utilization rate at about 12 hours a day. So, that means, in a year, the planes are in the air only half the time, the other half of the year they are sitting on the ground. We fly in excess of 17 hours a day; that's a big difference. How do we achieve this difference? For the past 50 years airlines have been thinking about the premium customer. The premium customer wants two things: they're very fussy about the time that they depart and the time that they arrive. So that's why you see most long-haul flights leaving Asian airports close to midnight. 'Boom!' – all the big jumbo jets are flying out at the same time so that the flights that leave Singapore arrive in London or Sydney early in the morning. The planes then just sit there and wait until they are needed again, clocking up hugely expensive parking charges in the meantime. A premium passenger does not like to wake up at 3 o'clock in the morning to catch a 7.30 am return flight back to Singapore, so the plane waits for a more convenient time for the passengers to fly back. That means a lot more down time than is necessary.

Change the business model

What we've learnt is that you just can't simply take existing low-cost models, not even AirAsia's, because the AirAsia, Ryanair and easyJet business model is about point-to-point traffic. Now, you can do that with smaller planes over short distances. But when you fly long distances, you physically have to use a big plane with the fuel capacity to take you over that range, and the economics only work when you can fill up the plane. The problem then is that there isn't enough premium point-to-point traffic from even London and Singapore, which is why all the airlines came up with this massive hub-and-spoke system – which carries a lot of cost. The other thing that is important for the premium customer is seamless connectivity. You need code-sharing partners, which means getting systems to talk to one another. The premium customer is also very fussy about feeder connections, so, for example, the flight from Sydney to Singapore connects with the Singapore to London flight with a minimum 90 minutes connecting time, allowing his bags to be transferred.

The industry thought we were mad

Our very first route on AirAsia X was to the Gold Coast of Australia and people thought we were mad. They thought we were mad on four counts. Number one, to start an airline. Number two, to start an airline with only one plane. Number three, to use an unproven low-cost long-haul model. And number four, to fly to the Gold Coast in Australia, which is a very tourist-focused destination and very sea-sonal during holiday periods. So how on earth are you going to fill up a very large wide-bodied plane flying to a very small beach resort 365 days of the year? Well, it actually works because a significant percentage of our passengers are not just ending their journey on the Gold Coast; they're flying off to a number of places including, interestingly, Sydney. Now, what's interesting about Sydney is our flights leave Kuala Lumpur at night, arriving in the Gold Coast at 7 o'clock in the morning and within 60 to 75 minutes they fly back to Kuala Lumpur. There is no flight from Sydney to the Gold Coast that will get you in early enough to catch our flight out of the Gold Coast, yet 8 per cent of our passengers were flying in from Sydney. What they were doing was flying in the night before and either staying with friends, staying in a hotel – some were even sleeping on the beach – to catch the morning flight. What was interesting is there was another so-called low-cost long-haul ser-vice flying direct from Sydney to Kuala Lumpur. When we asked our passengers why they chose to fly with us when the total journey time now is 20 hours instead of eight hours, they said it's because there is a A$150 dollars price difference. At a saving of A$150 per person, if you have a family of four you save A$600 and that is enough to cover your entire week's hotel stay in Malaysia. So, some people who travel are very price sensitive and time insensitive.

By serving this market we can keep the plane flying. We've perfected the art of getting over 300 people off the plane as soon as it touches down, getting it refuelled, restocked, 300 people back on and flying again. So the whole economics changes by utilizing our aircraft more, allowing us to offer low prices and good service.

Show us the data

When we held our first investment evening we had a number of private equity firms attend and they asked us, 'What's your market research telling you? Where's the data to prove that there's a demand for this?' We had none of that. So we said to them, 'You've been to travel fairs and seen that when someone's offered a £300 fare from Kuala Lumpur to London, grandmothers push and shove each other just to grab these few fares. So imagine if you could offer that fare consistently throughout the year.' We simply had this belief about price elasticity. That was our only market research.

Tony Fernandes, the founder of AirAsia and AirAsia X, then had to prove it worked. He brought in people from different experiences, different industries, different age groups, but with a skew to younger people. Our chief engineer is 35, our chief pilot is 41, our head of legal and HR is 36. So our team is made up of young people who otherwise would not get the opportunity to take on these responsibilities. I was brought in as CEO with no previous airline experience. The number-one reason is probably my ability to ask 'Why?' and 'Why not?' and keep challenging people. Coming from a very varied background in different industries allowed me to bring that to the table. Experience with start-ups definitely helped. Getting stakeholders – particularly prospective investors – regulators, government officials and, very importantly, internal people aligned is critical.

Keep it simple

One of our key values was making it very easy for everyone in the organization to really understand what this business is about. Still today, we share very simple KPIs. **We don't try to make decisions complex; we try to simplify**. I keep telling the team, 'Just remember "one, two, three".' Number one: we want to get to $1 billion within five years because thinking of top-line growth and reaching scale in this business is very important. Number two: we've got to get our cost structure down to 2 US cents per available seat-kilometre and keep everyone very cost focused because this is about breaking new ground. Number three: three out of every four seats must be filled and three out of every four hours the plane must be in the air. So that makes our strategy very easy for everyone to understand.

Using social media to sell an experience

A key difference from other airlines is our extensive use of digital channels and social media. AirAsia has about a 75 per cent share of sales coming through the internet, which is higher than most airlines. AirAsia X has 89 per cent, so it's very high and we are engaging people all over the world, from Australia, the UK, Europe, China, India and so forth. Another way we are different is we are selling an experience. We started with just one or two destinations yet we outspend Malaysia Airlines on advertising. They may have more than double the number of flights to Australia that we do, yet we spend more than double what they spend on advertising; selling the excitement of long-haul travel to exciting destinations. We're trying to sell the experience of faraway travel; it's not about people commuting for business. When we sell flights in Australia we tell them, 'You've got three of Condé Nast's top ten islands on your doorstep: Bali, Langkawi, Phuket. You've got exciting cities: Bangkok, Singapore, Kuala Lumpur, Hong Kong. So with AirAsia's cheap fares you can go shopping in KL; go to Phuket for a beach holiday; visit Angkor Wat for sightseeing. It is this multi-destination variety that is really changing the way people travel and you begin to get a community built up around your brand.

Changing the way people travel

One of the things I think is interesting is how people consume travel now. In the old days, if you wanted to go on a holiday, you would have planned for it months ahead, discussed it with your family and then you'd decide where and when you wanted to go. Finally you would find the airfare and hotel on the website or by calling a travel agent. But now we have a huge following of customers, with over two million people signed up as members of AirAsia. People now wait for special offers or sales before they make their travel plans. Recently we offered one million free seats and the whole world was abuzz. People log on, they don't know where they want to go, they don't know when they want to go; they just grab a seat. They might think, 'I'm going to try to get a free ticket to Bali.' But Bali's filled up – so they are offered a deal to Vientiane and they just grab it. 'It doesn't matter it's only available in October; I got it first. I don't even know where Vientiane is; maybe it's in Austria, maybe it's in South East Asia; it doesn't matter, I'm grabbing it.' And then they decide, 'Okay, now that I've got the ticket I'd better speak with my boss and take leave.' So our economic model totally flips the purchase process.

Building customer communities

We love the idea of building communities and try and focus on at least three specific verticals that relate to travel. Number one is sports; that's why you see AirAsia being associated with a lot of sporting events and sports as a lifestyle. People thought Tony was completely crazy sponsoring Manchester United in 2005 when we had no flights serving the UK market. Take the Oakland Raiders football team – again people say, 'What on earth is AirAsia doing with the Oakland Raiders football team?' But it's driven by the idea that if you make these brands part of

Tony, Azran and team

your global network people start to associate that lifestyle with your own. The second sector we associate with is music and entertainment, and the third is youth. Youth and university students and the whole lifestyle of travelling, learning and experiencing life are three things that we are very focused on. So we love the idea of flying people to London to catch the Rolling Stones concert at the O2 Arena, or watch Arsenal play live, or watch the MotoGP. It's about lifestyle, an aspirational lifestyle.

Leveraging the brand

The other major difference between AirAsia X and other brands is that we have set ourselves the objective of earning 50 per cent of our revenues from non-airline-related sources. That requires us to think of big and bold ideas if we want to stretch ourselves to achieve 50 per cent. The traditional way of looking at what we in the industry call ancillary income is earning money from small incremental things: selling food or merchandise or T-shirts. That might earn you 3 per cent or 4 per cent in revenue but it's not big and it certainly won't get you to 50 per cent. We don't have all the answers yet but we're thinking completely differently and looking at other opportunities. One is AirAsia Courier. We have seen how much people are paying to send packages on DHL or UPS or FedEx at what we think are unnecessarily high rates. If we could offer air shipping at 50 per cent, 60 per cent less than these brands, that would create more reasons for people to send packages. We think that could take off, particularly in Asia because it's not common practice to send stuff by air.

The second opportunity is AirAsia.com. Now that we've built a community we can be a point of access, where people can come for exciting, exclusive access to interesting events. Some may fly; some may not need to. But they start thinking about us as the place to get tickets to lifestyle events. At AirAsia we want to be more than just an airline that takes you from point A to point B; we want to be a lifestyle brand.

See AirAsia's access to music and entertainment: http://redtix.airasia.com/

The challenge of growth

We've experienced quite a few challenges. The big ones are the macroeconomic situation, what's happening with Europe and the Euro debt crisis, and whether we are going to have more volcanic eruptions. I'm less fussed about these things, though, because they affect all competitors equally. The airlines who are going to survive are the ones who are better able to execute, are more nimble, more agile and have the cost structure to absorb these shocks. So, while those things worry us, they won't change our strategy. For me the bigger challenges are sustaining the pace of growth, building a team that can take us into completely new markets. We were very deliberate in our early years of focusing only on Australia and China, so we added more cities and flights rather than spreading ourselves too thin. But now we've got to a stage of where the next market is India and that's a completely different culture. Towards the end of the year we're now looking at Korea and Japan, each with very distinct language, culture and distribution challenges. And that means building a global team from scratch.

Connecting people to a purpose

AirAsia has a slogan: 'Now everyone can fly.' The AirAsia X version is 'Now everyone can fly Xtra long.' People join us not because we're the greatest payers in the industry but because of this challenge of building something new that allows people to travel to faraway places and make the world a smaller place. There is the story of the grandmother who flew on an aeroplane for the very first time in her life to meet her granddaughter in Australia, whom she had never seen. We have families that remain united because of AirAsia X. A student living in London would not otherwise be able to afford to return home but now can come back home for his sister's wedding. These are the things that our people are really motivated by. **Let's keep connecting the world and make it a much smaller place.**

London Launch Bus

To connect with Azran on Twitter click here:
http://twitter.com/azranosmanrani

To hear Azran talk on how AirAsia X is changing the rules
of the industry, click here:
http://www.cnbc.com/id/15840232?video=1398864304

Moses Devanayagam – director of operations

Moses joined AirAsia X as director of operations after 41 years in the airline industry in a variety of senior operational roles.

The first thing I noticed when I walked in here was the simplicity. Simplicity is everything we do. For example, I had a small desk compared with a huge office with a big table and secretaries sitting outside. That was a culture shock for me.

Simplicity rules

From the office set-up to the way things are discussed, and to the way things are put into the system, **it's all very, very simple**. My old company had a very traditional way of thinking: lots and lots of meetings, rules and processes. Here we look at a problem or an issue; if we can resolve it among one or two people, it gets done: finished. For example, if we want to improve the boarding process for passengers, one or two people might get together, look at the problem and somebody will say, 'Why don't we have staggered boarding?' Someone else might say 'Okay, guys, let's do it,' and that's how it's decided.

Of course, some issues are more complex and we will consult with people from various departments. For example, despite the recession AirAsia has placed orders for 180 new A320s, 25 A330s and 10 A350s. Ordering over 200 new aircraft in a downturn is quite bold but we are looking at it from the point that we need aircraft for the future. We are always very positive about the growth of the airline industry, and that is why we decided that we might as well order planes now.

Multitasking is a way of life at AirAsia

We have talked about simplicity; the other thing I noticed as soon as I walked in was multitasking. **Everybody does everything themselves.** Never in my life, in all my years in airlines, did I ever need to photocopy something myself.

By multi-tasking, the numbers are greatly reduced throughout the various positions that normally other airlines would have filled. In other airlines, I had 10 guys directly reporting to me. Now I only have to have three or four people reporting to me. We have a very basic, simple reporting structure, with very few people in line, and that goes all the way down. A lot of things in the company are automated and that cuts down layers and the work that needs to be done.

Low cost doesn't mean poor service

Unlike some other low-cost carriers, service matters to us. We keep emphasizing to our people we must have repeat customers. If a person has a horrendous experience at our hands, even though it's through no fault of AirAsia because of weather or whatever, we don't want these passengers to be left with a bad taste in their mouth about our brand. The incident in 2010 when UK air space was closed because of the volcanic eruption is a good example. We had to suspend our operations for six days and because of that, lots of passengers were stranded in Kuala Lumpur. We knew that people at that particular point needed communication. They needed to know what was happening. So the first thing we did was update the passengers by asking them to go to our website for the latest information. We also took the e-mail addresses and mobile phone numbers of the passengers who turned up at the airport so we could contact them. We told them: 'Because this is beyond the airline's control, it's an act of God, we cannot provide you with hotels, but unlike the other low-cost airlines, what we will do is make the arrangements for you using our own contracted rates because we know you will be mercilessly overcharged by the hotels otherwise. We will even arrange transportation from the hotels to pick you up so that you do not get overcharged.'

Those who remained at the terminal were given water and meal vouchers for the first day and quite a number of them decided to make the low-cost terminal their home. As I walked around, I saw a lot of people, some with children, putting newspapers down and sitting on them. We sell comfort kits, blankets and so on, so we distributed them free of charge. They really valued that. When flights started operating we said, 'There are thousands of you here, but each flight can only take 286 passengers. We've got to prioritize.' We created additional flights, we managed to get more aircraft and we did what we could to treat our passengers as human beings. That was something many of the passengers appreciated, because they thought our being a low-cost carrier meant we were just going to dump them.

Low cost doesn't mean low employee morale

The feeling of being a family is very important here. People work for the best part of the day together in the office. **Our business model will only work if they pull together as a team** and, to do that, you have to be a team player. We keep telling our people, 'If you work solo, it only works once in a while. You're going to fall flat. If you work as a team, somebody will be there to pull you up.' That has been the success of AirAsia. They are like a big family here. I am the old grandfather; looking after them, their needs and requirements, working with them from Monday to Friday. I say to them, 'The week is done, have a good rest over the weekend and come back on Monday recharged. We still have a lot more to do at AirAsia.'

Datin Shelina Razaly Wahi – director of legal and people

Shelina joined AirAsia from Astro All Asia Networks and before that she was in the oil and gas industry.

Our heads of operations, engineering and flight operations are all highly experienced people with a very technical background. But if you look at Azran, who came from Astro and consulting before that, and myself coming from oil and gas, and our first CFO, who came from a construction company, it is clear that we have not restricted ourselves to just taking people from aviation. You do need people with the technical knowledge, but we have tried to be creative and attract people with other strengths. If you look at our corporate team, whether we're talking about our strategy people, some of our analysts, or even in finance, there are actually very few who have an aviation background. Moses is probably our most senior manager, both in terms of age and in terms of his vast experience in aviation, but the average age of the team in AirAsia X is only about 34, which is pretty low, compared with most other of the established airlines around.

So we have not been constrained by age or background, and we have recognized that it's important to give people the opportunity to prove themselves. We have a very young and energetic team for the most part, and we've found that **when you give people the chance, they tend to live up to it**.

A culture of openness

We're a very open company. If you look at the way our management meetings are run, everybody talks; there are no restrictions. It's not a case that I represent legal and HR, so I'm only allowed to talk on legal or HR matters. In fact, because of this I've learned a lot more about engineering and operations and flight ops than I ever thought.

We have a very open culture. Anyone can approach anyone else. You have engineers going up to Azran to ask a question. We've got this huge white board, right in the middle of our office, which has the key KPIs that the company is working to this year, and the reason for that is so that everybody knows what our targets are. It's not a case that you're an engineer and therefore you only ever have to worry about engineering, or you're in finance, so you don't need to know what engineering is doing. Everything is related, and the idea is to make everyone feel that we are all chasing the same targets, so you're not just working in your own little corner, but you're part of a much bigger picture.

As a result, when there is a crisis, for example, such as we had to cancel flights because of the volcanic ash cloud over Europe, it's not just the operations team who get involved, it's everyone. It was all hands on deck, engineers, finance people, even office administrators were coming down to see what they could do to help, whether it was supplying bottles of water to stranded passengers, or trying to help passengers who had difficulties because they were running out of medicine or whatever. I see teamwork here happening at a very different level from any other company I've been in. Now, the size of our business has grown, and so has the size of our staff, although I still think that if you compare us with other airlines, we probably have a much smaller corporate office, and even though we now have more people on board, and we're now more structured in terms of job divisions, we haven't lost that family feeling. There's still a lot of exchange of information, a lot of sharing, and that translates into everybody pulling together whenever we need them to.

Hiring for fit

In terms of bringing in people, what we've found is that in the past we've made some mistakes. We recruited some brilliant people from a technical point of view, but they were not able to fit into the organization. So more recently, **what we've been looking for really is fit**: a kind of personality that is AirAsia. So for example, we're taking on a new CFO, and one of the things that most of us liked about her is the fact that although she has a very strong CFO background, her current position is as a COO, so she understands business and operations, not just finance. When we asked her, 'What do you like about your current job?' she said, 'Oh, I like the fact that I'm learning about the business, that I'm exposed to everything and that I'm not constrained.' That's exactly the kind of person we're looking for. We're not in a hurry to recruit, particularly for senior hires, so we are trying to make sure we get the fit right.

Lean, not mean

Our highest costs are in relation to engineering. Another huge cost relates to the allowances of the crew, whether it's the pilot or flight attendants. Another big chunk is fuel, so if you add all that up, and then you look at the HR cost and head-count, they are not really a major proportion compared to everything else. So if you look at it from that perspective, we don't have to unduly constrain ourselves in terms of the way we treat our people. We recognize that there is a need to recognize outstanding performance. It isn't always financial. It's amazing how far just taking somebody for lunch gets you. If you take a group of people for lunch and congratulate them in front of their colleagues, it makes a huge difference.

Bold lessons

Challenge the current beliefs

Most of the airline industry works on the belief of the 'time-sensitive, price-insensitive' passenger. Observing how some customers would accept less convenience for a lower price led to the insight that there is a market of 'time-insensitive, price-sensitive' customers. This insight led AirAsia X to completely change the operating model, achieving utilization levels its competitors can only dream about.

Simplify your strategy

By having costs some 60 per cent lower than competitors, AirAsia X is able to insulate itself from short-term price pressure that its larger competitors might impose. The fact is that this differential makes it impossible for competitors to come anywhere near AirAsia X's fare levels. Having arrived at a bold strategy, make it easy for your people to remember it: as easy as remembering 'one, two, three', as Azran told us. It also makes it simple to measure.

Low cost doesn't mean low class

There is an old saying: 'You can have it cheap, you can have it fast, you can have it good – but never all three.' All too often organizations believe that there is a trade-off to be made between service and cost, speed and quality, focus on culture versus focus on customers. What we can learn from AirAsia X and the other bold brands is that in fact you can have it all if you think innovatively enough. AirAsia X's innovative products, processes and people all set the brand apart and work together to achieve low-cost, superior product and friendly service.

Innovative marketing

AirAsia has embraced innovative marketing techniques – from sponsoring Manchester United before the airline even had a presence in the UK, to having a six-figure fan base on Facebook.

Don't invent it if you don't have to

A high-profile flamboyant CEO, attractive stewardesses in striking red uniforms, high-tech entertainments systems, comfortable flat beds; sound familiar? You might think that we were describing Virgin Atlantic. In fact AirAsia X has adopted much more of the style of Virgin than it has its Asian competitors. No surprise then that Tony Fernandes, the founder of AirAsia, used to work in Branson's music business and Virgin owns 16 per cent of the Asian carrier.

Make the culture fit the business model

Hiring young people who are used to being self-sufficient and are unfamiliar with industry practices, breaking down silos, encouraging people to take responsibility; all of these practices serve to increase innovation and reduce costs. The fact is that your culture needs to be very carefully crafted to support your business strategy. When one is a mirror for the other you get a self-reinforcing effect.

Leverage the brand

When you have a powerful brand, make it work for you! A brand can become much more than the product you happen to start by selling. Ask Virgin or O2. By linking your brand to the lifestyles and aspirations of your customers you become a trusted friend to them. We believe that increasingly brands will become 'curators' for their customers, able to guide them on the many aspects of their lives because of the insight those brands have about them.

See AirAsia's access to music and entertainment:
http://redtix.airasia.com/

Another brand that is a portal to entertainment is Chilli Beans, the subject of our next chapter, which invites its customers to enter into its world...

Chapter Four
Chilli Beans

As we travel the world giving speeches and conducting workshops we are constantly looking out for new, hot, brands – the Virgins of the future. We were in São Paulo a year or so ago and were invited to the launch of a new advertising campaign for a brand called Chilli Beans, a fashion accessory retailer. The launch was held in a top night club and the venue was chock-full of employees, customers, franchisees and partners. The interesting thing was that we couldn't tell the difference between them – they all looked like they belonged to the same club. There seems to be a vibe about Chilli Beans that is mainlined into the music and fashion culture of Brazil.

The brand was started by Caito Maia in 1994. He had been studying music at the University of California and he observed how students would wear sunglasses as a fashion accessory rather than for eye protection. When Caito returned to Brazil he started importing and selling sunglasses to friends before becoming a wholesale supplier to retail stores and designers. In 1996, Caito decided to dedicate himself exclusively to the retail eyewear market. In 2006 he was chosen as the outstanding Brazilian in the 'Commercial, economic and/or business success' category of the Junior Chamber International Organization.

Today the brand has over 270 exclusive outlets in Brazil, in addition to points of sale in Portugal and the United States. It also sponsors shows, music festivals, sports and social events. The brand expects to have 500 outlets by 2013.

See:
http://www.youtube.com/watch?v=JrnoNRgbh1A

Sunglasses

Bold practices

Chilli Beans

- Chilli Beans uses a 'digital mirror': cameras fitted to flat touch screens to film customers and freeze their image, allowing them to compare sunglasses more easily and send images to their friends for comment.

- The brand sponsors music, festivals and sporting events.

- The Chilli Beans website streams its own music station.

- Ten new designs of sunglasses and watches are launched every week. There are so many designs that customers search for them on the website by launch date.

- They 'threw away' their procedures manual and relied on natural spontaneity and the 'brand essence' to ensure a consistent experience.

- No products are heroed in their advertising – instead adverts show the 'Chilli Beans universe'.

Caito Maia – the founder

Caito   © 2011 Chilli Beans

Caito started the brand in 1996 and is currently CEO.

I love sunglasses. I think they're cool, I enjoy wearing them. I've always worn them the same way as we now sell them; thinking about them as fashion items that can complement a particular mood or style. And that is our brand concept – to sell a range of affordable sunglasses as fashion accessories that can suit your style.

Create a strong brand

From the very beginning the idea was to create a strong brand. In my opinion, the most important part of Chilli Beans is the brand concept. Once you get that, you can do whatever you want; you can create a lifestyle. So our first step was to work with the brand to create an impact in the market. The second step was focusing on accessories to support the core business. Chilli Beans is already the biggest sunglasses brand with the highest sales in Latin America; our objective now is to become one of the five biggest accessory companies in the world.

The store is the experience

The store is a fundamental element of the proposition. We have a self-service, open-display format where the clients feel comfortable trying out new styles. We have 10 new models each week, every week. But it's not only about the glasses. A store must offer more than just product. Our customers come into our stores not necessarily looking for glasses. They're observing what's going on around them: our salespeople's clothes, the parties we sponsor, the music we play.

We're a 'mutant' company. I don't follow any stereotype; I'm not fancy, I'm not modern. I'm democratic and mutant. People like to define us as audacious, modern, but I don't really feel the need to be defined, I don't need a stereotype, a qualification. I believe it's a big risk for a company to create any sort of label for themselves because the world is changing so fast that if you become defined by a label you'll have very hard work for the rest of your life to live up to it and at some point you'll have market problems as a result. If you put a label on yourself you may get stuck with a concept that doesn't work any longer.

Spontaneity is key

We developed a booklet, a sort of procedures manual we were supposed to give to our salespeople. I took a look at it and said: 'Let's throw it away!' First of all Chilli Beans has got its own brand essence and we're constantly checking on it, and this checking covers everything from new products to how we say hello or thank you to our customers – treating them with respect. **We must also understand and respect our own people's personalities; we must allow them to be who they really are.** Their spontaneity coupled with their positive feelings for the brand is a perfect combination which ensures they do the right thing for our customers.

There's something very simple and honest about spontaneity. It's just something that happens naturally. I believe it's quite simple but people often make it very complicated. I don't deliberately set out to be innovative... I only want to use the things I like myself. I always ask my designers to be inspired by simple things, such as a picture, a toy. I want to know from my people what they like themselves. This is what I call 'the truth', and nowadays consumers are increasingly looking for that. Years ago, when we went to the mall our mental reference for sunglasses would be an image of Ray-Ban but I'm sure that if today you take your child to a mall he/she is more likely to take away the image of a colourful Chilli Beans store with all the products on display. So the intention is to take an idea that is already successful and then project it to the future to make it even more successful. In three years our objective is to have at least 500 stores. Every month I record some videos that are shown on our extranet site. But there's nothing better than being there in person. So every year, my team and I visit all of our stores.

Everything can be changed

I'm completely open to new ideas. I told the marketing director that everything in this company is changeable, and that includes me. Everything can change. Chilli Beans stores are top in sunglasses, so we'll create a different brand to develop new things. I launched the 'Four worlds' of Chilli Beans and I have no idea what will happen to them. Let's see how the market reacts. One of them has already become a branded music festival – Virus Chilli Beans. There are many business books in the market 'teaching' strategies to be successful but I believe that each company must have its own particular story. What works for you may not work for me, and I respect that. You have your story and I have mine.

Mario Ponci Neto (Marinho) – the expansion and new business director

Mario has been with the brand from the beginning and is responsible for marketing.

Since the very beginning Chilli Beans has had a sort of 'naivety' to it. I'll try to explain what I mean by that. When Chilli Beans started there wasn't a business plan detailing how big the brand would be or how many stores would be opened, there was nothing like that. Actually none of us, Caito, Vanessa or myself, had any financial background or resources to start a business. None of us had any money. I had some knowledge of franchising, Vanessa had a retail background and Caito had an entrepreneur's mindset. Caito used to buy glasses when he was studying in the States and sell them in Brazil to friends and to stores. He is a charismatic person; he has great ideas, values, and he's a guy capable of making things happen, but he needed the right organization to put the ideas into practice. So we decided to use our natural talents, plus good sense. We've always worked with good sense. But we didn't have good strategic plans.

Brand trust

We've always worked with the truth. We didn't want to sell the most expensive product; we wanted to sell what was really good for the customer. What we needed most was the trust of our customers and to eliminate the idea that retailers are out to 'cheat' their customers by selling them product that is not right for them. We would never do that. We know a lot about our glasses: which ones go with a specific skin colour, face shape, hair and so on, and we will always give an honest opinion. The sale becomes a consequence of that; we are almost a consultancy. We want to create the same trust with our customers that a doctor has with his patients. The brand needs this trust because we don't want our customers to think about buying sunglasses – we want them to think about buying Chilli Beans. Trust means that if you don't like our product for whatever reason you can return it. And we don't care about specific consumer laws: we'll change the product or give you your money back.

We have an internal joke that when a customer enters our store he or she is what they would like to buy. Talk to a person with, and then without, glasses and you'll know what I mean. Glasses give you a sort of protection. When you wear them you feel confident. People wearing glasses are more outgoing, they show who they really are. So when Caito is developing a collection he focuses on that all the time. He looks at the glasses and describes the type of person who might buy them: their face, their style, their attitude. From the beginning the collection came from Caito's mind, his ideas. The processes could not influence the person, the person needed to influence the processes. Now we produce 10 to 12 new designs each week in three or four colours and they need to be manufactured and distributed to our 270 stores. We opened 55 new stores last year and we will open at least 50 this year, so good processes are important to us, but they must not replace the creative insight that we started with.

Creating the Chilli Beans world

What we've built is not a company; it's our universe, our world. You must use your four senses to experience it and as you become part of the brand you'll have a visual experience, you will smell it, feel it or hear it. If I tell you something, it's completely different from letting you experience it for yourself. When you experience the Chilli Beans world, you become involved with the brand.

Our objective has always been building a brand, creating our own universe, and we have invested a lot in it. Customers want glasses with identity – that's why they won't buy copies or fake glasses. It is our high investment in the brand that keeps us protected. We've always focused and valued the brand. Our typical customer will purchase every three months or so and will own four or five pairs of sunglasses. We've got a Chilli Beans fan club and the members will purchase a lot more than the average customer, sometimes the whole collection.

When we advertise we don't show our products, we show our 'world' – our identity. In the last campaign we focused on our 'Four worlds': 'Play', 'Gasoline', 'Royale' and 'Virus'. 'Play' is more sports-like. 'Gasoline' is based on a street style; it doesn't mean you are like that necessarily, it just means you're in the mood for that style. 'Royale' is more formal, elegant. 'Virus' is more about fun, going to

Chilli Beans store   © 2011 Chilli Beans

a rave, a party. When we created the four worlds the idea was not that you are put into one of them, the idea is that you can be in the mood for any or all of them. So for each world we are creating products with specific characteristics such as colour, music, events. The worlds in our Chilli Beans universe allow you to be a part of any of them according to your mood.

> To experience Chilli Beans for yourself click here:
> http://www.chillibeans.com.br

Joining the Chilli Beans family

When we hire a new employee I keep in mind the following questions: is this person capable of being part of our family and will I enjoy working with this person? I want to see their eyes shining. All directors participate in the interviews, including Caito, who has an amazing feeling for the right fit.

We take a viral approach to induction: We need to influence the new hires, motivate them and introduce them to our world. We've created a network of trainers so that it becomes a daily exercise. It's a sort of infection; one person spreads the virus and so it goes on. As we grow it becomes more difficult but **Chilli Beans spreads like a very nice virus that we all like to have**.

Chilli Beans event   © 2011 Chilli Beans

Vanessa Rincon – director of products and supplies

Vanessa, like Caito and Mario, is one of the founders of the business. She has been responsible for product design and manufacturing from day one.

Constantly growing

Chilli Beans is a big family. This family is constantly growing and having more children but that is okay because the family takes care of the family. The family has grown, educated the children and sent them to college. You take care of your kids with all your heart; you want them to all have the same opportunities. That's the way we work here. It starts with the father, Caito. He created this energy, this concept of business. I've never worked for a company with a structure similar to Chilli Beans.

Constantly producing

We create, develop, buy, produce, follow the whole production process and deliver the products to the international trade department. And they take care of the whole logistics process until the product is delivered into stock. There are 10 new sunglasses models each week, every week – and now watches too. Watches used to be ordered every 15 days but now it's done weekly. So it's an intense flow and the operation must be working at full power all the time. If you miss one step on the way from creation to delivery you are in trouble.

Constantly selling

We bring so many new products to market each week because we found that the more you offer in retail, the more you sell. Every week customers will stop by to see the latest product, so there's a bigger chance of purchase. I've got a stock of 300,000 glasses here and they have to move. One moves in, one moves out. So the purchase of glasses, watches and headwear is programmed in advance.

The retailer closest to our operational model is Zara. We're not considered a store for sunglasses any more because we're beyond that and we work with different types of accessories. Our product lines have been growing to become fashion accessories. It doesn't matter if they're sunglasses, glasses, caps, hats – the concept is fashion. **Our intention is to make our customers' life better, more pleasant.**

Constantly communicating

We constantly communicate internally. We are completely integrated: the manufacturers, wholesale, retail, consultants, franchisees and our design team travel all over the world in order to check new trends. Caito goes on these trips and personally participates in the creation process. He's a constant source of great ideas, actually. During our trips – it doesn't matter if we travel for fairs, purchases, etc – we dedicate part of the trip to creating orders and another to developing new ideas. The synergy inside Chilli Beans is perfect. I 'am' Chilli Beans, including at weekends because that is when I work in my local store, which is a kind of laboratory for me.

Bold lessons

Brands are more than products – they are lifestyles

Chilli Beans is a complete lifestyle brand comprising fashion, music, events and sports activities. When you create a brand that resonates with customers they begin to look at it as a guide to what is cool. As we saw with O2 and AirAsia, the brand becomes a passport to those things that customers value in their lives. As Marinho says, 'What we've built is not a company; it's our universe, our world.'

Your employees are your customers

For retail brands particularly, the closer your hiring profile is to your customer profile the better. People buy people. We know from research that when empathy increases so do sales, and the fact is that we are much more likely to be able to connect with customers when we share common interests and values.

Be authentic

Customers instinctively know when they are being manipulated. Research has shown that consumers have declining trust in large organizations, so if your brand is 'real' that is a very strong asset. As Marinho says, 'The brand needs this trust because we don't want our customers to think about buying sunglasses, we want them to think about buying Chilli Beans.'

Create a branded customer experience

As with other brands we have studied, Chilli Beans has elements of being a little cult-like for the customers and employees that embrace it.
We believe that the more multi-sensory and distinctive the experience, the more likely this is to be true. Think of Harley-Davidson.

Innovation

It is hard to be innovative unless it is built into the very way you operate. Delivering 10 new designs every week forces innovation so that the organization is geared up for it. It becomes a way of life. Innovation is driven through continuous customer feedback by involving customers in events, technology like the digital mirror and processes that quickly turn ideas into products. Like other bold brands, Chilli Beans uses social media sites like MySpace to get its message out there.

Watch how people use the product

What you sell is not necessarily what customers are buying. Ray-Ban thought they were selling eye protection. What Caito realized was that students were buying a fashion accessory. This insight led him to create a business model that produced sunglasses of good quality but exceptional variety. Because of this, a typical customer will own three or four pairs of Chilli Beans and visit the store weekly to check out the latest models.

See:

http://www.myspace.com/chillibeanslosangeles

Caito is very hands-on and in touch with the way people use his products; it is a characteristic he shares with Sonu Shivdasani, the founder of our next brand, Six Senses Resorts.

SIX SENSES

Chapter Five
Six Senses
Resorts and Spas

Six Senses Resorts and Spas has taken a very different approach to luxury hotels from its inception in 1995. Refusing to adhere to the conventions and commonly held beliefs in the industry, Sonu Shivdasani and his wife, Eva Malmström Shivdasani, have redefined the way that luxury hotels operate. Their first resort, Soneva Fushi, transformed the tourist industry in the Maldives by merging six-star service with the unspoilt beauty that usually only backpackers experience. It has since become a haven for the rich and famous, from show business celebrities to US presidents and Russian billionaires.

But Six Senses cares less about who you are than what you stand for. If you are looking for 'bling' and status rather than getting back to basics and sustainability, it is probably not the right place for you.

From the very beginning, Six Senses has borrowed more from the natural world and universe for its inspiration than from the world of finance and business. Its organizational chart is based on the solar system, its name is derived from numerology, and guests are more likely to entertain themselves by looking at the stars in the firmament through the resort telescope than by seeing stars on the small screen, as Six Senses doesn't provide television in its resort bedrooms.

The company has won numerous awards, including the Condé Nast 2010 Gold List Award for its Soneva Fushi resort in the Maldives. It has 15 resorts and 27 spas that operate under a number of brands: Soneva, Six Senses, Six Senses Spas and Six Senses Sanctuary.

Bold practices

Six Senses

- On arrival, guests are greeted by name by their host, who invites them to remove their shoes. These are placed in a bag labelled 'No news, no shoes'.
- The resorts only provide television and newspapers by request.

- Guests are provided with a special hessian bag to take their plastic refuse home with them.
- Managers are recruited through a 360° interview process in which they can meet up to 40 people.
- The executive group rarely wear suits and often forgo socks and shoes.
- Hosts are empowered to spend up to US$2,000 per customer on service recovery to exceed the guest's expectations.
- Resorts are constructed and operated to be carbon neutral and self-sustaining.
- The company publishes a glossary of terms that defines the many words and phrases unique to Six Senses. The current version runs to 26 pages.
- Guests are invited to stay a further week for free if they volunteer to work in the local community.

Six Senses Spas

© 2011 Six Senses Resorts and Spas

Sonu Shivdasani – the visionary

Sonu Shivdasani started the Six Senses brand with his wife Eva, opening their first property, Soneva Fushi, in the Maldives in 1995.

How it all started

Six Senses Resorts started because, whilst I loved the geography of the Maldives, I hated the standards of hotels when I first visited the islands. The hotels then had white tile floors, blue plastic roofs, and offered burnt fish.

I told my wife, Eva, that I didn't want to come back if this was all that was on offer. But my resolve was broken about a year and a half later when we visited again. At that time we met a Maldivian who, over dinner, explained that there was an island that had been abandoned. So I said, 'Well, let's go and have a look.' So we took a boat for three hours to an island where Soneva Fushi, our first resort, is located now. It was very remote and it wasn't very accessible, as in those days there was only a boat transfer and in certain seasons the sea can be very choppy, resulting in delays of up to two or three days to reach the island. So it wasn't the obvious place to build a luxury resort. We changed all of that with the advent of seaplane transfers and the island suddenly became remote but accessible. This is now an important formula in our site selection today.

The Six Senses difference

What we realized from day one was that **we wanted to create something that was quite different from what other hoteliers were doing**. For example, we went to the bank for funding and they asked, 'Where is your tour operator bed agreement?' We said, 'Well, we don't want one because we want to attract guests from a mix of nationalities.' Then they said that our proposed average room rate was double the nearest competitor and this was not feasible in their view, so our loan applications were turned down.

We didn't do any research except that Eva called up every tour operator and travel agent that was featuring the Maldives at the time and asked them what customers complained about. There were things like the lack of fresh food: everything was imported and tinned. So we developed our own organic garden, which means we can actually offer our guests much fresher and more nutritious salads than they get in London. A lot of our innovations were based on gut feel and gut instinct, but it was always very clear that we were all about the 'experience'.

The Six Senses culture

We decided our HR philosophy and approach would have to be different as well because in a city hotel, the focus is on time and execution. Your guests are buying the product. They want efficiency along with some comfort and an element of prestige. You have to make sure that the guest checks in very quickly because they're on their BlackBerry. If they don't get the room service within five minutes or that drink within five and a half minutes or when they look up there's no one there to take their order they get very frustrated and they get even more stressed. So a military-style approach towards management works very well in a corporate-orientated hotel because you're trying to eliminate defects; your focus is on execution, and so a hierarchical system works well. The boss gives orders; the employees follow orders, and so on.

In a resort environment the guest will linger and they'll chat with the barman. They'll be here for 10 nights, not one night. They'll have every meal here, so they'll develop a relationship with the employees who serve them – whom we call 'hosts'. We call our employees hosts because what we want to do is create a sense of ownership. So if we have 4,000 employees, we'd like to act as if we have 4,000 owners rather than just one owner.

Of course, you do need processes. Without processes there is no organization and service fails, but the question is: where should the priority and the emphasis lie? For example, rather than Six Sigma, we have the 'SLOWLIFE line', a process of service recoveries. Saying that we will have zero defects or Six-Sigma level quality is fine for an engineering industry, where if you have a defect on an aircraft engine it's a bit serious when you're flying at 45,000 feet or whatever. But **with our sort of environment the service recovery can be much more powerful than zero defects**. You can either have the host focused towards never-ever making a mistake, which can lead to stress for the host and the guest, or allow a few defects in a thousand or two and that's good enough in our industry. But what's more important is that, when you do have a defect or make a mistake, you recover from it very well. So our whole service recovery philosophy and approach are geared to empowering the hosts so that they are encouraged to spend a discretionary amount to resolve a guest complaint.

A company is really the sum of its culture, its values and its philosophy. We call this the Six Senses Sun, because without it we are lost – just as the planets would lose their orbit and balance without the sun. We have our core purpose, which is to provide 'innovative enlightening experiences that rejuvenate our guest's love of SLOWLIFE', which is an acronym for Sustainable, Local, Organic, Wholesome, Learning, Inspiring, Fun, Experiences.

Intelligent luxury

The Six Senses group properties are further differentiated by what we call 'intelligent luxury'. We try to understand what luxury represents to a 21st-century traveller because the guests that visit us today live in London and Paris and Milan and come from a totally different context from that of the 20th-century wealthy individual, when some of the conventional 'language' of luxury was defined. And so of course what they now define as 'luxury' is totally different too. To be able to spend two weeks walking barefoot is absolute luxury. If you travel a lot, as I do, 400 hours a year or whatever, and you've got to pack for meetings, it's quite nice when you're packing for a holiday to take things for yourself, like sports shoes, fins, etc, rather than shoes for others to see you in. This is, in a way, intelligent luxury: to be able to do things for you. Our typical customer lives in London, so they can have the 1989 Cristal any time they like. But what they can't have is a fresh organic salad picked from the garden that morning. Most of the vegetables they eat have either travelled two days to get to the restaurant or are processed and vacuum packed. Another example is that light pollution in capital cities is such that you cannot see the stars very well. Intelligent luxury means we have an observatory at the resort so guests can see the stars in the absolute blackness of the sky because of the remote location.

Focus on the target customer

Our target guests are wealthy individuals from capital cities, who are sophisticated, well travelled, well studied, and who live stressful lives. They may be a politician, a celebrity, an actor, a musician or a businessman, but they all tend to travel a lot and lead hectic lives. When they come to our resorts the real luxury is to just chill, unwind, be with oneself, rediscover their partner, read a good book, but with access to wonderful service and like-minded people when they want it. When you read the

Cinema   © 2011 Six Senses Resorts and Spas

guest comments book they talk about walking barefoot on the beach or watching a movie in the open air underneath the full moon. So **intelligent luxury is really about giving people what they actually want rather than what hoteliers think they want**. Mainstream luxury hotel chain competitors offer air-conditioned restaurants with marble floors, which mean that you have to put shoes on and dress up every evening for dinner – which sometimes people may not want to do. In today's environment just being exposed to fresh air is a luxury in a way.

Vision of the future

We are now working on developing our resorts as zero-carbon-emission resorts. I think that's going to be the next trend. The challenge is to generate all of your own power from sustainable and carbon-free sources and we're looking at various options. If we achieve our aim, then everyone else is going to have to follow suit and to be zero carbon will no longer be a differentiator; it will become a qualifier, because I think as people start to feel and see the impact of global warming and how it affects them at home, they'll make the choice to stay at a resort that is carbon neutral. Our Soneva brand is already carbon neutral and we are on track to make Soneva Fushi zero carbon by 2011.

Conscientious consumption

We are developing a new approach called Evalution. 'Eva', of course, is the name of my wife and she is our conscience when it comes to environmental issues, but it also conjures up innovation and forward thinking. We have built an eco-suite at Soneva Kiri which has zero-carbon emissions. It's a 200 square metre guest villa with its own pool. There was no cement used in the construction as we've used earth as the basic material. The foundations are formed from rocks taken from the site. The timbers have been sourced as locally as possible, so there's very little carbon input in the building. We've got this natural cooling system where the power it consumes is just 10 per cent of a normal air-con. We also use water from underground sources to pump cool air into the building. Then there's a solar pump that moves water from the main pool into another pond which cleans the water and purifies it naturally through oxygenating plants, so we don't need chlorine either. Finally, the water tumbles back down into the pool and that helps to generate energy as well. The Zero Carbon and Evalution strategy is very relevant today in a 'post-Lehman' era where the reality of global warming is starting to dawn on people. There is a shift away from conspicuous consumption to conscientious consumption.

Purpose is the compass that guides you

Our purpose also requires us to have respect for nature. For example, our chefs have proposed the idea of the live fish tank experience: you can choose your fresh fish and then they cook it for you. It's very fresh and it's a concept that's really successful in Singapore, for example. But we've said no, it's cruel to animals because they are confined to a tank and that is at odds with our purpose, despite the fact that some of our guests may want it. So we've got two values, one is around our concern for the environment and the other is around the guest experience, but the environment comes first. We couldn't provide a guest experience that wasn't environmentally sustainable because then we would be undermining our core purpose. There's always a little element of bravery when you start a new project. It's a bit like jumping in at the deep end in a way. You don't know exactly where you'll come out so **you need to stay true to your core purpose – it becomes the compass that guides you**.

To hear Sonu Shivdasani speaking more about these issues click here:
http://www.youtube.com/watch?v=JGfvKGH-1Hw

The Hub   © 2011 Six Senses Resorts and Spas

Bernhard Bohnenberger – the managing director

Bernhard was one of the very first hires for Six Senses, coming by way of a classic hotel school and then experience with a number of high-end hotels in Asia.

It's all about having fun

The initial very small team that started Six Senses was always determined to make the entire experience fun, not just fun for the guests, but fun for ourselves and fun for anybody who would work with us, and it's still one of our core values. We felt it was extremely sad that millions of people who go to work every day hate what they do, count the minutes until they finish, wait for their days off, long for their retirement: it's very sad. The whole passion and drive of the company come from the fact that we really do enjoy ourselves every minute and we hope to make that possible for everybody who works with us, even business partners and clients, because then there is no work. It's all fun!

Dare to be different

Our approach has always been to dare to try new things. I come from the traditional hotel business and, perhaps, the most traditional hotel management school in the world. But that training has simply provided me with the tools to be able to do things differently. For example, the traditional resort business started by building city hotels at the beach, which is totally inappropriate, so we challenged that and asked 'What do guests really want in a resort holiday and what do we need to do to deliver that?' The answer was certainly not the 'corporate city hotel on the beach experience'.

It starts with the destination. Our first flagship resort hotel, Soneva Fushi, challenged the prevailing wisdom because we opened a very high-end luxury resort in what was an extremely downmarket charter destination at that time. The Maldives is such an amazing environment, such a paradise, that we believed it could become a destination for luxury guests. It was tough in the beginning, because the only way into the Maldives was via charter flights. There were three or four charter airlines out of Singapore, which was the wrong direction for our European market, or from Colombo on Air Lanka, which was not considered a very good airline at the time. But we felt that if we created something special, the guests would come. Nowadays every luxury chain is in the Maldives, with at least one if not more properties. It was the same thing when we opened in Vietnam. It was purely a backpacker destination and the bankers and consultants said, 'It's not done. Nobody does it.' We said, 'We'll do it, we dare,' and again we were successful.

The Six Senses service concept

After the destination comes the concept. We took this idea of luxury and then tried to be very creative with it. There are a lot of advantages to backpacking and staying in tiny little huts on the beach, because backpackers typically find the most amazing spots that are not yet discovered by the mass tourist market. The problem is that you have mosquitoes, you don't have running water, the food is not safe, the service is not good; in fact, the whole experience can be dangerous. So we took all of the ingredients of a backpacking holiday and packaged them into a true luxury environment with wonderful service. At the other extreme, it may be sensible to have a palace-like hotel in Paris, but it's not intelligent to have a palatial hotel on the beach in the Maldives. What is intelligent, though, is that there is a place where you can stay that offers wonderful fresh local food and where you are totally at one with the environment, where you can dine barefoot in the sand, yet still have amazing service and space. So this is the concept we call 'intelligent luxury'.

The Six Senses solar system   © 2011 Six Senses Resorts and Spas

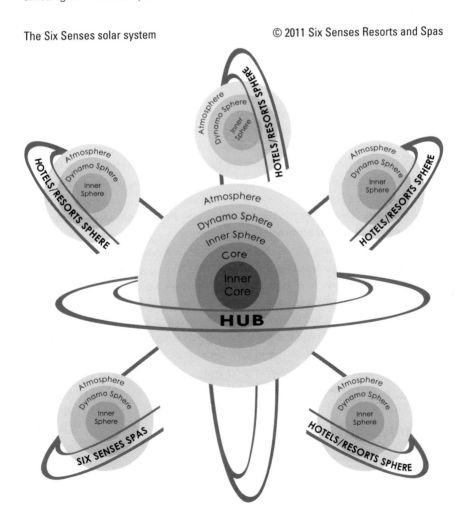

The Six Senses culture

If you promise intelligent luxury, your service and therefore your people are key.
The traditional hotel business is based on a very strict military style, with a highly
hierarchical and disciplined culture; we never enjoyed this or thought that it would be
appropriate for our purpose. If I go to a resort, I want to be served last; I want to make
sure the guests are taken care of first. I don't need a huge show of attention and
people almost jumping to attention when they see me. That's the last thing I want.

So we based our culture on the model of the natural universe, not on military
structure. We decided on the stellar model, where you have at the core the 'hub'
with the planets that radiate out. We talk about 'spheres of influence' rather than
job descriptions. Originally we had the 'core', being the key directors. Then as we
grew we added what we call the 'dynamosphere', which comprises all our middle
management, who are responsible for translating our ideas and communicating
these to our people. Finally, and most importantly, there is the 'atmosphere', which
is the environment our hosts create for our guests.

Our recruitment process is also a bit unconventional. We do a 360° interview,
which exposes the applicant not only to superiors but also to peers and to future
reportees. So a general manager will be interviewed by senior people from the
hub, they will meet people from the regional areas, and they will meet the department heads that will be reporting to them and even some more junior people. We
gather everybody's input and we form an opinion based on this. Equally, the candidate will have met at least 20 different people in the organization and will have
had time to speak with them. He or she will have had time to make up their mind
whether it's an organization they would like to join. Now it's much easier to find the
right managers, because people have heard about us and buy into our philosophy.
They aspire to join Six Senses, because it's not your boring, dusty, military model
where you have to work because you need the pay. **People join us because they
aspire to a lifestyle and embrace our philosophy.**

The next step is a very, very thorough induction process that takes the new hire
through company culture, values, philosophy, the things we do and don't do. This
induction gets the new hire really 'Six sensitized', as we call it. Part of this is a
training programme which we call 'The thin red line', which teaches our hosts to
be casual, to be relaxed, but to show respect to the guest. How do I know if a guest
wants to chat? How do I read the signs that a guest actually wants to be left alone?
What should we point out to the guest? What shouldn't we touch? Should we
disturb them or not? So the training programme teaches hosts to be casual yet
still give top-quality service through developing high levels of empathy.

Measure what matters

In order to keep our finger on the pulse, we are extremely diligent at collecting
guest comments and also host comments. Typically, at most of our resorts, about

80 per cent of guests will reply to the guest questionnaire, which is a very high response rate for the industry. This is because at the Soneva resorts we have very high attention to detail, fewer guests and a high loyalty factor; so, for example, Soneva Fushi has about 35 per cent repeat guests.

We also strive for employee retention. Our newest resort, Soneva Kiri, is now our new standard for employee accommodation. It has a pool and even spa services for our 'hosts'. They have an amazing canteen and enjoy lovely, really nicely decorated rooms that don't feel like a compromise. The reason we do all of this is that, physically, it's quite easy to copy our model. You can copy the look of the pool or a room type or a spa. There are a lot of resorts now that look like ours. I look at the brochures now and I say, 'Is this ours or somebody else's?' But, in terms of the culture, I challenge competitors to copy us – but you know what? I welcome them trying, because it's better for the people, better for the community, better for the environment.

Anand Rao – the chief talent officer

After his extensive experience in working in human resources for a luxury brand, Six Senses presented a culture shock for Anand.

There was a big discussion about my title before I joined the group. Our CEO wanted the title to be 'chief happiness officer' but it ended up as 'chief talent officer', which I was quite relieved about – but in both cases my division's main goal is really to ensure that we bring passionate, talented, committed, caring people into the company and that while they are with us, their talents are developed and their dreams fulfilled.

Challenging the norms

I worked for a luxury hotel brand for 13 years before joining Six Senses and for me it was a huge change, because in my previous company, for most of its history, people were told what to say and how they should say it. At Six Senses we don't have these kinds of rules. **We tell our hosts what Asian hospitality means and what our philosophy of caring for the guest is all about and then we leave it up to them.** Our leaders are very informal. They don't dress up. They don't wear suits. They dress in harmony with the environment in which they are meeting people. They are very approachable right from the very top. Sonu hardly ever wears socks and is usually in shorts and a cotton or linen short-sleeved shirt. Our hosts see this, they see a relaxed, informal style of leadership, and they reflect that in the way they interact with guests.

Recruit for fit

At Six Senses we try to recruit people who have that natural desire to serve and to make guests thrilled with their experience, but also there is a secondary aspect to our philosophy, and that is the responsibility to the communities in which we operate and to the environment. These are the two big overarching things that cover everything that we do. We believe that our guests choose to come to us because they are more and more concerned with these things too. These are people who have the money to be able to stay with any luxury operator they wish but choose to come to Six Senses instead because they feel that they have a certain responsibility too in the luxury experience that they're getting, and they feel good about that.

Our resorts are usually in pretty remote locations. As far as possible, we try to recruit from the population as close as possible to our resort. Often these people are simple people, who very quickly understand the philosophy of Six Senses, which is basically to make the guest feel at home and extend a helping hand to the community. We build hospitals, we build schools, and we take care of serious illnesses, so they get that part very quickly. The fact that we reach into the community to find the people, first ensures that we get people who are in tune with the environment in which we are operating, but secondly, if they have never worked in a hotel before, which is often the case, they are like a blank page, and it's much easier to teach them what Six Senses is all about.

Take your vitamins

When someone joins Six Senses they are given what we call our 'Sun card', which summarizes our purpose, vision and values. You know, many companies give their employees cards summarizing the company vision or values, but few companies do a great job of keeping their vision and values alive, so for about the last 18 months now, we have sent out an e-mail every day that reinforces one of the items within the Six Senses sun card. We call these e-mails our 'Vitamins' of the day.

We have several processes in place to foster our philosophy. One of them is called 'NIBI', which stands for 'New idea, better idea', and every resort is required to implement at least three new ideas every month, and they report this as part of their balanced scorecard to headquarters, or what we call our 'hub'.

This isn't a company that is just superficially committed to the community and the environment. It's not just talk. This company lives it, breathes it and believes in it, all the way through, from resort design to the materials we use, community involvement and in the delivery of environmental consciousness, through our hosts to our guests. I have worked for some great hotel companies over the years but they did not even talk about any of this, let alone do it. That's what makes Six Senses really different.

Alasdair Junor – the COO

Recruited as one the first general managers for Soneva Fushi, Alasdair was challenged to bring new thinking to the brand.

Sonu is a fantastic visionary and really wanted to create a product and a level of service that were second to none. He was incredibly bold and very courageous to start a venture which he knew very little about. But of course, as an hotelier this was an opportunity for me in that I had to fully understand where Sonu was coming from, what he wanted to do, and that he wasn't familiar with boundaries or limitations, or concerned with them. It opened my mind to what is possible.

No News No Shoes

© 2011 Six Senses Resorts and Spas

Break the barriers

Most hoteliers think within the box and say that they can only do X, Y, Z, because of perceived limitations, be they human or other resources. Sonu constantly tried to break those barriers. He was very accustomed to five-star hotels as a guest and felt that the service didn't really go beyond the call of duty. The first very innovative thing he came up with was our 'No news, no shoes' service, which means that when clients arrive, their shoes are automatically taken off them and placed in a bag which says 'No news, no shoes'. They are returned when the guest leaves. We wanted to create an environment which allows guests to escape back to nature, but luxuriously back to nature. The resort was designed by Eva and she wanted to create a very unpretentious, unostentatious environment for wealthy people, which, at the time, back in the early to mid-1990s was unheard of. Sonu was entering into something which hadn't really been tried and tested, but he firmly believed in the concept.

Of course, we need to make sure that guests are comfortable with our 'intelligent luxury' concept. Our marketing and website make quite clear it is a luxurious but back-to-nature type of property, so I would hope that 95 per cent of people expect that it is going to be no shoes, and no news: no television, no CNN, etc.

But I do remember a couple coming to see me to complain. The wife was wearing a Gucci twinset, pearls, matching high-heeled shoes – the whole works. She basically just wanted to walk around in her high-heeled shoes all the time and didn't really understand the concept of the hotel. I had to explain to her that this was very, very different from Four Seasons and Ritz-Carlton. From her reaction I knew that it probably wouldn't get any better for her or for us and that she would be much happier somewhere else, so I arranged and paid for flights for them. I am sure she had a wonderful time.

Innovation is hard but execution is harder

Creating the vision and culture is one thing but implementing it and making sure that it is followed by all of our people are quite another. I tried to take Sonu's vision and the culture that he was trying to instil and built it into the business plan, so it became an integral part of the operation. I would involve all the heads of departments with the compiling of this business plan, so they were very much a part of it and took ownership. We then created an A5 version which the general managers would use when sat down with all their people to go through the business plan with them. Explaining the purpose, goals and objectives, explaining the vision, explaining the culture, explaining what we need to achieve, and explaining how we are so very different from our competitors in terms of involving all our people in every step of the business would take two to three hours. We then created a condensed book, about 16–18 pages, which was a smaller version of the business plan. This was written in very simple English for all our people to fully understand. The feedback from the hosts was just mind-blowing. They were so happy to be a part of the whole process, and that I was willing, as a general manager, to take the time with them to explain the whole business plan and identify how important they are to the business, whether as a manager or as someone cleaning the pots and pans or the toilets, or whatever. You know, **in this industry it is all about attitude**; if you don't have the right attitude you will never instil a service culture.

Overcoming resistance

Probably every initiative that we come up with has had some resistance from our owners. We need to convince them of these initiatives because they have to fund them. These green initiatives are going to save money in the long term, but that might be two or three years down the road. Because of this there are, inevitably, some occasions when we disagree with owners over various initiatives, so we usually drive all the initiatives in our own properties and test them there first. We'll play with the initiative and refine it, with the intention of rolling it out in eight, nine or ten months across the other properties. So really it's all a timing issue more than anything else, but we try not to let it affect our end product because, if a client goes to Soneva Fushi, they're expecting the same service and similar facilities at Soneva Gili, so we have to provide a consistent experience.

We have a history of innovation. We were one of the first resorts to offer pools with each villa. And we were also one of the first to have spas. Back in the mid-1990s it was very rare to come across a five-star property that actually had a spa attached to it – now spas are a qualifier for five-star properties. So we've always taken the lead on initiatives that every other operator has since adopted, because we've set the trend and, for them to remain competitive, they've had to follow our lead.

Making a world of difference

I think the latest innovation, although very small now, will come to have a huge impact on the world. We are refusing to buy any imported bottled waters for any of our properties. So we produce our own water and even mineralize it. It's probably better for you than some of the branded waters. There are about one billion people in the world who do not have access to fresh or clean water, so we refuse to import and sell branded waters and instead sell our own water, and 50 per cent of the proceeds of these sales go to a water charity to provide clean water in India, etc. In the years to come we're hoping that our competitors will feel compelled to follow suit, which will then make a huge impact on the world, when you consider that **one year of not transporting water across the world could actually provide enough fresh water for every human being on the globe**.

Rochelle Kilgariff – the general manager

Rochelle joined Six Senses as general manager of Soneva Fushi. She now runs the Zighy Bay resort in Oman, which was recently voted 'The Middle East's Leading Luxury Beach Resort' and 'Oman's Leading Resort' at the grand final of the World Travel Awards – also known as the travel industry 'Oscars'.

Intelligent luxury is creating a guest experience that gives them something that they desire, but without being detrimental to the environment. So for example, take our 'Robinson Crusoe picnics'. We take the guests to a deserted island. We provide a picnic box with all the wonderful delights we can, but we also include this lovely little hessian bag with a tag that says, in effect, 'Sometimes a little bit of rubbish washes up on the island, so would you help us out and remove some of it when you leave?' So it's about giving guests an experience whilst they're on the island that they wouldn't be able to find in their normal day-to-day world.

The Six Senses experience

The Six Senses experience starts when you arrive on the island from the boat or seaplane. You are greeted by this lovely lady or gentleman who is your 'Friday' or host, who takes your shoes, pops them into a bag, and then walks you to your villa. We don't have a reception desk. They will show you to your personal bicycle. You know, most of our guests haven't been on a bicycle since they were 12 years old – they drive everywhere – so you've just knocked away another barrier. The rest is about having your privacy. You can disappear here, completely. You can go to the main restaurant in the evening and seated right next to you could be a prime minister or the owner of a Fortune 500 company, but the way the lighting is designed, you wouldn't really know that they're there, so... it's all about your experience, not who is dining next to you.

A lot of the guests come from a very privileged environment. They will live in a very elegant home, so when they come here, we try to provide an experience that's unexpected and yet very practical. So, for example, the table that is provided in front of your villa is actually an old wooden cable drum turned on its side. We have an amazing carpentry team on the island, who pretty much make about 80 per cent of the furniture we have. But then you're resting on a sunbed that has the fluffiest, most comfortable mattress you will ever have experienced, with a beautiful little matching pillow chosen from a pillow menu based on your preference.

What's in a name?

Traditionally, luxury hotels always address guests as Mr Smith, etc, but here in the Maldives people often refer to others by their first name, as in 'Mr Shaun', which is a little less formal. We ask the guests for their permission to do that in the resorts too. But most guests, who are wanting to feel even more relaxed and laid back, will actually ask us to just use their first names.

Our model introduces a little more risk to the service offer but also allows us to be very flexible as well. We have a goal every month to give what we call 'service recoveries'. We actually aim for about 40 service recoveries every month, which means we've not met the guest's expectations to the extent we feel we should have, so we empower every host to provide value of up to US$2,000 in service recovery. Now to put that in context, we are asking a host who only makes perhaps US$400 a month in salary to feel good about spending US$2,000 to provide an experience to a guest that will exceed their expectations. It requires excellent training to get this balance right. We have a company goal to give every one of our hosts nine hours a month of training. We have a full-time English teacher to help them with conversational skills. We have the 'Sixth Sense', a great week of classroom and outdoor training which is all about the company and its values. We have our own marine biologist to provide training to them about the environment that they live in so that they can explain it to guests too.

From rhetoric to reality

When this company was conceived 15 years ago, 'sustainability' was probably not a word most people would have ever heard of, but it's the basis on how this company has been developed. We don't usually advertise it because we're too busy getting on and doing it instead of just talking about it. I perceive this as a huge differentiator between Six Senses and other companies. There are a lot of companies developing properties now who are making sustainability a key marketing focus but we've been doing it for so long, we forget to talk about it. **It's not a marketing tag line; it is just what we believe in.**

The beauty of my job is that I have interaction with so many guests, because I meet them all on arrival and departure. I see the pleasure on the faces of the guests that are visiting for the very first time and those that visit us time and time again. It is particularly gratifying on departure when they say, 'I'm coming back. It's a wonderful experience,' and it's then that you can tell that ours is actually a very successful formula. Maybe that is why about 35 per cent of our guests are repeat guests, and some of them visit us eight or nine times. One guest has been here 20 times. To put that into perspective, the industry standard for retention is about 17 per cent.

Authenticity and being 'real'

I guess there's always the threat of someone trying to copy the Six Senses philosophy, but moving around the world as I do and seeing what Soneva and Six Senses as a company bring to the resort or a hotel operation, it's something that I don't worry about. Six Senses is about going in the opposite direction to the rest of the industry; with guests, with community, with the environment. It's about finding those destinations that are hidden away in a world that's becoming increasingly commoditized. It's then about building in those destinations and helping the local communities. It's about giving the guest an experience that they would not be able to normally buy or touch in that region. Guests are still being completely wowed even if they have come from a resort that tries to be like us. They say that ours is the real deal.

The Six Senses virtuous circle

There's a huge level of pride working at Six Senses because of the virtuous circle concept we operate. **It's about giving back to the community, giving back to the environment, giving back to the team and giving back to guests.** It's all about giving and taking in a continuous circle that is, in itself, breathing in order to sustain itself – a constant, perfect balance.

To see Soneva Fushi click here:
http://www.youtube.com/watch?v=7S10yp6Vd-o

Christopher Bailey – the customer

Christopher Bailey is the chief creative officer for Burberry and a typical Six Senses guest. He has a high-pressure job involving a lot of travel and spends much of his time in the glare of the media.

I think the biggest factor about Six Senses is that it has a point of view. It's about welcoming, it's about comfort, it's about privacy, it's about quality, and most of all, it's about forgetting about everything else apart from you... and it's a luxury experience because of that. Not because it might be expensive to stay there or because you arrive there by seaplane or all the other things. It's the philosophy that it's built on that is the true luxury. Taking your shoes off the second you get there because you don't need them any more: it's the core of what they're about.

Six Senses Virtuous Circle

3. FAR EXCEEDING GUEST EXPECTATIONS, RESULTING IN STRONG CUSTOMER LOYALTY

2. GENERATING ENTHUSIASM AS WELL AS PRIDE AND LOYALTY IN OUR HOSTS

4. A PROFITABLE AND SUSTAINABLE BUSINESS AND A FEELING OF SATISFACTION AND SELF-FULFILLMENT

1. CREATING A UNIQUE CORPORATE CULTURE AND A SPECIAL EXPERIENCE AND CONCEPT

Virtuous Cycle

© 2011 Six Senses Resorts and Spas

Bold lessons

The lessons can best be summed by the Six Senses
'Virtuous circle' diagram. It has four elements:

1 creating a unique corporate culture and a special experience
   and concept;

2 generating enthusiasm as well as pride and loyalty in our hosts;

3 far exceeding guest expectations, resulting in strong customer loyalty;

4 a profitable and sustainable business and a feeling of satisfaction and
   self-fulfilment.

Start with a consumer insight

The big idea underpinning the experience concept is 'intelligent luxury'. The
prevailing wisdom in luxury hospitality is that guests want 'conspicuous
consumption': being seen in the finest surroundings. The Six Senses insight
was that the 21st-century consumer is now more concerned about being
seen to be environmentally aware; in other words, 'conscientious consumption'.

President Nasheed of the Maldives said whilst outlining his government's
10-year carbon-neutral strategy: 'Soneva Fushi … will become the world's
first carbon-neutral tourist resort. It will host a symposium to demonstrate
how, through a combination of technical wizardry and common-sense
solutions, it has slashed carbon emissions, putting to bed the myth that luxury
necessarily equates with environmental degradation.'

Focus on what customers truly value

But the management also realized that although wealthy customers may be
willing to accept a simpler product, they would not wish to accept less than
excellent service, so they focused on creating a culture that exceeds guests'
expectations. This is done through creating a less formal, friendlier and
flexible service style that narrows the social difference between guest and
host but without ever compromising the appropriate level of respect.

Don't force it: be natural and embrace empathy

The success of Six Senses is in large part down to the way that they
encourage their hosts and their guests to be themselves and to 'get in
touch' with their natural feelings of empathy for others and nature.
They're making a business out of living, as much as a living out of
business. This is impossible to fake but it is surprisingly easy to encourage –
simple but iconic actions help: for example, the leaders of the business
dressing down and encouraging informality; or paying for a guest to leave

the island and stay at a more traditional luxury resort, which sends a strong signal to guests and hosts of what the Six Senses experience is and is not, while at the same time empathizing with a guest who just should not be there. Few organizations in our experience have the courage to recognize when customers do not fit the profile.

Moreover, adapting recruitment processes and selection to the local community, working with the culture and environment of the locale, however difficult that might be, mirrors the way that communities naturally evolve.

Arranging their internal organization around the metaphor of a solar system rather than a traditional organigram has enormous cultural and operational significance.

Internal culture must support the strategy

This in turn requires a similar relationship between management and employees so that the culture operates much more from shared purpose and values than management dictat.

Finally, the sustainability of the enterprise is ensured through creating a harmonious and continuous win–win relationship so that the customers, the employees, the company, the shareholders and the environment all gain from their involvement with the brand.

For more on values see:

http://www.sixsenses.com/About-Six-Senses/
Core-Purpose-and-Core-Values.php

Perhaps the biggest lesson we can take from Six Senses is that companies in the 21st century may have as much to learn from the natural world as they do from business schools.

For more about Six Senses click here:

http://www.sixsenses.com/

Six Senses demonstrates a new approach to luxury, an approach that challenges the stereotype of conspicuous consumption. It is fitting that Christopher Bailey is one of its guests, because he is the chief creative officer of our next bold brand, one that also has a unique approach to luxury, which it describes as 'democratic luxury'.

Chapter Six
Burberry

Burberry is a brand that is 155 years young. Young, because despite being chosen to support Sir Ernest Shackleton's expedition to the South Pole and despite being the maker of trench coats to the military in the First World War, Burberry is now better known for its cutting-edge fashion and for dressing modern-day icons such as Emma Watson and Orlando Bloom.

This is a brand of contrasts, exclusive yet inclusive; high fashion yet very down to earth. Check out its line of wellington boots: stylish yet practical. Few brands in our experience have managed to retain such a strong sense of their heritage whilst being completely contemporary.

The year 2009 saw the biggest decline in luxury sales for as long as anyone can remember. Most retailers dropped prices, cut back on staff and hoped for the best. Burberry took the view that a storm was no reason to change tack and kept on with its strategy. In fact, it increased its investment in brand-building activity, customer-facing initiatives and improvements to the customer experience. The recession provided an opportunity to tackle a number of operational issues like reducing supply chain costs and improving efficiencies. As a result, in spite of the recession, sales increased, employee morale rose and, in April 2010, the Luxury Institute published independent research that found Burberry offered the best customer experience in the luxury retail sector. It was no surprise that the company reported record profits for 2009–10 despite the challenging market conditions.

We have worked with or written about many great brands over the years, but what impresses us most about Burberry is the vision, passion and conviction of the leadership team to do what is right for the brand and trust that everything else will follow.

Burberry is now leading the way in the digital medium, taking its brand to millions of new consumers via the internet whilst still maintaining its stylish, sophisticated and, above all, sensory approach.

Artofthetrench.com

© 2011 Burberry

Bold practices

Burberry

- The management team significantly increased their investment in the customer experience as the recession hit.
- The Burberry runway show is now reaching a potential audience of a million customers through streaming live over the internet.
- Burberry was the first luxury brand to attract more than three million fans on Facebook and now has over 4 million (**http://www.facebook.com/burberry**).
- Its social media site attracted over 9 million page views in the nine months after launch (**http://www.artofthetrench.com**).
- The Luxury Institute reported in April 2010 that Burberry offered the best customer experience in the luxury retail sector.

Angela Ahrendts – chief executive officer

Angela Ahrendts   © 2011 Burberry

Angela Ahrendts became CEO of Burberry in July 2006. She has extensive experience in luxury retail, having held senior appointments with Liz Claiborne and Donna Karan International.

For me, the journey began four and a half years ago when we created five key strategies that have become the company's strategic pillars, underpinning almost everything we have done with the business since that time. These were to leverage the franchise, intensify non-apparel development, accelerate retail-led growth, invest in under-penetrated markets, and pursue operational excellence.

Interestingly, the most misunderstood strategy externally was leveraging the franchise. The franchise is simply the Burberry brand and it was clear to us that for everything else to work we had to have one company, one brand.

Building the brand

Burberry had grown into a federation of local licensed businesses before my predecessor began 10 years ago acquiring back the Burberry trademark around the world. Our new strategy was simple: with one share price we had to connect all components in one focused vision, which we could then leverage across every region, every product category, every channel of distribution – basically tighten control over anything the consumer sees. So it was taking this federation and just making everybody understand there's only one Burberry brand.

Our priority has also always been to keep the focus on our core businesses. The Burberry brand was born from a coat and has highly visible icons like the check and the Prorsum horse to innovate and to protect; these must underpin each of our strategies. They are the foundation and the greatest differentiators which need to be as respected and revered as the brand itself. At the heart of building our strategy and culture is how closely Christopher Bailey, our chief creative officer, and I work together. He is the 'art' and I'm the 'commerce'. But we are both brand builders first and foremost, and we will always begin with intuition and then confuse ourselves with the facts before we make a decision.

Christopher and I were fortunate to have worked together prior to Burberry, so we too had a solid foundation to build on and a huge level of innate trust and respect for one another. I'm from a small town in Indiana, the heartland of America; he's from Yorkshire. We both had a strong family upbringing. For us sharing the same core values was just as critical a component as sharing the same vision.

It's funny, often during interviews or investor presentations, I'll pick up something that maybe he forgot on product or marketing, and he'll mention a business strategy he considers relevant. So our minds are aligned and we're sharing the same brand vision, while our hearts are so aligned and we're sharing the same values. This is how we want the Burberry teams everywhere to work; this is what we want all employees and customers to see and feel.

In order to ensure we are creating the transparent trusting culture we dream of, we share our results and key messages verbally and visually with 6,000 associates around the world quarterly. Very early on we said that we didn't just want Burberry to be the greatest luxury brand, but we also wanted to be a great company. For us that is simply how the customer experiences the brand and how the company employees behave at all levels. We always say it's not about what's best for me as CEO or about Christopher as chief creative officer. At Burberry today it's not about any one individual – it's about 'what's best for the brand'.

Redefining luxury

The idea of 'democratic luxury' was for us an innate reaction to how we as luxury consumers wanted to shop; yet this was in contrast to the prevailing wisdom in the industry. We felt luxury should be inclusive, not exclusive, inviting, not intimidating. This positioning came from truly knowing the target customers we wanted to connect with on- and offline, and envisioning the interaction and experience we wanted them to have with our brand. Externally, we have consistently focused our energy into high-profile, broad-reaching initiatives such as our runway shows, digital initiatives and retail stores.

Internally, our focus was on what we called the 'soft strategies', which all centred on the culture. We believed that if we balanced our more traditional 'hard' strategies equally with these 'soft' strategies and our core values, we could double our revenues and profits in five years. We knew intuitively we needed to successfully implement both to achieve this vision: it couldn't just be one or the other. You have to do both.

Connecting people to purpose

To reinforce our soft strategies further, in 2008 we created the Burberry Foundation, with the aim of helping young people in the communities where we work realize their dreams and potential through the power of their creativity. For us, this was the connecting piece, the thing that would give a different dimension, an additional purpose to Burberry.

The Foundation works with partner charities in five cities globally to help young people gain confidence, build connections in their communities, and envision opportunities to achieve their dreams. We assist through financial contributions and product contributions, and our associates contribute by volunteering and mentoring. Last year alone they gave over 3,500 hours of their time to help the next generation of talent.

Our initial financial vision was to gift £5 million in five years, and two years on we are on plan with £2 million. For us, the Burberry Foundation is part of what makes this not just a great brand but a great company, and that's right at the heart of my and Christopher's aligned vision.

http://www.burberry.com/foundation

Staying the course

This consistent, balanced focus on hard and soft strategies also served us well through the recession. When the financial crisis hit, the senior team became more united than ever and agreed to stay the strategic course that served us so well. We believed so strongly in our vision and the type of company we wanted to be. And we took a bold decision: to keep investing in the brand and not to cut a dime from anything consumer facing. We didn't cut our sales and service programme – in fact, we invested more in enhancing the customer experience. We doubled our digital marketing efforts because we got 10 times the reach for the same cost. At the same time we took £50 million of expense out of the business by acting swiftly to tightly manage costs, drive efficiencies, improve inventory management and generate cash.

There is always this balance between hard and soft strategies, investment and intuition, but if you have a greater purpose that can serve as the focus it becomes relatively easy to make those calls. At Burberry the brand is our beacon. In 2008, when we were asked 'Why are you moving into this new headquarters, why don't you cut that cost?' we said, 'Because that's not what's best for the brand.'

When the whole world went into recession, we did anything we could that was brand enhancing. In 2008–09 we actually moved into three new headquarters.

In New York we locked into a 20-year opportunity for a 100-foot Burberry sign lighting up Manhattan. In Tokyo we moved into new headquarters and hired a new team. And most importantly we moved into Horseferry House, our global headquarters, in London. We closed many local facilities to consolidate all brand executives under one roof. This investment was absolutely the right thing to do at the right time, and further united and connected our teams. This not only formed a new physical expression of the brand where the vision was now reality, but reaffirmed and created a new energy hub which further ignited the culture. We didn't have to make this investment but we knew, long term, that was best for the brand, and would enable us to achieve our hard and soft strategies.

With half of our business wholesale at that stage it was critical to share the brand vision with our large partners. How do you talk about the purity, energy and excitement around your brand and then have people come to a tired showroom and offices? We intuitively knew we would get a very tangible return on these brand investments and by doing so in a down market, a greater return in the long run.

Embracing digital

The other bold initiative was to embrace aggressively the digital medium. Very early on, when some of our peers were saying the internet was the enemy and 'You can't sell luxury online,' we said, 'It's just another channel.' We knew our brand experience was now pure and compelling. We focused on where our customer was going, thinking that maybe we could leverage our content in this exciting medium which would in time impact all customers and channels.

We also knew that this brand experience had to then be consistent across anything and everything the consumer sees. From the store windows, the store touch points, the website, social media or a magazine, it has to be one pure customer experience, not just to gain market share but to gain mind share. In this medium, the customer would now clearly see, hear and feel the brand vision; this would be the ultimate brand experience: our million square foot store if you will – that more customers will see and visit than all customers in all stores combined.

It's all about the brand

I told the team very early on when we hit £1 billion turnover, 'We are too big to be an individual sport; at Burberry it's a team sport. It is not about what's best for you; it's about what's best for the brand.' Burberry has been around for 155 years and as CEO I get to write a couple of chapters of this great story. My job is to write the most exciting chapters that I can and leave a greater and more compelling novel than when I arrived. That's how I see my role; it's not about me, it's all about Burberry and keeping it strong and relevant for another 150 years.

Prorsum show   © 2011 Burberry

Christopher Bailey – chief creative officer

Christopher Bailey can perhaps be thought of as the yin to Angela Ahrendts's yang. Together they make a formidable team. Christopher joined Burberry in 2001, having been senior designer at Gucci and womenswear designer at Donna Karan. Christopher is also the customer we interviewed for Six Senses Resorts.

My vision for the brand has always been to have authenticity: to respect the heritage and the history, but not to be limited by it. Our heritage is our foundation, but we continue to grow and develop.

I often talk about or think about the brand in terms of it being like a beautiful diamond. When Angela and I first arrived here we found that it had been slightly trodden into the ground, it was a little bit dirty, and it was a little bit dusty. Our role has been to take the diamond and just clean its facets and make them sparkle again, challenging people's perceptions about the brand whilst ensuring that we don't veer away from its soul.

The yin and yang of the brand

Our idea was to unite the brand, in terms of both the product and the culture. We have an attitude in the company of anything is possible if we all get behind it. I often describe the company as a 'young old company', because it's 155 years old, it's historic. But it has a very young attitude. In fact, the company is one of contrasts: young and old; inspirational and inclusive; luxury and democratic; global and yet local. We are big but we can act small.

Another contradiction is on the one hand being really focused on what our customers tell us they want and on the other hand having a clear point of view around design. If we speak to 10 customers, they will all tell us something different about what they want or what they think of Burberry and the way they perceive the brand. So it's hugely important to listen but still to follow our own path because we have such a strong idea of what the brand is. If we simply listened to everybody, nobody would have a clue about what the brand stands for, including me.

The reason why it's so important to have this clarity is because a consumer doesn't cherry-pick what they see of the brand. If they have different experiences of the brand that have nothing to do with each other, they become very confused about the brand's identity and point of view. And when you have no point of view people don't remember you. **That's what a brand is; it's about having a voice and a vocabulary, an attitude.** So if I'm online buying something, I want to have a pretty similar experience to going into one of our stores or showrooms.

Challenging conventional thinking

We are challenging some of the conventional thinking in the luxury industry by introducing a new global store that exists only on the web. It is going to be the biggest store that we have because it will cover the whole world; so that's a big deal. When everyone around the world can buy from the same store it changes that dynamic. For example, everyone can now buy straight off the runway – we call it 'Runway to reality'. So you can view our runway show online and then buy an item straight away for delivery to you six to eight weeks later. That is a seismic change

Worldstore

in the industry because all of a sudden the old model of spring, summer, autumn and winter collections with delivery between four to eight months later will become obsolete.

> To see the Burberry world store, click here:
> http://www.burberry.com

I think a web experience can potentially be even more enriching than a store experience because if I walk into a store, hopefully I'm welcomed with a smile and so on... But with the web I can be enveloped: in music, in attitude, in movement, in video: things that I might not experience in a store environment. How do I see that garment on a real person? How do I see it from every different angle without having to ask the salesperson? So for me it's not one channel or the other; it's making sure that you get a richer experience in both.

Being bold is instinctive

I would say that **being bold is about believing in your instinct**. You need to keep going back to that, because it's your instinct that drives you forward. The other thing is not losing sight of the fact that the brand is more important than the moment. You see, there is a legacy – it's going to last a long time, this brand. I sometimes describe my role here as being a drop in the ocean of time. I've only been here 10 years and the brand is 155 years old, so it's our role to look after this brand for the future. We are privileged to be looking after this beauty and we need to make sure that it lasts for a long, long, long, long time.

> To hear more from Christopher, click here:
> http://www.youtube.com/watch?v=PKN47vzg-sk

Sarah Manley – chief marketing officer

Sarah has been with Burberry for 10 years, having worked in a number of market-ing roles with the brand. Prior to Burberry she held positions in marketing and communications at Polo Ralph Lauren and Yves Saint Laurent.

We have four regions: Americas, Europe, Asia and Emerging Markets; and we have heads of marketing in all those regions. They are responsible for developing a plan, based on our marketing strategy, appropriate for their region. But there are certain things that we create centrally under Christopher's direction that will never be created in the regions.

The reason we do this is because we're striving for consistency: one vision, one point of view and one marketing approach. So if a customer comes into a store in New York or Hong Kong or Milan, they will have a consistent experience.

The old young company

We are a company that is old but new. We have 155 years of history, but we try to behave in a very modern way. Our digital marketing strategy is a great example of this. There are many brands out there that are nervous and prefer to watch and see before they actually do anything in this space because it's new and sometimes untested. By contrast, we're trying to be bolder, always innovating and testing new approaches, while staying true to our values and our heritage. Take our social media site, artofthetrench.com, which allows our customers to upload images of themselves wearing their trench coat and comment on the photographs they see there. We took the very core of our brand, our iconic trench coat, and used it in a very new way to entice, excite and entertain the consumer. And it's working – the site had more than 9 million page views in the nine months after its launch in November 2009.

See http://artofthetrench.com/

Engaging with customers

We're introducing the brand to lots of young, new customers who weren't really engaging with Burberry before. We're giving them content that is compelling and interesting: we're entertaining them. And so we're growing a new customer base and building awareness a lot faster than our competitors. In fact, in autumn 2010, we became the first luxury brand with more than three million fans on Facebook. And yet retaining our luxury sensibility online is really important to us, and so it's not just about throwing everything you possibly can onto your website, or onto your social media sites. We position ourselves as luxury online by not behaving like we are online.

Burberry Acoustic: http://www.burberry.com/acoustic

This concept of being an old new company permeates all our communication. For example, the way in which we shot our autumn/winter 2010 advertising campaign was an industry first, using immersive digital technology that allowed customers to manipulate the images and products online. This was truly innovative and took the luxury customer experience online to a new level.

In many ways we are behaving much more like a media brand than a luxury retailer. In 2010, 40 per cent of our marketing budget was spent on digital and content creation because we believe that this is the future in terms of building awareness and educating the consumer about Burberry. So whenever we think about marketing strategy now, the first thing we think about is how we do it digitally, before we think about offline. Offline remains important, but the balance has definitely shifted to digital.

If you go back to February 2009, we were showing our women's collection in Milan, at Milan fashion week where we had been showing for the past eight years. That show was attended by 1,300 people. In September 2009 we decided

Burberry Autumn 2010 Advertising   © 2011 Burberry

3D   © 2011 Burberry

to celebrate 25 years of London Fashion Week by showing in London instead and, for the first time, we decided to stream the show live. Doing this meant that around 55,000 people actually watched the show. So the difference that digital marketing made was that it enabled us to move from reaching 1,300 people in February to 50,000 plus in the space of six months. And it wasn't just a passive experience – viewers were engaging with the show at a new level, thanks to the ability to post comments in real time.

In February 2010 we decided to take it a step further and to film the show in 3D and show this simultaneously at private events in five different cities around the world. These, together with the live streaming, meant we reached 120,000 people with this show. However, if you take into account the reach of the 80 different websites around the world that partnered with us to stream the show live on their websites, this number increases exponentially. We believe that we have the potential to reach around a million consumers in this way, and so the way in which it raised our brand awareness was truly huge.

Runway to reality

We also realized that it wasn't just about entertaining people in a room any more. If you go to a fashion show it never starts on time. **We realized that we needed to entertain the people online** waiting for the show to start. So we had 20 minutes of pre-show content, interviewing people as they arrived, watching people arrive on the red carpet, wearing the Burberry product. Add to this the launch of 'Runway to reality', whereby we enabled people to click immediately and buy what they were watching – something we now do for all our shows. No other brand had ever done that.

Understanding changing patterns of consumer behaviour is vital for us, and so keeping at the forefront of digital marketing is central to our overall strategy. Through this, we're developing new ways to entertain our customers while helping them to understand more about the Burberry brand.

See 2011 spring/summer show:

http://www.youtube.com/watch?v=n51LNPrBOIU

http://uk.burberry.com/store/content/experience/
spring-summer2011/index.jsp?WT.ac=LP_MW_B1

Reg Sindall – executive vice president, corporate resources

Reg Sindall joined Burberry after senior customer service and HR appointments in multi-brand organizations and hospitality companies.

There is a very clear and distinct sense of brand within the business. **The company and the brand are indivisible.** There is no sense in which people within Burberry distinguish between the brand and the company and perhaps this is one of the fundamental differences between Burberry and other major companies in which I've been employed. This single focus is so powerful because there are no dissenting camps; there are no thoughts of 'Our brand is better than your brand.' In multi-brand employers that I've been with there are always times when one brand thinks it's the top dog and another one isn't. There are always times when one industry sector has the dominant position. Sometimes it's because they have the best people or the best products. More often than not it's because the industry itself is going through a positive cycle and so they are doing the best. But in Burberry we rise or fall together, and I think that's part of the fundamental difference between this and other businesses.

HR as a strategic partner

The HR function was similar to the way that the rest of the company had operated historically. It was disjointed; it didn't take a global perspective. People lived in their own little boxes. And so, as **the strategic changes in the business focused on creating one pure brand, so HR had to change and reflect that as well**. You can be the best HR person in the world but if you're going round touting solutions looking for problems, then you're going to fail. And all too often that has been the case with the HR function: people have thought of a great idea and then they've gone round looking for a problem that this solution can solve. That isn't the case here.

There were very clearly identified business needs before I arrived and what we've done is to help shape and structure the HR strategies and the nature of the team to deliver against those.

Three golden rules

Three very basic ground rules were the foundation for this. The first one is that you are a part of a team, and that team, ultimately, is the brand. So make no bones about it, there is no room for being partisan or sectarian in any way. The second one is that there is no point in having a hospital without doctors, so you need to be the best technical experts you can be. If someone from another function comes to an HR specialist and says, 'I want your help or advice on something,' you'd better know what you're talking about. But if you just do that then there's a danger that you'll offer the latest theoretical advice. And so the third simple rule that we introduced is that, above all else, you've got to be commercial. You've got to be grounded in the business needs. And those three simple rules have made a major difference in terms of changing and transforming the way in which the HR function has operated.

This is a business which is over 155 years old, and so our higher purpose is to make sure it stays around for another 150 years at least. So the long-term vision for the business is to continue to build on our heritage, to continue to innovate but to still be around in future. Now, clearly, we won't be around to say whether we've been successful or not but I think if we've done the right things we should have a pretty good view that Burberry as a brand is likely to still be around in another 150 years' time.

The three words that we use to describe the culture internally within the business are to protect, to explore, to inspire. Those words are just as relevant today as they were when Shackleton and Scott wore Burberry clothing on their polar explorations.

For example, we're inspiring people to understand their potential, inspiring people to deliver better service, inspiring people to want to produce new products, new ideas and new perspectives to our customers. That's as relevant today as it always has been. Inspiring people in a business which is growing at the rate that we're growing is absolutely critical in order to fulfil and fuel that growth.

It's still within our product focus to make sure that we protect our customers in what they wear. Our outerwear and iconic trench coats are a great example of this. But, actually, it's just as important that we protect the brand; it's important that we protect the heritage; it's important we protect our people, our customers and our reputation.

And we continue to explore, be it through our geographical expansion into new markets, our experiments with new means of communication and new ways of working, or in striving to bring still better service to our customers and development opportunities to our people.

The perfect storm

We went into the recession on the back of a period when we had been sailing along, all sails out, with a perfect following wind. The recession and the credit crunch changed all that and we found ourselves sailing into the perfect storm. That didn't mean, though, that we had to lose our momentum. We just found different ways to keep moving forward. And that was very much what we were determined to do. We weren't going to let this recessionary time and the credit crunch stop the growth of the Burberry brand. That was absolutely clear to everybody. And so we took the decision to continue to invest in those things which are customer facing in order to continue to fuel our growth. You know, there's an adage which you'll often hear people in Burberry talk about, which is: '**Nobody ever cost cut their way to prosperity.**' Of course, we're very prudent with our use of money, but we're using it to fund growth and that's quite a different proposition from many other businesses.

There were a number of positive consequences to this. The first one is we did not experience the drop in morale that many other companies faced. We have had remarkably low levels of voluntary turnover. In fact, our reputation as an employer and the desirability of Burberry as a place in which to build your career have shot up. The other thing is by continuing to invest in those customer-facing activities, whether it's been through digital marketing or the Burberry experience in the stores, what we've done is to send a strong message to our people, which is that we haven't lost momentum. We are still growing and there's still a brilliant future for you here with this business. And that's a very powerful message few companies have been able to replicate over the last couple of years.

The Burberry experience

One of the real challenges for us as a brand is to make sure that that sense of welcome, that sense of aspirational, democratic, approachable luxury becomes a reality for more and more customers. One of the things that should make Burberry different from the competition is the fact that no matter how little someone has to spend, if they want to buy something, even if it's a key fob, they should still come into the store and feel so welcomed, and go away with such a brilliant customer experience, that they will forever cherish that product, and they'll forever remember that experience. And as they continue to be successful in their life they'll continue to be loyal customers.

The fundamental issue that we've worked on is to really change the way in which we approach the customer and to build a service culture that is set to become, in our view, unique in this business.

Burberry Store

© 2011 Burberry

Bold lessons

One brand, one company, one experience

The key thrust of the management team has been to unite the organization around the brand and ensure absolute consistency in the way that it is managed. The danger of the franchised model for so many organizations is the difficulty in getting the franchisees and owners to share the same priorities as you do. Burberry overcame this by buying back the brand. For companies that cannot do this, aligning stakeholders behind a common vision and strategy is imperative.

Think of the company holistically

The yin and yang concept tells us that there has to be a perfect balance between hard and soft strategies, old icons and new ideas, maintaining the heritage of the products but in a contemporary context and thinking about individual channels as seamless customer experience. So many organizations think about all of these things in isolation with different departments, with different priorities vying for scarce resources. In these cases it is usually organizational politics rather than what is right for the brand that will determine the outcome.

Have a point of view

Christopher Bailey is intensely focused on his target customers and what they value but also has a very clear understanding of what he believes the brand is about. If you don't have a strong point of view about your brand then you should not expect your customers to either. Being all things to all people is a recipe for mediocrity. The lesson for consumer brands particularly is to understand at a deep level what your brand really stands for: its DNA. It is this understanding that brings true authenticity through tone of voice, imagery, product design and the nature of the customer experience.

Embrace digital but don't get distracted by it

The internet is just another customer channel. It may be capable of so much more than traditional channels but that is no reason to treat it as a separate and disconnected part of your marketing mix. It should be integrated with all other marketing activities and work with them as an integrated whole. At the same time, because of its power to actively engage and involve consumers, as Burberry has with the 'Art of the trench', it should not be seen as merely a 'moving catalogue'. Find ways to get your customers to become part of the brand community.

HR practices that support the strategy

We have found through our own research that there is approximately an 85 per cent correlation between the way your employees feel about the brand and the way that your customers do. It goes without saying, therefore, that the employee experience must mirror the customer experience and the brand must present the same values to both audiences. 'Democratic luxury' means welcoming stores and an inclusive experience. Those same attributes must ring true for employees too. What Burberry did was to align the HR strategy with the business strategy and ensure that the employee and customer experiences were the same.

For more on Burberry visit **www.burberry.com**

Burberry shows the importance of knowing your brand, staying true to it and making sure the decisions you take are to support it, not devalue it. It's appropriate therefore to continue our story with another brand that stays true to itself and has taken decisions to protect its distinct approach over the years. BBH is our next bold brand.

· ·

BBH

Chapter Seven
BBH

When Bartle Bogle Hegarty Advertising opened its doors in the mid-1980s it quickly established a remarkable reputation in the marketing and advertising industry. Its bold decision to refuse to do any creative pitches (ie produce speculative advertising campaigns as part of pitching for a client's business) went against existing practice and caused much debate. It was part of a broader philosophy the founders had about the importance of strategically grounded and effective work. Their belief in the marriage of creative, strategy and client management as three equal and interdependent pillars was a vital part of their approach and quickly won them high-profile clients.

Within a decade, BBH had become one of the most admired agencies in the world. It now employs nearly 1,000 people in offices around the globe, including Shanghai, Singapore, Mumbai, São Paulo and New York. It has won numerous awards over the years, including twice being named Agency of the Year at Cannes (the big annual global advertising industry event), winning 32 Institute of Practitioners in Advertising (IPA) Effectiveness awards, becoming the only agency to win both IPA and APG (Account Planners Group) Effectiveness Awards at the same time and being named the Global Agency of the Year by *Advertising Age*.

Despite selling 49 per cent of its shares to the Leo Burnett Advertising group, it remains fiercely independent; its symbol is a black sheep. More importantly, in an 'industry' so often criticized for being superficial and wasteful, for having high levels of employee turnover and huge levels of ego, BBH continues to win plaudits for its effectiveness, has notably long tenure among its staff and remains committed to its basic recruitment policy of finding people who are 'talented and nice'. In 2009, during the depths of the recession and the swingeing cuts in advertising budgets, BBH employees voted for a pay cut to try and avoid redundancies, a sign of the strong sense of culture which has defined the company from day one.

Find out more about BBH here:
http://www.bartleboglehegarty.com

Bold practices

BBH

- Refused to do creative pitches – against the standard practice of the advertising world.
- Pioneered the 'micro-network' approach to building the agency globally.
- Offers sabbatical to all staff with 10-year tenure.
- Pioneered financial transparency so that clients could see where their money was being spent.
- Provides doctors to visit staff in the office – as well as beauticians and therapists!
- Refuses to work in certain sectors such as tobacco and politics.
- Refuses to compromise on creative work – even re-shot an advert out of their own budget, rather than present work they thought was simply 'good'.
- 'Resign' clients for whom they do not have respect.

Nigel Bogle – founder

Nigel Bogle founded BBH in the mid-1980s with John Bartle and John Hegarty; his background is in account management, the client service side of advertising.

It is very important in the first year of a business venture that you have a clear vision of what you stand for as a business. If you don't do it in the first year, it becomes increasingly difficult to be very clear about what you are.

Get the first year right

In our first year, we had a number of principles of how we were going to run our business: the importance of the founding client, the fact that we weren't going to do speculative creative work in pitches – which everyone thought was lunacy – the fact that we wanted to enjoy ourselves and that we wanted like-minded relationships, the fact that we were each from a different discipline and that we believed that great advertising comes from the effect of those disciplines working together as a team, the fact that it was a fireable offence to sell a piece of work that hadn't been signed off by the founders. All the ways of working were hammered in within the first 12 months and are evidenced in how this company is today. There were tangible manifestations of the fact that we wanted to be the best advertising agency in the country.

Our 'founding client' philosophy is very important to us. When we started we had no business. We were eight people. We had an overdraft from Barclays in Hanover Square and we felt that our founding clients, our first three or four clients, would inevitably define the way we were seen. And founding clients tend to be much more entrepreneurial and risk taking than clients who come to you 20 years later. Therefore we were very keen to say to those founding clients, 'We will commit to you in a way that we won't commit to any other clients; we will be on your business for as long as you want us to be.' And we got Audi, Whitbread and Levi's in the first four or five months. They are fantastic brands and they helped us to become quickly visible in the marketplace.

Build long-term partnerships

We have quite a lot of long-term relationships. Audi has been with us 27 years, as had Levi's until very recently. Unilever has been with us for over 15 years. The key to that has been our two core values of stability and restlessness, which are very odd bedfellows. Ours is a stable business in terms of vision and personnel and I think that is reassuring for clients. We don't have lots of 'guns for hire' coming in and changing this place every three years. We grow our own management. But we are very restless; we like to do new things for our own business. There is a very strong fear of failure at BBH and I think that is what drives us on. We are always better with a mountain to climb. You're three phone calls from disaster, is the mantra I live by. So I don't think we ever take for granted that any of our relationships are ever secure. We never sit there and go, 'We can take it easy here.' We are constantly trying to move the thing forward, to do new stuff. We don't spend a lot of time wining and dining. Our relationships are built through our work.

In a productive client–agency relationship there is a sense of partnership. The most important thing for us at the front end of a relationship is chemistry and like-mindedness or the ability to become like-minded. We can't work for a client who is constantly telling us how we should do what we do. We work well with a client who is constantly telling us what they want.

Stay true to your own brand

We also think about our brand image and what kind of clients will help us develop that image. There are certain categories where advertising is a formula and it's very effective. There is not a lot of interest for us in working in those categories. We can't bring anything new to it. We are more interested in working in categories or with a brand where things need to be changed. We used the statement '**When the world zigs, zag**' to reflect our desire to change the nature of advertising in a category. In fact, we set up a brand innovation business called 'Zag' that is imbued with that spirit.

Levi's zig zag ad

© 2011 BBH

The black sheep is a very important part of our identity and the black sheep is about going your own path, doing your own thing. There has been a very strong belief from the beginning that BBH is a company that likes to be in control of its own destiny. At the same time, as we went global as a business, we wanted to have a partner who could shepherd us into markets that we didn't know and stop us making mistakes that we might have made on our own. We also had a lot of people who had worked with the company for a long time, who we felt deserved to capitalize on their investment of time and commitment. So we sold 49 per cent to the Leo Burnett Advertising group (now Publicis Group). The minority deal meant we would get the support which we wanted and they could work with us on certain pieces of business, like Johnnie Walker. Almost every agency group who wanted to buy us would say, 'We've got this great idea. We're going to do this with your business.' Leo Burnett was the one company who actually understood our business. They didn't want to buy the majority. They understood that we were the black sheep and they understood that we wanted our freedom.

Retain independence of thought

The great advantage we have as a private company is that we do not have to have quarterly results. We do not have to answer to the City every three months, if we've done well or we've not done well. We have very long-term views about building business. So when we went into Singapore, I remember saying, 'This is going to take 10 years to build the business.' In America, 'This is going to take 10 years.' And it does take a long time to build a business like BBH because we're not opportunistic, we don't chase after everything.

Having said that, we run our business like a public company, with the same kind of disciplines, reporting targets, hitting targets, making sure we make our numbers, driving our margin, etc. We are very disciplined about our financial performance and the way we run the business. And we are very proud of the fact that we are seen to be a very well-run business financially. If you look at our business over time, it is virtually uninterrupted growth over the last 15, 20 years; and every year we've made a profit.

The biggest problem with growth in the advertising industry is you don't know when it's going to happen. Because you don't know when a client is going to pitch, it's quite difficult to control the growth. But my learning is **you should never grow faster than your ability to hire the best people**. So if you suddenly get huge amounts of new business, it is almost inevitable you are going to have to hire a lot of people quickly. If you hire them quickly, you may not get the same quality. More importantly you won't have time to induct them into your business and so they won't really understand you. When we had won a lot of Unilever and BA business together, we shut the doors to new business for a while to bed that work down, otherwise we would have had to hire a lot of people. That's the big risk when you grow fast. That's when your company starts to lose focus.

Let the talent flourish

The most important thing about growth and growing a business, if you are a founder, is knowing when to delegate and when to release responsibility, when to empower more people. I think a big mistake that one can make, and we made it to some extent, is that you don't release that early enough.

There were times when John (Hegarty) and I were still signing off all the work and quite clearly the process was not working because there was too much work in not enough time. We were holding onto it because it was symbolic rather than because it was the right way of doing things. Now we have a very decentralized management structure. So, for example, the guys running Shanghai are responsible for everything that comes out of Shanghai. We make them accountable and responsible, and give them the right kind of support and inspiration.

Increasingly, in creative business, I think you **have got to be prepared to release the potential of your young talent**, to give them a lot more authority and accountability than one might have done 10 years ago. You have to say, 'I know he or she is only 23 but that is the person who needs to take responsibility for this because they are a digital native.' You have to remember the guy who started Facebook was 23 and the guy who started Bebo was 22.

Embrace change fast

Our world is changing out of all recognition but we still can't see the future as clearly as we should because a lot of us have come out of a broadcast culture and are now into a digital culture. And the biggest challenge will be to change fast enough. That is going to be huge. We are doing well because we want to change. I just realized you've got to love change. And the advertising industry doesn't. It's frightened of doing things differently. There is too much reverence for what has gone before. I find that quite frustrating because I fear that I am going to leave this business and we still won't have got it as modern as it should be. My advice to my 26-year-old self would be, '**Work harder at embracing change**.' You have got to be prepared to fail a few times. So don't be frightened of failure. Don't think because you fail once that it's wrong. Don't always get risk averse if you don't get it right first time. We've had lots of things that have failed. Lots of things that haven't worked out and cost us a lot of money. We always learn from that. We go on putting money into things that might not work but we believe they might.

It's all about the people

But one thing that won't change for us is the importance of hiring the best possible people we can. We have two principles in hiring people: they must be talented and nice. We look after them, we hope, pretty well. We have around 50 shareholders in the company, we have good bonus schemes, and we pay well. We offer a range of benefits: a company doctor comes in so people don't have to go to their GP and waste half their day; there are beauticians who come in; there is a culture club that organizes events all the time. We spend a lot of time training. We have a global head of talent department. We have very good HR functions to make people feel that they are really cared for. We have always had a sabbatical policy to reward long service – so for every 10 years you work with us you are entitled to a month's sabbatical.

I see my prime responsibility as a manager as being to create the sort of environment in which people can excel, in which people can fulfil their potential. I say to every new joiner, 'This is a two-way street. My obligation to you is to help make you the best you can possibly be by creating an environment in which you can do that. And your obligation to me is to make us better by the fact that you have come from a different place. You know things we don't know, whatever job you'll do.' And diversity, in that sense, is really important. And then, giving people great brands to work on, making people feel proud to be part of it. The feedback we get when we do staff surveys is that people are very proud to work at BBH. They believe in the business because they know what the business stands for. And, as I said, we were clear what our business would stand for, from our very first year.

John Hegarty – founder

John Hegarty is one of the most respected figures in the advertising world; he is the creative force behind BBH.

'All roads lead to the work.' As soon as you, as a company, stop putting the work at the pinnacle of what you measure, then you will fall apart. In our industry you have to consistently come to work every day and have a new idea and that new idea can't be like yesterday's idea. I can't think of any other industry that is quite as relentlessly creative. There is a saying, 'You're not as good as your last ad, you're only as good as your next ad.' It's a business that recognizes talent very quickly and forgets it very quickly. So it is relentlessly creative. Managing a creative business where you require constant freshness, constant innovation and constant change is very difficult. I can't come in and go, 'Here's a John Hegarty idea... it's like this,' and everybody goes, 'Yeah, it's a John idea... fine, we'll take that.'

Create a creative environment

When you're in an environment such as ours, it is fundamentally important that the creatives feel that what they do is the most important thing in the company, that they are being encouraged to do what they want to do. We put different things together to make something else. And from that something else we create a piece of magic that has a value that other people get attracted to. To create a great idea you've got to make creative people feel positivity. It's easier to run through a field in lovely sunshine than it is to go through a tangly wood where it's pouring with rain and you're slipping and sliding.

If you don't have that, you won't get them pushing themselves to create the kind of work that they want to create. So it is fundamentally important that I encourage an environment of constant innovation, and that they know that when they do creative work, I am going to take it seriously and I am going to sell it as best I can. They need to feel that there is a circle of confidence around them. We sold 49 per cent of our company and kept 51 per cent because we determined that, if we were not in control, we couldn't genuinely say to people, 'Don't worry, we will resign that piece of business if it can't produce the kind of work we believe in.'

Listen to the clients

To sell great work you've got to let the client know that you've absolutely understood and listened. That's fundamentally important because they've got to feel: 'I've been listened to. They've understood the problems I'm facing and they genuinely are going to come up with a solution that is going to solve the problems I've got and the opportunities I have.' We always say to clients, 'Look, it's a partnership.

We've got to be open and honest with each other.' If I feel they are being absolutely open and honest and they just say, 'Look, I really don't like the work,' then I tend to continue. When we were working on Häagen-Dazs, we were on our fourth campaign and we didn't really like it; there was a feeling that the client just didn't want what we wanted. But we paused and asked ourselves, '**Have we really listened, have we really understood**?' And we went back one more time, with something else and the client said, 'That's absolutely it,' and we produced one of our most famous campaigns.

Häagen-Dazs ad   © 2011 BBH

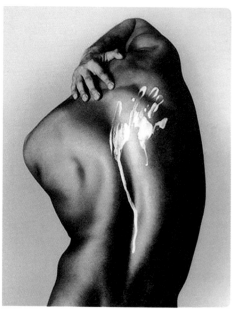

Stick to your principles

Bill Bernbach, who is the man who created modern advertising, has a famous saying: '**A principle isn't a principle until it's cost you something**'. And we've tried to live by that. We started by saying we wouldn't do speculative creative work and that cost us. But actually, in the long run it paid off. It cost us in the short run but I think the principle in the long run is supposed to pay back. The problem is it isn't an instant payback and so you've got to believe in it. Obviously if it instantly paid back, that would make life very easy!

We've also avoided types of work on principle. We always said we wouldn't work on cigarettes and we wouldn't work on politics. We made that call because of a rule which somebody, wonderfully, expressed once: 'I would never promote something I would not wish my children to partake of.' I thought that was a great way of expressing it because it put a moral component into that decision-making process that was very personal. So for everybody it would be different. I felt that if I was going home to my kids saying, 'Whatever you do, don't smoke,' and coming into the office promoting cigarettes, it would be hypocritical. The best creative work has an element of integrity to it. It is an expression of a truth and that's what makes one creative idea better than another – that it touches that truth and if you're not able to do that, you will compromise your creativity. So we said 'No' to cigarettes.

We said 'No' to politics for different reasons. We have this saying here: 'None of us is as good as all of us.' But politics is divisive. We thought it would be very, very difficult for people to be able to put away their very deeply held beliefs about certain political parties when they were coming to judge work. We feared that it would divide the agency and we wouldn't be able to say, 'Would you work for such and such?' So we couldn't guarantee to use the best of BBH if we were to work for a political party.

We've also had to make decisions about resigning a client, which is always a hard thing to do but sometimes you just have to. Sometimes new people join companies and change the point of view. They come in and say, 'I'm now the marketing director and I think the way it's being sold is completely wrong.' And you're faced then with the dilemma of 'This man's a lunatic. This is completely wrong and destroying what the brand's been building for years. So, do we resign it? Or do we try and work with that person? Or do we say, "In 18 months' time, someone will clock that this is really stupid and he'll be gone"?' Managing that dilemma is very difficult.

The importance of being lucky

People often ask me, 'What's your biggest mistake?' It's hard to answer, actually. I think so much of what I do is luck – and that's very hard to put into a business presentation. There are campaigns we've done which haven't been as successful as I'd hoped. There are people I've hired who have been a disaster, while other people I have hired whom I wasn't sure of, have turned out to be brilliant. My father, who was Irish, said, 'John, there's no point in being Irish if you can't get lucky.' For example, we did two commercials to launch the Levi's 501 campaign – which were tremendously successful and really cemented our reputation at the time. One was called Laundrette and one was Bar. Now all the judgement of the creative people here was that Bar was the better script. And, there was a debate as to whether we should make two commercials or one. The client was thinking, 'If I only make one of the ads, I can save production costs and spend more money on TV spots.' But in the end he went, 'No, we'll make two.' And so we made Laundrette. And that was probably the most iconic and talked about ad of its time, and it's still remembered today. It was his instinct, there was no research involved. And you go 'Wow! Now there's a decision.' There's no way you can quantify that. And that's the truth. Of course, business doesn't want to hear that. That's why research is so used in our industry.

The fact that it's sometimes completely useless, the fact that it often doesn't help to get great work is neither here nor there. Business will listen to it because it believes that it actually is necessary. It's a bit like religion – people believe in it because they want certainty but actually luck is fundamentally important.

To watch the seminal Levi's advert, click here:
http://www.youtube.com/watch?v=wT4DR_ae_4o

Turn intelligence into magic

I think we've had a fairly charmed existence and I think that is because we have applied that basic principle that it is 'all about the work'. To do great creative work, you must get the strategy right, understand the brand; like a building, you need a foundation before you put up a building. A phrase I use is, '**We are constantly trying to turn intelligence into magic**.' That magic... it is genuinely, genuinely hard.

Therefore you have to have managers who genuinely understand and have enormous sympathy for the creative product and the creative process and know how to work with creative people. The great creative minds are able to take complex problems and turn them into simple statements. And I think that's one of the great conundrums of great ideas. They look stunningly simple. And the reason they are stunningly simple is they open out inside your head. That's where I want an idea to open out. The means of painting or writing or film-making or advertising, or whatever it is, are just the means by which we get an idea into your head. It's just a route into your brain and the only space we're buying is the space between your ears. That's the space we're really trying to occupy. And the simplicity of putting that idea in there so it opens out is what we want to try and do. The brilliance of a great idea is that it's amazing how it diminishes problems and accelerates opportunity.

Gwyn Jones – global chief operating officer

Gwyn Jones joined BBH in London from university. He has been the CEO of its New York office and is now its COO.

When I joined this business, it had a real sense of purpose, a real sense of mission. It wasn't driven by what you might call conventional shareholder concerns. It was driven by a belief in the kind of work it wanted to do and the kind of company it needed to be in order to do that kind of work. And that made it stand apart from the crowd. And it's an odd thing because it makes you fiercely proud of your way of doing things and your state of independence. But it makes you a bit separate from the industry. You know, probably to an outsider we looked pretty much like lots of other advertising agencies but inside we felt like we were doing it differently. And that was a very powerful motivator and mechanic, I think, in the business.

Go your own way

The 'no creative pitches' rule was an example of that right from the start. A little later on, we pioneered 'open book accounting'. This was when the fee relationships between clients and agencies were starting to break down. Historically fees had been based on commissions that were derived from the media income that agencies generated when they were full-service businesses (ie they both created the ads and planned and bought the media that broadcast the ads). How the revenue flows were coming into the agencies based on their media deals was pretty opaque to clients. So we saw an opportunity to say, 'We're going to be completely transparent in how we engage. We want to be paid fees in a way that you understand what you're paying for.' That was a bold move at the time. Later on, when it became clear that for us to grow we were going to have to go overseas, we said, 'We want to build this organically.' The rest of the industry said, 'That's nonsense. You will never get to build a global business and partner with global brands by doing it step-by-step, organically. It just won't be quick enough and you need to do a deal – you need to become part of one of the big networks. That's the only way that will work.' But through a combination of naivety, arrogance and self-belief, we thought, 'Well, no, we don't want to do it like that.' So we started what is now referred to by the analysts as the 'micro-network' – wholly owned independent businesses in hub locations (New York, Singapore, Shanghai, etc) that has been a model for other agencies to follow, like Wieden and Kennedy, and Mother. And it has proved to be an effective way of servicing our global brand relationships. It may not be relevant for all brands; maybe there are lots of brands where on-the-ground presence from your agency partners in all 88 markets of your operation is the most important thing. But, in terms of finding the most efficient structure for delivering advertising to increasingly global consumers, there's a big enough slice of the market that is attracted to the way we do things. So, again that was a sort of step where the market said, 'No, that's not how global advertising works. You need to be a network.' And we said, 'Well, we're going to try and do it differently.' And it's proved to be a successful model.

Know when to adapt and embrace other cultures

When the agency was born we were part of the UK industry. So the way we set out was to say, 'Right, here's how we're going to be different from the industry. That's the way you create premium – by establishing your difference.' When we went to New York, it probably took us a while to get it right because I think we first went in there going, 'Yeah, we know how the US ad scene works. Well, this is how we're different.' And then there was a rude awakening because our reputation didn't precede us there. It took us a while to find the right balance of being different but being so in a way that was appropriate, acknowledging the ways of engaging in the US. And getting the right balance of leadership – so that it was an embodiment of the culture of the company itself, but it had leadership that was born out of the culture of the US market. Those are all things that took a while to evolve. And it's more of a roller-coaster ride in the US because the scale of national accounts there is so huge compared with a market like the UK. You tend to get much bigger shocks to the system in the States. You can win an account that will double your size in two months, followed by a knock that will have a dramatic impact. So it's a much more white-knuckle ride in the States. And that's something that it took us a while to adapt to.

The nature of the employment market was different too. Working within the UK – and probably much of Europe – London has a reputation as the single primary source for international advertising. Whereas in the States, there are other centres than New York, like Chicago, where big businesses were built up around the Mid-western farming belt, or the West Coast, where agencies built up around the entertainment scene. If you look at the great agencies in the US over the last 20 years, they've been in San Francisco, in Portland, Oregon, in Minneapolis, in Miami and in Boulder, Colorado. The centre of creative and commercial success in market-ing services is not focused on New York. And because of that, the people that work in the industry tend to be much more mobile. I can remember one of the first things that happened to me when I was there was that an account manager who worked on Levi's resigned. I naturally assumed there was something wrong and sat her down in my office and said, 'What's the problem? I hear great things. You're doing a great job. Clearly we're doing something wrong.' And she said, 'No, no, you've got it all wrong. I just want to go back to San Francisco. You know, I've done a few years in New York.' And I found that transient approach to business and New York very different from being in London.

Our way of doing international development has taken a lot more time and cost a lot more money than would have been the case if we'd simply done a deal to jump into a network. And that has had implications for shareholders, doing it that way. But we feel we've built businesses in those markets that are part of our business and genuinely part of the brand. So I think one of the things we find now as we develop businesses in other parts of the world, is that some of our newer offices feel like the most ardent advocates of BBH culture and values because they're adopting it afresh in a new market. So, if you were to visit our office in Brazil or in Shanghai, they are in no way watered-down expressions of something that thrives in the mothership. **They are absolutely the most vibrant expres-sions of our brand** as a business that you could hope to find. And the sense that

Boddingtons cone ad

they're touching new ground and establishing markets really reinforces that pride in a positioning that's born out of difference.

Always look for where to make a difference

There's no question, it's got tougher working in this business. I look back at some of my early clients who had an instinctive understanding of how creativity added value to the business. They had more latitude to operate in because the means of measuring performance and accountability were that bit more lax, the ease with which people made brave, instinctive decisions was just more apparent. It's a harder thing to be a marketer now in cultures of absolute precise measurement and accountability. John Banham (the former head of the Confederation of British Industry) had a great quote: 'In business we value most highly that which we can measure most precisely.' Whilst that's entirely legitimate and understandable, it's also hard not to let it be a constraint in a business that's supposed to be about creativity. Because what that kind of culture delivers is more sameness; fewer unique selling points in the world than there used to be; the ability for retailers to quickly copy each other and for the high street to look the same in each season. But at BBH we think, 'God, the opportunity for difference must be more profound than ever.' It's hard to get it out there but if you can... it should be great.

Charles Wigley – chairman of BBH Asia

Charles Wigley joined BBH as a graduate recruit at the same time as Gwyn Jones. He left the company to travel the world but rejoined in Singapore, becoming Chairman of BBH Asia.

We were a business that was anchored in London and it proved very successful and then the challenge was to extend the model without becoming another network. I mean, there was no point us replicating the big network agencies that had 60 plus offices worldwide. We needed a different model, so we landed upon the whole notion of creating hubs – regional centres of excellence. We were quite open about that. I think everybody expected us to go west first to New York but we decided to go east, in a typical zag-like piece of thinking. It gave us an opportunity to bring something distinctive and new to the market.

The importance of a common culture

Our hub approach has a huge advantage because it encourages a cohesive culture. Clients walk into our offices around the world and are universally surprised by how they know they're in BBH. If they go to another one, they say, 'This is very similar.' Our management around the world get together frequently. Account teams around the world know each other. It's such a huge competitive advantage in pitches when we're competing against big international firms where it's quite clear that their people have met for the first time a couple of days before.

I think one of the things we've learnt globally is for our culture to be consistent in its principles and overall approach – not necessarily in the specifics of its output, which will vary. I think one of the big challenges we've had to overcome is moving from a very UK-centric culture and set of judgement criteria to a more international culture. And that's been quite a big transition for us. That's an interesting challenge for a creative company with some very strong creative voices in it around the world. There are different aspects to it, certainly in Asia. First, the way you do business here is more relationship based, in terms of depth and length of relationships. As a creative partner to companies, you're allowed to do more and more over time as you win trust. It's very rare to be able to do high-impact work from the get-go. Then there's the whole area of 'What is good?' I mean, what is good to me as a middle-aged, UK-educated British citizen may be very different from what is good to, say, a young Chinese man living in Shanghai, working in finance. We may wear similar brands, he may be very plugged in and Westernized but don't be fooled by that. You scratch the surface and what people actually enjoy, what they like in terms of communications, can be quite different. So if you have a very strong creative culture like BBH's in the UK, where I trained, there's kind of an in-built set of guidelines in your head about what constitutes a great piece of advertising. That is highly culture specific – go somewhere else and they may look blankly at you and say, 'No, it doesn't constitute something that's great.' You have to start understanding from different perspectives what really talks to people. Now, sometimes you can create essentially the equivalent of a Hollywood hit that travels everywhere. And we've become quite skilled at doing that. But quite often you're not in that world.

But I think the key thing, in terms of our cohesion, is based around the company DNA – its spirit, its values – as opposed to the specifics of 'Well, this ad is good and this ad is not good.'

Good and nice

We have a global policy which is very simple: we want good people and we want them to be nice; good and nice are slightly saccharin but it's worked for us over the years. You want smart people but you want ones you can actually spend 10, 12 hours a day with. I mean, our industry is slightly blighted at times with quite unpleasant people. They don't tend to last too long in BBH. So, the fundamental thing is you hire the smartest people and you make sure that they're the kind of people that aren't complete egocentrics and can get on with others. The industry is going through a revolution now, and there are many different craft skills, even from 20 years ago when I was training. So we're looking for people increasingly who are T-shaped people: the downstroke of the T being their specialism – they have to be brilliant in their specialism – but they also have to have the horizontal T bar too: to be open to and actively interested in learning about everybody else's specialisms as well. Because, you know, we've got teams now with technologists, you know digital technologists, who sit in the same room with an old-school long-copy writer. They are going to have to make something that works online. So both of them have to be quite open to what the other has to offer.

Honesty is the best policy

A key differentiator for us in Asia is that we're distinctly non-pragmatic. I think we're one of the few agencies in this part of the world that resigns business. Being globally an independently owned company still enables us to do that. If essentially you have a disagreement with a client that you're not going to get past, then politely parting ways is the only option. Now that, in a UK or US context, is fairly normal. It's not in Asia. Recently, the Singapore office walked away from Tiger beer, which is part of Asia's biggest brewery. It was talked about for weeks in the marketing community and stood us in good stead in terms of differentiation. **We're also incredibly clear about what we do and what we don't do.** Whereas, I think, a lot of our competitors attempt to do everything and not all of it particularly well. We won one of the biggest clients locally a year and a half ago, the Singapore

Tourist Board. Our opening line in our first meeting was, 'We'd love to work with you but we certainly don't want all the business you put on the table.' They said, 'What! Nobody says that to us!' And we said, 'No, it won't be cost effective enough for you to do that.' I think almost every other agency was fronting up with, 'We'll do all of it. This is how we'll do it. Here are our 15 different departments, blah, blah.' We said, 'We really won't be cost effective for you on that but we know some people that can do it very cost effectively.' That focus and brutal honesty around process and what we are really good at were a massive point of difference.

SJA ad   © 2011 BBH

A grape stuck in my throat. I couldn't breathe. It was really scary. But I knew a grown-up would help me. Who was clever at first aid. Who knew that all I needed was some hard slaps on the back. Because grown-ups always know what to do. Don't they?

Abigail West 2005-2010

You can be the difference between life. And death. To find out how search 'life saved'.

David Gates – global category director for whisky for Diageo and BBH client

David Gates was the global marketing director responsible for the Johnnie Walker brand; BBH was the agency working on that account.

BBH are inspiring. They're curious, they're opinionated and they're infuriating. They have an opinion about everything – which is something that's special. Some agencies exist to sell work and really what they care about is selling the work and getting the fees in. BBH care deeply about what they do and they care that it's right for the brand. That means that they hold really, really strong opinions about what excellence represents. And they'll stand by that opinion. Sometimes to the point of being irritating because if I have an alternative opinion or one of our markets has a different view, we'll get into real conflict. But that is partly what I respect about BBH. I think businesses tend to be quite conservative and there are parts of our business that are really, really very conservative but I think BBH believes so much in creative brilliance that they will at times create tension because they will be constantly pushing to be new, to be antagonistic, maybe; but most of all to be noticed. In a world of so much advertising clutter, being noticed is actually critical. There's one quote that is attributed to John Hegarty which I have repeated many, many times to people because I think it is my philosophy as well as theirs. It is: **'I'd rather be noticed once than missed a dozen times.'** BBH really do live that philosophy.

Be committed to the best possible work

You can tell very viscerally when you're talking to agencies whether they care or not – whether the brand and the creative output matter to them. The difference in somebody who cares and somebody who's wanting to make a sell is, at least in my mind anyway, really obvious. I think nearly everybody at BBH cares about both the brand and the creative output.

For example, we agreed a script recently for Johnnie Walker. It was a fantastic script and all the stimulus looked like it was going to produce a brilliant film. The agency went off to Kiev and shot it but, when they came back, it wasn't delivering the promise of the script. They kept working at it, putting us off and we were getting more anxious, saying to them, 'Show us the film!' In the end, they said, 'Look, we are not happy with this. It's not good enough. It's not up to our standard. We want to throw it away and start again at our own expense. We promised you something that would be great and this isn't good enough.' So they literally threw it away and they started again. The irony was that it wasn't nearly as bad as I was expecting. Actually, if they had brought it to us in the state that it was in and tried to convince us that it was okay, I think we might have been persuaded. I mean, it wasn't so ridiculously awful that you would go, 'Oh, God!' I think many other agencies would have tried to sell us that work. But in the end they were right and the final work was far superior.

Crisp thinking, creative excellence

BBH have a good combination of some very charismatic people who are, in inverted commas 'very nice', and some more introverted, sometimes prickly, characters who are massively respected. Their 'niceness' is important but it doesn't distinguish them for me. There are plenty of nice people in all of our agencies. What distinguishes them is the crispness of their thinking and the excellence in their creativity.

Be constantly curious about the world

When we appointed BBH, it was quite an edgy thing for us to do because in the past we'd worked with JWT, Leo Burnett, Saatchi and BBDO – who were all big global agencies. And BBH weren't. They only had offices in London, New York and Singapore. Shanghai wasn't open, Tokyo wasn't open, Brazil wasn't open, and India wasn't open. But we took the view, at that time, that what was important was going to the best creative shop that existed. Obviously, the distribution of advertising can be achieved through a big network. But what we wanted to buy was the best planning, the best creative that money could buy regardless of where it was. I remember being in Brazil at the time when BBH came out as part of the pitch process. They were three Brits who knew nothing about Brazil but they invested the time in understanding the market and they were intellectually curious people. If you are a global brand, like Johnnie Walker, nirvana is finding a global insight and a global idea. Because it drives scale, it drives stature and it drives efficiency. Great thinkers combined with great creatives will produce great work for you. Then it's a question of either adapting it or, in some cases, distributing it.

I guess if I'm looking at the BBH case study from our own perspective, we would say this approach has worked really well for us. We don't want agency networks with dots on their map. We want incredibly insightful, intellectually and culturally curious thinkers who can find the common insight that binds your brand with your consumers.

Johnnie Walker 'The man who walked around the world' advert: http://www.youtube.com/watch?v=pAVv23DrD-I

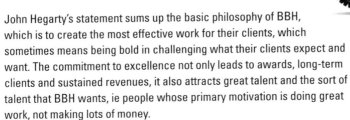

All roads lead to the work

John Hegarty's statement sums up the basic philosophy of BBH, which is to create the most effective work for their clients, which sometimes means being bold in challenging what their clients expect and want. The commitment to excellence not only leads to awards, long-term clients and sustained revenues, it also attracts great talent and the sort of talent that BBH wants, ie people whose primary motivation is doing great work, not making lots of money.

When someone zigs, zag

Differentiation is essential in brand building but often the differences between one brand and another can be relatively minor and occasionally cosmetic. BBH's example demonstrates the importance of being demonstrably, and occasionally bravely, different. Whether it be in challenging their industry's conventions on creative pitching or growing an international network, or in pursuing work which transforms perceptions of a particular category for its clients, BBH is determined to ensure standout for their clients and themselves. Again, in John Hegarty's words: 'I'd rather be noticed once than missed a dozen times.'

Look for some simple attributes in your people

There are numerous tools used by HR departments and recommended by management consultancies to recruit people. From psychometric tests to simulation exercises, there is a 'science' that has grown up around recruitment which can often seem complex and impersonal. BBH have grown successfully because they have kept their recruitment policy simple. They are effectively hiring for DNA and use the basic criteria of 'good and nice' as their mantra. Like other of the businesses we have covered in *Uncommon Practice*, in *See, Feel, Think, Do: The Power of Instinct in Business*, and in this book, they have yet to find a replacement for the good old-fashioned interview and the use of their intuitive sense to determine who is and who is not a BBH person.

Protect your independence

Whether it is financial or operational independence, the bold businesses work best by being allowed the freedom to do what they want to do in the way they want to do it. Freed from the shackles of short-termism and able to invest time and money in risky ventures, they have been able to innovate, create great products, build people's careers and earn sustainable profits. BBH's decision to sell only a minority share in the business to Leo Burnett proved a shrewd one because Leo Burnett – once the largest independent agency – was subsequently taken over by the Publicis Group, an amalgam of various advertising and marketing agencies. BBH has thus retained their independence while Leo Burnett has not.

Being brave

One of the characteristics that the bold brands share is courage and it's a trait BBH has repeatedly shown. It takes courage to know when your work does not meet your own high standards and refuse to release it to the client. It takes courage to 'resign' a client and walk away from good business because the chemistry is not right. It takes courage to walk into a pitch and say, 'We are not the most cost-effective people for that work,' as BBH did with the Singapore Tourist Board.

Stay true to your brand

At its best a brand acts as an organizing principle for a business, a 'North Star' which guides decision making during good and bad times. BBH – as one should expect of practitioners in brand building – has an almost intuitive sense of what its brand should be about and acts accordingly. The symbolic black sheep represents the notion of independence and standout that has guided the business in its choice of clients, categories, work and strategies for growth. Staying true to your brand is a belief that BBH shares with one of its iconic clients, the fashion house Burberry that we profiled in the previous chapter. Staying true to your brand is also demonstrated by the company you keep.

http://www.bartleboglehegarty.com/#/europe/news/
burberry-celebrates-25-years-at-london-fashion-week

BBH is a brand that shows the importance of a founding vision and how the founders have stayed true to it as the business has grown dramatically. It's a lesson that our next bold brand also teaches us. The Geek Squad is a great example of the single-mindedness of one man.

Chapter Eight
The Geek Squad

Brands don't get much bolder than The Geek Squad, the technology support company. From a one-man start-up in 1994 the company has grown to become an internationally admired brand offering technical support for home users and small businesses when their computer hard drive crashes or they get a virus. But that was just the start of their ambition. The Geek Squad, with just 100 locations, merged with US retail consumer electronics brand, Best Buy, in 2002 and absorbed Best Buy's then 700 stores on its path to global domination. If there was ever a case of a minnow swallowing a whale this was it. Today the company numbers well over 1,000 stores and 150,000 employees, and has recently bought 50 per cent of the UK's Carphone Warehouse to bring the Best Buy brand to the UK.

Despite the 40 per cent year-on-year growth rate, the company feels small, with Robert Stephens, the founder, still actively involved in hiring and training new people. One of Robert's favourite sayings is: 'We only have temporary custody of talent,' and the enormous lengths that he goes to in creating a bold, zany culture where 'geeks can feel at home' is testament to this belief.

The whole organization dramatizes the Geek Squad experience through language, organizational structure, titles and even the uniforms the Special Agents wear. It has created an enormous word-of-mouth effect. As Robert says, 'Marketing is a tax that you pay for being unremarkable.'

Bold practices

The Geek Squad

- The Geek Squad brand promise is 'We'll save your ass.'
- New hires are presented with a 'Mission Impossible' task to test their ability to navigate around the city in which they will be working.
- Organizational titles, structure and roles are all designed to change the way people think about themselves.
- Above-the-line marketing until recently was a measure of last resort, with word-of-mouth recommendation being the primary source of new business.

- Despite never being visited by customers, Agents working in the call centres all wear the Geek Squad uniform to preserve their identities.
- The words 'Geek Squad' are moulded on the soles of the Agents' shoes so that in the event they are walking in snow they leave an imprint of the logo as free advertising.

Robert Stephens – founder and chief inspector

Robert Stephens started the Geek Squad in 1994 with $200. His vision for the company is 'global domination'.

Robert Stephens
© 2011 The Geek Squad

The thing that was uppermost in my mind when I conceived The Geek Squad was starvation.

I tell people that the best thing that ever happened to me when I started my company was that I had no money because otherwise I would have paid someone else to come up with a brand and a name and a logo. **The reason start-ups are often so innovative is because of what they don't have; what they don't know**; which allows them to see things through fresh eyes and take chances.

The Geek Squad mission

When I started out I had never created a company before, but, you know, I'd heard some of the things you were supposed to do. You should have a mission statement. Well, what's a mission statement? Okay, well, it really clarifies why the company exists, what its ultimate end goal is. My problem is that most mission statements are so corny, and yet, when you have no money and you're about to drop out of college for the second time, you kind of figure, hey, this had better work or I am going to have a pretty nasty reputation as a quitter or a person who doesn't really finish what they start. So I said, okay, really, the goal of every company is global domination.

I believe if Microsoft had just told everybody 'We would like to dominate the operating system,' and said so in that clear, unambiguous language, they would have at least earned respect for clarity and consistency. So we're very honest, our goal is simple: 'Complete global domination of the technology services market.' Of course, this doesn't mean physical domination, rather domination by reputation. You need to be clear about what your goal is and that's ours. Notice that our mission says 'technology services'. Our plan was always to support screens and networks but when I first started in 1994, there weren't many networks around so it was mainly screens. Now there are screens in your pocket, on your mobile phone, screens in your car and screens in your living room. Now you can kind of see we're just going to be doing the same thing for the next 20–30 years as more and more screens proliferate on more and more networks.

In the early 1990s, as normal people started buying computers, there was such a rush to keep up with the demand that Dell and Microsoft and the other manufacturers just focused on moving boxes and product. Service was an afterthought. But when commoditization occurs, as it does in every industry sooner or later, service becomes a great differentiator. Now hardware commoditization has occurred and it is increasingly happening with software. Commoditization and complexity are creating too many choices for consumers, too many buttons to push, too many software updates to keep track of, and customers like their lives made simple: one number to call when they need help. So that was my big idea.

There is what you do, then there's how you do it

My intuition was my research but whenever I fixed computers to make extra money in college, I did start noticing a pattern. First, there is what you do in business and then secondly there's how you do it. **What you do is your function but how you do it becomes your reputation.** I noticed that showing up on time is a form of advertising and being polite is a precursor to word-of-mouth recommendations, and explaining what you're doing and not talking down become just as important as fixing the technology. And it wasn't just that the manufacturers like Dell Computers were not offering enough customer support, it was also that the technology support companies who were supposed to provide service were rude, showed up late, did not keep their promises or just didn't do the job right the first time. This created the opportunity for one company to come in and become the brand that represented the ideal of how it should be. And that was really the basis of the business model.

The DNA

Then I said, 'Why don't I give it a name that's generic and that implies intelligent people banding together in the service of whatever support you need and the name itself is the advertising. It tells you everything you need to know about the brand, the organizational culture, what the people are like and what they do. It's a kind of paradox between the individual smart person – the geek – but then the power of the network – the squad. No one individual in this company will know everything but together they know everything.' And so that was the genesis of the DNA. Once I went down that path, it kind of liberated me to say I'm going to go with a name that is also humorous. So we became The Geek Squad.

You know, humour is a subtle form of self-confidence. If you poke fun at yourself, it means you have knowledge about yourself and are comfortable with what you are. It is also very useful in my industry, which often gets criticized for being arrogant, talking down to customers and not revealing their knowledge. So this is going to be a company that is comfortable with itself, it knows that the 'geek' is in the social ascent and the 'jock' is reliant on the geek to get their technology to work. But the way to win over the public is to make fun of ourselves because a company can humanize its brand by using different forms of humour. We employ a kind of British dry wit, which is essentially comedy with a straight face. The name's already funny, so we're not going to be silly when we get to your home. In fact, it works even better if we don't acknowledge the humour at all: we just show up on time, we're dressed smartly, we get the job done efficiently. So **behind what may look like marketing gimmicks are some very intricately woven brand elements that are inseparable from the actual function we perform**.

The Geek Squad promise

I never did much advertising in the beginning, but somebody gave me free advertising for fixing their computer. So I had to create an ad. I've got the name 'The Geek Squad', I've got the logo. But we needed a tag line and kept coming up with stupid saccharine phrases like 'We solve problems,' 'We help you' and so on. **This is where companies go wrong – they don't take a bold enough point of view.** That's what brands are for, to make you distinct from other entities. So I said, 'We'll save your ass,' and that became our brand promise.

I often say that **marketing is a tax that you pay for being unremarkable**. If people know you're using traditional advertising, you're going to pay traditional advertising rates. But if you come up with new ways to get your name and message out there, the chances are that prices have not yet been set for those new channels and therefore they are less expensive. In fact, now having gone from one employee to over 19,000 in the Geek Squad worldwide, my advice is – and parents will understand this – even if you have the resources to provide cash for the organization, you should occasionally starve them so the organization learns to fend and learn for itself. The danger is, the bigger you get the more resources you have and the more you get lulled into a very lazy way of thinking that is dangerous.

Keeping the creative hunger

As we have gotten larger and merged with Best Buy and now Carphone Warehouse, keeping this creative hunger is very important. The way we sustain our culture is through a natural network effect. I think we all would agree that social networking is nothing more than a technological version of a very primal human need to connect with others, and a very natural tendency to maintain relationships. The larger a company gets, the more diluted its culture can get, but you can avoid this by putting a few things in place.

If the DNA is protected properly as the organization grows, it carries a copy of itself in every person. That's why it is so important to have a strong point of view, to have a clear vision that is unambiguous in its language, so that if competitors copy you, it's very clear whose DNA they've copied. When people try to copy the Geek Squad, it's usually done poorly because if you are going to copy me, I'm going to make you stick your neck all the way out. But the kind of person bold enough to do that would probably do something original anyway, so, either way, it ends up not being competitive. The DNA helps the organization withstand the scaling-up of the entity so that the more geeks there are, the better the squad becomes. If you take five employees in one city and you spread them around the world, you've diluted the culture. But if you go from five employees in one city to 100 and then in another city you go from 100 to 500, you've actually increased the nodes on the network; you've increased the strength of the DNA and the network because the connecting points have all increased.

Agents   © 2011 The Geek Squad

The importance of language and metaphor

Then you have to deal with what I call the 'Founder's dilemma', and that is that the organization will begin to weaken if it relies on a central point, which is me. A founder, a strong leader, must work to fake their own death, as I refer to it, meaning get the network to be self-healing, self-replicable. And the way you do this is through the use of archetypes, myths, stories, rituals and your own unique language. All industries, whether pharmacists, firemen, law enforcement officers, all have their own language that helps to protect their culture, because language moves like a virus.

In our case the fundamental unit of the Geek Squad is 'the Agent', and the use of the word agent is very carefully chosen. In the US there's a company called Target, a very well-known retailer, and they refer to all their customers as 'guests', which changes the tone and context – which I think is brilliant. I did the same thing. I'm not interested in perpetuating the stereotype of the word geek. I never use the word geek outside the phrase 'Geek Squad' because there are other companies that use the word and they are diluting the meaning of it. That's why I refer to them as 'Agents', or they're 'Counter-intelligence agents', or they're 'Double agents'. In fact, we define any of our channels where a computer is fixed on a bench and not in a customer's home as technically a counter-intelligence operation. So we have a master brand with distinct subcultures which are named accordingly. This allows me to treat the departments as separate but equal. We have a group of people called our 'Secret Weapon'. The reason they are secret is because customers don't know this department exists within the Geek Squad but all the Agents do. When the Agents have trouble, they can call this number and it is the tech support function for the agents. The calls are very quick because providing tech support to another agent is very easy, it takes two seconds – versus an hour to explain it to a customer. It's a very efficient model that saves us a lot of money and helps to bind the culture together. It's our secret weapon. So the way we use language and titles simultaneously respects the individuality of the department or the individual, but it also prevents company politics or comparisons of power because you can't really compare a Secret Weapon to an Agent, to a Public Defender, to a Counter-intelligence Agent, all of which are real titles. They're not chosen just for the sake of humour. The words actually have functional meaning and define who we are.

What do you stand for?

The most important thing a company can do is to stand for something. The values the company possesses should be distinct and define the DNA. They should be impactful, with specific language used to define those values; not the saccharine, sugar-coated terms that are meant to please anybody and everybody. Brand is just as much about what you do as what you don't do. So the values are the light source that attracts people to a company. I think people are drawn to Apple, they're drawn to Virgin; we have an intuitive sense about what we think their brand values are and they'll be pretty close to what the founders probably intended; that's what makes them strong brands.

Then the next question is, how true are you to those values? In the company name, in the design of the logo, in the uniform, in the call centre experience. If you have a phone number, if you have a website, if you have an e-mail address that you communicate to customers; you are in the service business; the rest of what you do is merely those things that help drive that experience. I realized early on that you cannot *design* a customer experience because it is whatever the customer perceives it to be. What you can do, though, is to influence that experience through the people you hire. So what I began to realize is that I had a company name and logo that were created to be distinct and supported by the uniforms and the cars, each taking a functional role in creating our image, but that **the key to success was that I had to hand off that responsibility to each new employee and trust them to deliver our brand**.

Recruit for the experience

The brand became a filter. Some people turned down working at Geek Squad, they didn't want to be called a geek, or they didn't want to wear a clip-on tie. Wearing our uniform, if you think about it, is a type of forced humility. You really can't have an ego, wearing our uniform, and that's when I began to realize that the brand is almost more important in terms of how it attracts employees than customers. I recruit for the customer experience I want to deliver. So that's why in the last year I have moved away from the notion that we manage employees and distilled my philosophy to the concept that **we have temporary custody of talent**. That concept totally changes the management mindset away from management of employees to one of 'servant leadership'.

The question then becomes, 'How do I find the talent that will fit my brand?' I am currently negotiating with a film company in Hong Kong that owns the rights to the old Shaw Brothers Kung-Fu movie collection, and my hope is to create a Kung-Fu Film Festival in London and Minneapolis and eventually every city where I hire. Why? Because how you hire people begins to tell people what you stand for and what you're going to expect from them when they work for you. So it actually costs less money to rent a movie theatre and to hold a film festival where you show maybe an interesting double feature of the kind of films that only geeks would be interested in watching, mainly sci-fi films and kung-fu films. The result is you attract the kind of people who fit your brand and create a novel way of talking to them. There are only two types of people that will show up for this type of film festival: geeks and people who know geeks. So it is actually an efficient way to attract people from our target employee market and it costs less than an ad on monster.com. I would argue that recruitment should be your most authentic form of advertising.

Hire for values, train for skills

I believe if you ask enough questions you will pretty much come up with the same three values that it took me 15 years to discover, and these are 'curiosity, ethics and drive'. Those are the three attributes that I cannot train for and therefore I must hire for.

I'm teaching these to my recruiting department, which I call the 'Inhuman Resources department'. I call it that because HR departments can feel inhuman, so let's call a spade a spade and transform the typical meaning and bring it to the forefront, which enables us to have a different kind of conversation with our people.

Once I realized that the key to a great customer experience is to recruit for the employee experience and that you only have temporary custody of talent, I then realized that you have to figure out how to motivate them to stay with you. Our goal while you're with us, whether that be for six weeks, six months or six years, is to increase your value. How do you increase your own value? By showing up on time, doing it right, doing it fast, doing it well, engaging in curiosity, ethics and drive. If you do that, our brand will mean something on your CV, and therefore if you leave us, you will be able to command a higher rate of pay. So our litmus test is this: If you leave us and you go to work for a competitor for the same rate of pay, we have utterly failed you as a company. That is the benchmark that you can hold us to. We know that people leave managers, not companies, so you should expect inspiring leadership. I tell the leaders, 'Your job is to inspire employees, which means you must uphold curiosity, ethics and drive in service of that talent, and if you don't increase their value, then you as a leader are not being effective.'

The Geek Squad doesn't have my name on it, it's about the squad, it's about the network, it's about the crowd. We're seeing these trends towards self-organization. I've already started fading into the background. So now my focus is to detect talent and then position them where they'll have the optimal effect. And that's really my long-term plan.

Being bold can be as scary as hell

The boldest thing we did as a company was acquiring Best Buy. It's easy to be creative when you only have 50 or 100 employees or even 500, but it is as scary as hell when you have 15,000. The boldest thing I did personally as a founder was to remain with the business. I have ideas for 10 other companies in my head, all branded, all ready to go, but my work here is not completed yet. The world is

populated mainly by boring businesses but for creative people,
that's where the opportunities are to
contribute. If you think you're bold,
then I dare you to try and influence
150,000 people around the world
and get them to care about quality.
That's what I'm doing. It would be
easy for me to walk away and thumb
my nose at the leaders of the big
evil empires and say 'It's all their

Best Buy logo   © 2011 The Geek Squad

fault, they made the company mediocre,' versus saying, 'You know what, there
are two ways to change the world. You can either picket across the street from
the government office or you can take a job inside and begin to change the culture
one brick at a time.' I've chosen the latter because I think it's a more creative
challenge.

For more on Robert Stephens and the Geek Squad story,
click here:
http://www.youtube.com/watch?v=EeZLfy_
C254&feature=related

Jeff Severts – the promise maker

*Jeff is 'minister of propaganda' for the Geek Squad and currently working in
London on the introduction of the Best Buy brand into the UK market.*

I call myself the 'promise maker' in this business. We have 'promise makers' and
'promise keepers' and my team worries about the promises we make to customers. So what should the customer experience be like? What price will we charge
for it? How should we communicate the promise? How do we talk about it with
our employees? What levels of quality do we expect from the promise keepers?
Our job is to answer all these questions.

Our most powerful channel for making promises is through our 150,000 retail
Best Buy employees. We have millions of customers walking into our stores
every year and coming into contact with those 150,000 employees. **What those
employees say and believe about the Geek Squad is far more important than
any television ad that we might run.**

The Geek Squad difference

We have 20,000 Agents across the country. It's hard for me to promise the customer that the individual Agent they're talking to is always going to have the answer for every problem for every type of technology in every circumstance. So we try not to make that promise explicitly. The promise we do make, however, is that our network of Agents can find you every answer to every technical problem every time. They can do that because they're connected to each other, and somewhere within our huge network of employees we've got that answer. And that's what differentiates us from our regional or local competitors, or maybe an independent proprietor who is fantastically technically adept but is just one person. No matter how smart you are, there are limitations to how much one person can know.

We have a couple of ways that we use the power of the network to deliver our promise. We have what we refer to as 'Geek Squad Forums', which are web-enabled meeting places in which thousands of our Agents can log in and share information about challenges they're struggling with or insights they've discovered. We also have our 'Secret Weapon', which is the collection of our best agents across our different technical capabilities, who sit in Minneapolis waiting to take calls from our Agents in the field, who might be stuck with a particular problem. And our promise to the Agent is that either the Secret Weapon will know the answer or they will find it out very quickly.

Relentless pursuit of a crazy vision

When I think about how the Geek Squad is different to other places I have worked, I would say there's just a great audacity in some of the things we have done. So asking thousands of employees to dress up in a uniform that most people would view as ridiculous is audacious. Most business people would reject that idea as something that employees would not be willing to do. I can imagine the conversation: 'You are asking employees to wear pants cut three inches short above the ankles in order to show off their white socks? To wear a ridiculous short-sleeved white shirt with a black clip-on tie? And carry a police-style badge? Forget it!' Had I been at a former employer, I would have been on that same side of the argument, saying this is going to upset employees, hurt employee morale and consequently retention. But the conventional business logic was just ignored because of Robert's obstinacy and his relentless pursuit of this crazy vision he's always had, of what the Geek Squad could look like.

Geek Squad cars   © 2011 The Geek Squad

Geek Squad City

Another example is that we built a repair centre in Louisville, Kentucky, and by any conventional business wisdom this repair centre would have been called 'Repair centre number 12' and would have been in a dingy building somewhere. The people working there would have been allowed to wear whatever they wanted to work because they are not meeting customers. Instead what we did, mainly through Robert's encouragement, was create Geek Squad City. The head of Geek Squad City is naturally called the Mayor and our 700 or so employees wear the uniform, every day. Conventional business logic would never lead you to do that because the argument would be, 'No customer is ever going to walk into this repair facility. So why are you going to the expense of putting on this big show, when nobody is going to see it?'

But this kind of thinking is what enables us to preserve our authenticity. **There are things we do today that we could do far more economically but might sacrifice our authenticity** and so we choose not to do them. For example, moulding a Geek Squad logo on the bottom of our Agents' shoes so that if they just happen to walk in snow, the imprint of the logo will be left behind and people will see that the Geek Squad was there. Consultants would take a look at the things we do and describe them as waste. But they would be missing the point. We generally believe that we have two icons that dramatize the brand. They are the Geek Squad uniform and the black and white car. These are what consumers remember and describe as differentiating us from competitors.

Measuring the experience

We pay enormous attention to measuring how well we are delivering our promise. To put this in context, the Geek Squad represents roughly 5 per cent of Best Buy in terms of size, yet we spend more money measuring the quality of the customer experience than the whole of the rest of Best Buy put together.

We have a virtual customer council of several hundred customers that we consult monthly. We'll put out new concepts to them. We'll ask for current pain points and get feedback on the experience from them. We'll ask for any new ideas that they might have for us, on services we could offer against emerging technologies or existing technologies. So we have sort of a constant virtual dialogue with an established set of customers. And then we depend very heavily on our Agents to help us develop new services, so they channel the customers' needs to us, because, you know, they're dealing with customers eight hours a day.

Our ability to stay ahead of competitors also comes straight out of the Agent community. I'd like to say we are all strategic geniuses up here at the corporate office, figuring out exactly what we should do to maintain our competitive edge, but the truth is we are not, though we do have the luxury of having this community full of energy and vitality that's always looking for ways to improve and grow. So a lot of our best intelligence about what's going on with competitors just bubbles up through the community and a lot of our best ideas for how we can compete with new entrants comes from our community. It's just a natural part of the dialogue we have.

Turning employees into heroes

Part of the magic that Robert discovered when he first built this business was that there was already a community to tap into: this community of geeks, if you will, who share the same values, who share similar life experiences, who share common needs. And he created a kind of home for them: a place they could feel part of and had been searching for. Robert says we have created a place for people who, for most of their lives, may not have felt like superheroes but knew inside they had superhero-like qualities. In coming to the Geek Squad, they felt like they came to a company that understood and appreciated them.

I believe that this should be possible in nearly every business context if you ask the question, 'How can I create a culture that makes employees feel like we understand and appreciate them?' And whether you are selling dental supplies or cars it should be possible to create a culture that feels right for the people who work there.

We have a tradition of using real Agents in almost all our advertising. For example, take our proposition 'Geek Dreams', which is about promising to find a solution to your technical challenges. Say I want to watch my home theatre underwater in my pool, is that possible? Our Agents will see if they can build a system that would be capable of being viewed and heard underwater. This is consistent with our culture of geeks rising to the challenge of whether or not technology can be used to deliver an experience. We feature our Agents doing heroic things for customers. This is just one example of how we use the Agents as our main marketing weapon.

I am sceptical that senior management in a large company can ever really be close enough to their customers. We all do our best to make sure we're getting out to the markets enough and that we're talking to enough customers. Any good manager will do that, but there are just physical limitations in running a large organization that prevent you from ever being as smart as you should be. But if you allow your employees to have a very loud voice on how you're running the business they will take care of that for you.

If you're lucky enough in business to have your original visionary leader, make sure you value their contribution appropriately and give them the right voice in setting the direction for the company and maintaining the culture. You so often read about companies starting up, getting to a certain size and then parting from their founder because that person is an entrepreneur, not a professional manager. I think it's a very short-sighted approach that ends up costing the company dearly because the value that that original visionary creates is very hard for an accountant to capture, though it is real nonetheless.

We have a real community that people are proud to be part of in a way that's very difficult to find in a lot of business environments. For example, I was talking to an Agent in one of our stores recently who was among the first generation of Agents who were hired. He was telling me that he had his badge framed and fastened to the wall in his living room. I can't think of any other business where an employee would be so proud to be part of that business, that they would take a piece of their uniform and frame it and put it on a wall. That story made a big impact on me because it sums up what the Geek Squad is all about.

Lee Williams – the Double Agent

Geek Squad Badge   © 2011 The Geek Squad

Lee is an Agent with the Geek Squad covering central London. He has been with the brand for four years.

I'm a Double Agent – Double Agent 5235. This means I go to customers' homes and fix their computers or any other problems they may have with their technology, but I also work in the store supporting our Carphone Warehouse customers when required. When people say 'What do you do for a living?' being able to reply 'I'm a Double Agent' is pretty cool.

Mission Impossible

My first impression of Geek Squad was the recruitment experience. I came up from my home in Bath to London and the recruitment day was structured like a *Mission: Impossible* task. I had to meet the interviewers for a briefing at an advertising agency in central London which was kind of a daunting place to meet for this little boy coming from Bath. Then we went for a drink somewhere and they said, 'Okay, the next person you need to talk to is waiting at this location, so off you go.' And then when I got there I had to find my way to another location.

All I had was my phone to rely on but I found my way round London quite nicely. I then realized that this was all part of the process: to see if I could navigate around London and get to a place by a certain time just by using my phone. In the end I was interviewed by seven people and **that was the first time I felt a company had taken the time to make it an experience rather than just an interview**.

The interviewers were different too. Some of them were just chatting about technology, so I guess they got a sense of how genuine I was with micro-technology, others just asked about movies and stuff, it was pretty cool. It was mostly 'How you hanging, dude?' – you know, getting to me rather than looking at my CV and going, 'Hmm, you've got this qualification, when did you get that?' So yes, it was quite cool.

Special Agent training

My training as an Agent was mostly culture training. There was not much technical training as such. It was mainly learning about the brand and about Robert and his philosophies. He came to our class and spoke to us mostly about how to treat customers.

Robert says our uniform is like a filter for people. If you think you're too good to wear short trousers and white socks, you probably don't belong in this company anyway, so most people feel quite humbled being part of the Geek Squad. A lot of technical people can be quite arrogant about their knowledge, so it's really important to understand that it just so happens that we're experts in computing but it's not that special; customers pay us to impart our knowledge, not be spoken down to. I think most guys think it was pretty cool to dress up like an FBI agent for your job and be called Double Agent.

The training was good but generally I think the company just attracts some really prime people. The way we treat our customers is just the way we treat people normally in our lives and that just happens to be the right thing to do.

The thing with most computer repair people is that they don't look at actual solutions, they just look at the end result and the quickest way to get there, which I can kind of understand from a business point of view. But the thing about the Geek Squad is the extra time that we spend to fix your computer, so we sort out the culprits, the repair people who can give us a bad name, and get rid of them. We have a warranty so if anything goes wrong within 30 days of us fixing it we come back out and fix it for free. So you know you're genuinely paying for the solution rather than just paying for the time that we're there. We have a flat-rate pricing scheme, whereas other people charge by the hour and that leads to some sneaky people taking longer to do things than they need to. So our flat rate takes the pressure off the Agents to perform quickly and gives them the time to achieve a proper solution.

We are encouraged to think outside the box. For example, there was a customer whose computer was overheating and failing each time he tried to use it. We needed to get his data off the hard drive but each time we started it up it died because of the overheating problem. So the Agent opened all the windows in the house to make the house as cold as possible and then tried again. It worked; he was able to retrieve that important data for the customer.

Getting the badge

After the training and induction period you are awarded your badge but only once you have earned it because people really do have to prove that they're worthy of it. Generally it's around the three- to six-month mark. Our standard practice is to be five minutes early to appointments to show customers that their time is valuable to us. So often our supervisor, who is called Deputy Field Marshal will show up at the appointment and if you are there at least five minutes early you are awarded your badge but if you are later than that he has gone!

Most of our bonus is based on the customers' opinions of us. So we'll say to our customers after we've visited them, 'How did you find the experience?' and the big question is 'Would you recommend us to a friend?' And if we get a no to that – bad mark. If we get a yes to that – a good mark, so depending on how many of those you get a month that's what your bonus is based on.

The motivation for this job is definitely not money or anything like that but just seeing how you can change people's situations. It seems quite simple to us to fix something that can make such a difference to someone's life. So, you know, **being a hero is the big reward here...** when you save somebody's childhood pictures or something like that, it's quite awesome.

Baby Geek   © 2011 The Geek Squad

Casper Thykier – the customer

Casper is CEO of VEEMEE LLP, a computer gaming company based in London and an enthusiastic advocate for the Geek Squad brand.

I came across Geek Squad about 18 months ago through positive word of mouth from other people. I never really saw any marketing, I'm not even sure if they do any. It was one of those brands that had a mythology about it and friends said to me, 'Hey, have you heard of this company called the Geek Squad? You really should try them, they're amazing.'

I'm not that technically gifted and there is a growing anxiety about the amount of electronic equipment that you have in your home and the fact that you don't know how to use any of it and can't get the different bits to talk to each other. So friends who've had the Geek Squad treatment became evangelists about it. I guess the notion of having someone come to your home and solve all your technological problems in one fell swoop was just a huge gap in the market that needed filling.

Expectations and experience

I think my first experience of the Geek Squad was **one of those very rare occasions in life where the reality exceeded the expectation**, because it's such a singular message and such a pared-down approach that you can't believe it will be as good as it is. Thinking about the customer journey I had, it was brilliant at every single stage. So, from going on the website to making the initial phone call, where the person I spoke to was extraordinarily helpful... you know, when trying to figure out a time normally for support people you end up having to fit your diary around theirs, whereas this was, 'When is it most convenient for you – morning, noon, night?'

I was told who the Agent was who was going to turn up, what his name was, where he was coming from and why he was coming. Lee Williams is his name. (Editor's note: the same Agent who was featured in the previous section.)

Double Agent Williams

He was actually late for the appointment but dealt with it brilliantly because he had the courtesy and the common sense to phone to say that he was late but on his way and he apologized despite the fact there had been a big issue with public transport, which was out of his control. Normally somebody else would have just turned up late and said, 'Oh, yes, sorry,' but that would have mucked your plans up anyway.

He came in. He was in the gear, and, you know, his demeanour is one of someone who clearly knows that he is a geek and I don't mean that in a derogatory way. So you got an instant sense that there was going to be no problem that he couldn't solve. Our stress levels with the technology at that time were really high, so it was like the knight in shining armour coming in.

You know, I can see how people can get cynical about the Geek Squad thing, the uniforms, the badge, etc, because that's just the British way. But what I like about it is that it does what it says on the tin, it reassures me that these people are not like the rest of us. It just reinforces the fact that they are the guys who are going to know what to do to solve my problem.

It's very hard to gain a level of trust with a brand, and a level of advocacy, especially when you're a service business, because you're only as good as the person who walks through the door or answers the phone. For example, we have ADT come to our home to fix our security alarm. I don't know when they will turn up or who will turn up. One of their people upset my wife. I phoned ADT to request that this person does not come to my house. They still send him every time. They come late, they don't fix the problem, the problem recurs once they've visited and it costs the same amount to call them again. I feel ripped off by ADT because I hate the experience, whereas by the time Lee had come round and worked his magic, I'd have happily paid his charge twice over.

It's lovely to see someone from the Geek Squad come in and say, 'We can make all this very simple for you. Don't worry about the details, because that's why we're called the Geek Squad.' You know, that's the kind of service everyone should aspire to.

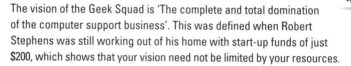

Bold lessons

Think big

The vision of the Geek Squad is 'The complete and total domination of the computer support business'. This was defined when Robert Stephens was still working out of his home with start-up funds of just $200, which shows that your vision need not be limited by your resources.

Be the brand

Robert Stephens is indistinguishable from his Agents. He wears the Geek Squad uniform and is ready to swing into action at a moment's notice when there is a computer problem. Shaun was giving a keynote speech at a conference and had a problem transferring the file. Robert immediately came to the rescue and provided a complimentary Geek Squad USB drive. Problem solved. Ass saved.

Engage with customers

The Geek Squad monitors social media like Twitter to identify when people are having computer problems. When it does so it sends a tweet to the person, offering to help. Robert was concerned that this may be construed as spam and so sent a tweet himself asking for people to let him have their views on whether it was okay or not to contact people directly.

The brand has used mainly viral marketing and word of mouth from happy customers to create awareness but as it has grown larger it has begun to use television ads to get its message across.

To see a Geek Squad advertisement, click here:
http://www.youtube.com/watch?v=q4l_
RIWs3TM&feature=related

Dramatize your brand through the experience

The strategy has been to create a distinctive end-to-end experience that screams 'The Geek Squad'. Each and every member of the organization is a walking, talking advertisement for the brand. By stretching the Geek superheroes and police squad metaphors to the extreme, the brand makes it impossible for anyone to copy them without it being obvious they are doing so. The experience is distinct, recognizable and memorable.

The importance of language and tone of voice

Although the Geek Squad's success is founded on its excellent customer service, it is its innovative use of language (both verbal and visual) that has distinguished it and built its memorable brand personality. Robert Stephens intuitively understood that language could be used not just to point out function or highlight a selling point; it could be used to organize the business, attract and deter recruits, shape and reinforce culture, and both set an expectation of experience for the customer and enhance it. It has been a remarkably successful form of corporate neuro-linguistic programming (and a geek would know what that means!).

Relentless authenticity

Many companies will take their marketing ideas so far, until they cost too much money or until they perceive they have performed their useful function. The Geek Squad are different; whether it be the logos on the soles of the shoes or the naming and uniform of non-customer-facing staff, it pursues its distinctive approach relentlessly regardless of whether any tangible return on investment is generated. It does so because its entire approach is founded on a culture of authenticity – geeks behave like geeks even when the customer isn't watching.

Super-heroes need super-tools

One of the most customer-friendly innovations has been remote support, where an Agent accesses the customer's computer remotely and is able to carry out maintenance or repairs without ever having to visit. For a small monthly fee, customers can call up for help and get this service at any time.

To see remote access in action, click:
http://www.youtube.com/watch?v=cluHXQAIN2k

The company DNA is the foundation for growth

Enormous attention is paid to the culture and the DNA of the brand through hiring, training, titles and performance management. One of the ways that the culture is reinforced is through a 24-hour hotline that Agents use to record and share their customer stories. Another is through 'hiring people for personality and their ability to innovate rather than technical ability – they can be taught that'. The firm has steadied at a year-on-year growth rate of 40 per cent, but the firm will not hire people unless they are right. The Geek Squad understands that the company DNA is as important for the effective running of the company as the source code is to the efficient working of the computers they repair.

For more on the Geek Squad, click here:
http://www.geeksquad.co.uk/about-us

The Geek Squad's insight was that you could turn people's fear of and dependency on technology into an opportunity to entertain as well as reassure them. They created a 'wow' experience by emphasizing a very human approach. Our next bold brand, Zappos, has similarly taken what could be a remote, technologically driven experience – shopping online – and found a way of ensuring it has a high human factor. It's made the provision of 'wow' its mantra. Like the Geek Squad it encourages its people to be 'humble'.

part of the
Zappos
family

Chapter Nine
Zappos.com

Nick Swinmurn founded Zappos because he couldn't find shoes one day in a San Francisco shopping mall. He went home and tried online but without success. So, on the spur of the moment, he decided to quit his day job and start an online shoe retailer. This was his vision:

- One day, 30 per cent of all retail transactions in the US will be online.
- People will buy from the company with the best service and the best selection.
- Zappos.com will be that online store.

The company required funding and one of the investors was a young man named Tony Hsieh who decided that selling shoes was more fun than being an investor. Over the past 10 years Zappos has grown to over $1 billion in sales annually, and has been included in *Fortune* magazine's annual Best Companies to Work For list. In November 2009, Zappos.com Inc was acquired by Amazon.com in a deal valued at $1.2 billion. In 2010, Zappos.com Inc was restructured into 10 separate companies under the Zappos family umbrella in order to enable the brand to 'sell anything and everything'.

The Zappos strategy is to provide customers with the very best service, what they call 'Wow' service, and to ensure the items get delivered to customers as quickly as possible. In order to do that, the company invests in its own warehouses, and everything they sell they ship themselves, unlike most other online retailers. This process costs more but enables the brand to have absolute control over the customer experience. This in turn builds trust in the brand, which has enabled the company to expand from selling shoes into other categories.

For more on Zappos, click here:
http://about.zappos.com/

Zappos

- Zappos handles all of its own warehousing and shipping to control the end-to-end customer experience.
- Prospective employees are asked: 'On a scale of 1 to 10, how weird are you?'
- Zappos offers new hires $2,000 at the end of their first week of training to leave as a way of testing their passion to work for the brand.
- Zappos's core values are:
  - Deliver 'Wow through service'.
  - Embrace and drive change.
  - Create fun and a little weirdness.
  - Be adventurous, creative and open-minded.
  - Pursue growth and learning.
  - Build open and honest relationships with communication.
  - Build a positive team and family spirit.
  - Do more with less.
  - Be passionate and determined.
  - Be humble.
- Zappos allows call centre representatives to do whatever it takes to deliver 'Wow through service'.
- Employees are encouraged to use Twitter any time to communicate with colleagues and customers.

Tony Hsieh – delivering happiness

In 1999, at the age of 24, Tony Hsieh sold LinkExchange, the company he co-founded, to Microsoft for $265 million. He became an investor and one of his interests was in a small online retailer called Zappos. He soon became CEO and the rest is history...

I was running an investment fund with Alfred, who is now our COO/CFO. We invested in about 20 or so different internet companies and Zappos just happened to be one of them. What made it interesting was that it was an online shoe retailer. Footwear in the US is a $40 billion market and about 5 per cent, or $2 billion, was being done by paper mail-order catalogues, and so, in our minds, from a purely

Tony Hsieh   © 2011 Zappos.com, Inc

investment point of view, it seemed like a good bet, because, at the very least, we thought that the web would catch up to what was already being done by paper mail order catalogues. That was pretty much the only thing that got us interested. But then I soon realized that investing was pretty boring for me and I really missed being part of building something. So I joined Zappos full time and have been there ever since.

The big idea

Our initial strategy was 'Let's just offer a large selection of shoes,' and that was pretty much the extent of our thinking. The original business model was actually 100 per cent 'drop ship', meaning we wouldn't actually hold any inventory ourselves. Instead, any time a customer placed an order, we would actually send the order to the manufacturer and they would ship the product from their warehouse direct to the customer. So that was the original idea and, on paper, it seemed like a great business model, because there was no inventory risk, but the reality ended up being a little different, which is that we weren't getting accurate inventory information and a lot of times the manufacturers didn't have the best products available in their warehouse. So we ended up doing a hybrid approach for a little while, where part of what we sold was inventory that we bought and held ourselves in our own warehouse, and part of our business was drop shipped. It eventually got to the point where about 25 per cent of our sales were coming from this drop-shipped revenue and that was pretty easy money because there was no risk on our part. But in 2003, after about four years of being in the business, we asked ourselves, '**What do we want to be when we grow up? Do we want to be about shoes, or do we want to be about something more meaningful?**' And that's when we decided we wanted the Zappos brand to be about best customer service and the very best customer experience.

Once you know your purpose, everything else follows

Once we had made that decision, the next decision was kind of made for us – but it was probably both the easiest and hardest decision we've ever had to make in the history of the company. It was to walk away from that easy, low-risk, drop-ship revenue. At the time it was a tough decision, because we weren't yet profitable, we couldn't raise funding, but we just knew it was the right thing to do if we were serious about building our brand for the long term around the very best customer service. So we took a deep breath and overnight literally flipped a switch and turned off that 25 per cent stream of our most profitable revenue.

Our decision wasn't really based on any analysis; it was more about '**What are we going to be proud of building 10 years from now?**' We've been focused on customer service ever since. It's actually made a lot of the subsequent decisions of the company much easier, because everyone in the company knows that story and so they know that we're willing to sacrifice short-term revenue and profits if it's for the long-term benefit of the company and our brand.

Having made the decision to focus on service, our number-one priority in our company became our culture because our whole belief is that, if we get the culture right, most of the other stuff, like delivering great service or building a long-term enduring brand, will just happen naturally on its own. **Our view is that a company's culture and a company's brand are really just two sides of the same coin.** Brand is just a lagging indicator of culture.

Hiring for fit

It starts with our hiring process. Everyone hired in our headquarters here in Las Vegas – it doesn't matter what position you're applying for, you can be an accountant or a lawyer or a software developer – has two separate sets of interviews. The hiring manager in his or her team will do a standard interview looking for a good fit within a team, prior experience, technical ability and so on; but then our HR department does a separate set of interviews, purely for culture fit, and the candidate has to pass both in order to be hired. So we pass on a lot of really smart, talented people that we know can make an immediate impact on our top or bottom line, but if they're not a good fit for our culture, we don't hire them. And the reverse is true too. We'll fire people even if they're performing their specific job function perfectly well, but if they're not good for the culture we'll fire them for that.

Training for fit

Everyone hired here, again regardless of role or position, goes through the same four-week training programme that our customer loyalty reps go through. It includes the importance of our company culture, our company history, customer service, and finally training on customer service tools. Then they're put on the phone for two weeks, taking calls from customers. Again, it goes back to our belief that culture and branding are the same thing and our conviction that if we're serious about customer service being our brand, then customer service shouldn't just be a department; it should be the entire company.

As a result, we tend to be a pretty flat organization, and regardless of what your specific job function is, we really encourage employee involvement. If an employee has an idea that they're passionate about, then they just run with it, even if it isn't part of their job description.

We use social media a lot but we didn't do this originally for customers, we did it for employees. We train new employees on how to use Twitter, and if you go to twitter.zappos.com you'll see a list that links employees and then there's another page that you can click on that aggregates all of their tweets together. It is just another really great way of helping build our culture, which is our number-one priority.

Click here:
http://twitter.zappos.com/

Doing things differently

We run our customer service centre differently from most call centres. We don't measure call times, we don't try to up-sell, we don't have scripts. We really care about each telephone interaction and treat it not as an expense to minimize or an opportunity to get revenue but as one of the best branding opportunities out there. What we've found is that, if we get the interaction right, then customers will remember that for a very long time and tell their friends and family about it.

I think our biggest challenge is making sure that, as we grow, not only does our culture not weaken but it actually gets stronger and stronger. A lot of what we do is trying to figure out these things as we go along, but a lot of it is based on employees coming up with ideas – it's not me coming up with ideas. Right now we have about 1,500 employees and if I came up with one great idea a day, that's 365 ideas in a year, whereas if all our employees came up with even one great idea a year, that's still way more ideas than I could come up with on my own.

Departments also have their own culture initiatives. They just come up with some idea they're passionate about and then go and do it. So last week our developers decided to do a parade in honour of Twitter and they had someone dressed up as a Twitter bird and they went parading around all our departments. Last year, our HR department decided to do an Oktoberfest kind of celebration, where they went around and distributed sausages to everyone. None of this is really mandated or planned; it is just each group coming up with its own ideas.

Our secret sauce

We have two locations now, Las Vegas and Kentucky, so it won't be exactly the same as we grow in new locations, but they're going to be based on our core values, so there will definitely be a lot of similarities and the things that make us Zappos will be the same wherever we are.

The thing we have realized is that customer service is about making customers happy and culture is about making employees happy. We also try to make our vendors happy. So the thing that kind of ties all of this together, **our secret sauce, if you will, is that we're really just about delivering happiness**.

To hear more from Tony, click here:
http://www.youtube.com/watch?v=oYNssS_DCPo&feature=player_embedded#!

Tony has recently published his first book, *Delivering Happiness*. Click here for more:
http://www.deliveringhappinessbook.com

Wendy Fitch – the happy customer

Wendy Fitch works for a marketing company and is involved with brands every day. That is partly why she became such a passionate advocate for Zappos.

I was actually looking for some shoes for a friend's wedding, and I found some at a store here in Omaha that I liked but they didn't have my size. They were also pricey at this store so, although I had never shopped at Zappos before, I just hopped online and found they had the same shoes with no sales tax or shipping. So I decided to buy them and that was my first purchase from Zappos.

That was easy!

A few days later I was online, showing the shoes to a friend on the Zappos website. She made some reference to the brand and she said those are good shoes. And I said, 'Well, I hope they are – I just spent $90 on them!' My friend then pointed to the price shown on the web, saying that they were on sale at a lower price than I had paid. I was initially impressed because the customer service number was on that page. I didn't have to go digging, it was so easy to find. So I called the Zappos call centre and said that I just bought these shoes and they are now on sale and advertised at $18 cheaper than I had bought them for. The agent looked at my account and she said, 'Yes, we do make price adjustments, but we can make the lower price to you within 10 days of purchase.' So she said, 'We'll credit your card right away but it's going to take a couple of days to be reflected in your account, but you're credited and you're good to go.' It was a matter of minutes. And then she ended the call – and this is my first purchase – by saying, 'I'd love to provide you with a link to our VIP website, where you can bookmark us, and then you get free shipping all the time and other perks.' I was just amazed that they offered me that incentive as a one-time customer. I hung up the phone and I remember thinking that was the easiest customer service interaction I've ever had.

The charity walk

Some while later I was participating in a three-day 60-mile charity walk for breast cancer. Whilst I was away I created an out-of-office notice on my personal e-mail account – saying something along the lines of 'Thank you for your message. I'm currently hitting the pavement walking 60 miles in three days to put an end to breast cancer.' After the event I return home and I'm going through stacks and stacks of mail, and I see this handwritten envelope from Zappos.com. Since it had been a couple of weeks since my shoe purchase I assumed it was a thank you for the order or something. I opened it and it was this handwritten letter from a customer relations rep at Zappos. I get their e-newsletters and it was sent out while I was away and so they obviously received my out-of-office reply. This customer relations rep decided to open the out-of-office reply, read it, and then act on it. And so she wrote me this note that said – I'll just read it verbatim right now:

FIGURE 9.1

'Hello, Wendy, while working through e-mails from our amazing customers, I came across your auto-reply. Normally we mark them as auto-replies but yours caught my eye. I just wanted to let you know what an admirable thing you are doing. We at Zappos are proud to have you as a customer and as a part of our family. Thank you for being a wonderful person'

Ashleigh

And it was signed 'Ashleigh'. It took me a couple of minutes to figure out what had happened and then I was floored. I couldn't believe that she took the time to read my out-of-office e-mail, respond to it, look up my contact information and write me a handwritten note. I was just amazed. I think it's the best thing ever!

The power of word of mouth

I write my own blog and I related this story on it because I was so impressed. I must admit that I don't have a huge following on my blog but one of my best friends reads it. She works in customer service and happened to be at a conference in California late last fall. There was a Zappos representative on the panel and they were talking about how you can get your customer service representative to live and breathe the brand. Anyway, they told this story about me and used the customer relations rep from Zappos as an example of customer focus. So my friend called me, freaking out, and she went up to the Zappos people afterwards and said, 'You know, that's one of my good friends.'

I still have Ashleigh's note on my bulletin board.

Weird

Alexa Farnes – the happy employee

Alexa joined Zappos as a phone representative in 2008.

I heard about Zappos for about two years before I decided I was going to give it a try. I was working as a loan officer at another company and I just kept hearing how great Zappos was. A really good friend of mine worked here and would talk about it so much but I didn't believe it. I thought there's just no way that there could be a workplace like the one she described at Zappos. But I got really tired of all the corporate BS where I was, so one day on a whim, I gave her a call and I said, 'Look, if this place is really like you're telling me I want to be a part of it.' So she referred me.

These people are really weird

I went through the hiring process, which was like nothing I have ever experienced. It was absolutely amazing. It was such a refreshing experience for me. You go to selection at most companies and are nervous because they are super-professional, ties, dresses, rigorous and almost scary interviews. You get such a different feeling when you go to Zappos and they start going through the application form and the questions that they have. You think, 'Are they serious, is this a trick question?' And then you start to realize that it's all about being different and about having different perspectives on people and how they look at things. One of our core values is creating fun and a little weirdness and that's one of the first impressions that I formed during the interview. For example, one question was, 'If you could be a superhero, what superhero would you be?' I chose Superwoman because I like to think that there isn't anything that I can't do or can't learn to do. The second question was, 'If you could have a theme song, what theme song would you have and why?' I chose 'Don't Worry, Be Happy'.

> Check out Alexa's theme song:
> http://www.youtube.com/watch?v=wnj_8k6xUlg

Don't worry, be happy

When you walk into this building, everybody's just smiling, everybody is happy. You can really feel it. It's like an aura that surrounds the entire building. You walk in and everybody smiles. The philosophy here is that if the employees are happy, the customers are going to be happy – it's kind of a trickle-down effect.

The initial training was absolutely amazing. You think of training in most companies and in my experience it lasts about two or three days and then they throw you out there and you have to fend for yourself. You get that sink-or-swim type of feeling. When I arrived here I went through a month of training and then started what we call the incubation process, where we come out of training and are assigned to a different group and they continue to make sure that we are developing the skills that we need to assist the customers at the level that is expected and continuing to have the resources that we need to succeed. After a month of incubation I came onto the floor but I felt so prepared and so ready and just so helped that the first time I ever took a call I was not at all scared.

Focus on the customer – no limitations

Zappos is like no other company... the culture here is so different. Our customers are important. We want to make sure that their experience, not only with the services that we provide, but with the products that we sell, is the very best. A lot of companies care about service but not to the degree that we do. We go out of our way to make sure that not only do we build and maintain our customer base, but we try to keep track of all the feedback we receive and we really, truly take that feedback and try to learn and to grow from it. I think that **whereas other companies are more focused on the bottom line, we're focused on the long-term picture**, believing that if we take care of our customers we will be successful.

In the recent economic downturn, our whole feeling was that we never wanted to look back and say we should have done this or we should have done that, so we took measures to ensure that we covered all our bases. One of our core values is doing more with less, so we really took that to heart. For example, there are no call-time targets here. We don't have limitations on how long we spend helping a customer, every customer is important no matter how long we need to be on the phone with them. That being said, though, we have become so efficient that we don't have a lot of abandoned phone calls. So efficiency is important, but there's never been a situation where we've been told, 'Hurry up, get that person off the phone.' There is no limitation here.

Wow through service – what would Tony do?

Our main objective is to deliver 'Wow through service'. Everybody here is empowered to do what whatever they need to in order to ensure that the customer is satisfied. We have a catchphrase here: 'What would Tony do?' If we're ever in a situation where we're unsure what to do, we say 'What would Tony do?' and 'If we were in the shoes of that customer, how would we want to be treated?' Because of this attitude 90 per cent of calls usually result in the customer saying 'Wow,' so we offer 'Wow through service'.

It all comes back to word-of-mouth advertising and Zappos has grown because of the service that we have provided and how much we have been recommended by satisfied customers. We care so much about this that it's very important to us to know what our customers feel about us, so we like to monitor social media, and Twitter is one of the channels we use to communicate with our customers. **When a customer has a problem they have two needs: the practical and the emotional**; I think that we look after both. For example, we can send flowers to our customers; we can do little things like sending handwritten cards so we have had that personal connection with them; we can send them one of our 'Wow packages'... Our main goal is to make sure that the experience is 100 per cent and more – that we get our name out there and make sure that people know that they can trust in us for not only products but also service, that we meet those standards and go above and beyond.

I really feel blessed to be here and I'm glad that I finally listened to my friend. I came and I experienced Zappos for myself and, honestly, that was the best decision that I have made yet. I hope to be here for a very long time.

Rob Siefker – the happy manager

Rob has worked with Zappos since finishing college in 2004. He joined as a temporary employee answering telephone calls and is now senior manager responsible for the call centre.

Mostly my job is about helping create a fun work environment for our employees in order for them to provide the best services for our customers. The number one thing we think about as an organization is our core values and our culture, so no matter what your department, you're still bound by that value system. A lot of call centres are very restrictive in terms of what their employees are able to do for the customer, so if there's a problem they're not necessarily able to resolve it to the level that they would like. We allow our employees to do whatever they think is in the best interests of the customer. We talk a lot about connecting with our customers in a way that's a lot more personal and emotional than a lot of call centres would think about in terms of the interaction. We don't think of them as just transactions, **we want to connect with people**! It's a great opportunity to represent Zappos to our customers and we want our employees to really have a good time with it, enjoy it and not feel restricted by a script or a process. We want to do whatever we can to make sure that they feel they are representing Zappos. So it's their job to connect and to relate.

Learn and grow at Zappos

We have lots of opportunities for employees to learn and to grow within the department; we have different speciality groups and teams and we have what we call our Progression Plan, so employees can learn new skill sets and earn a pay increase by learning that skill and adding more value. We have a Pipeline Team, which is our corporate training team, and even our call centre employees are able to go to classes, so that they can learn and grow in ways that maybe they wouldn't have the opportunity to do if they worked in a call centre in a different company.

We didn't have a lot of training early on; it was just 'Go out and wow the customer and take good care of them.' So now that we have 400 people, how do we know that we're operating as efficiently as possible? We do have a lot of metrics like any call centre would, but we manage them differently. We manage things more through our culture and through the fact that our number-one core value is to deliver 'Wow through service'. So if there are things that we need to do operationally, we explain the reasons why as a team and then we make the necessary improvements. If we are not providing a Wow experience for our employees and a Wow experience for our customers, then we wouldn't be acting in line with the commitment we've made as a company, and so **we don't have any tension between overall operational efficiency and Wow service**.

We survey our customers that have contacted the call centre. We ask them if they would recommend Zappos to a family member or friend. We also ask them, '**If you were starting your own service company, would you hire the person you spoke with?**' So hiring is very important to us.

How weird are you?

When we hire our people we ask them, '**On a scale of 1–10, how weird are you**?' It's not necessarily about the answer or the number that they give; it's about how they respond to a question like that. Do they play along with it, have fun with it and feel comfortable with it, or does it make them ask, 'What the heck is going on here?' Our recruiters have been here for years and they know what Zappos is all about, they know what kind of candidates we're looking for and they can get a good read on that just by asking questions that may be a little bit out of the ordinary.

If you want a strong culture then you need to have intolerance for things that are outside it, so we offer people a substantial amount of money to leave at the end of their training period if it's not what they thought it would be. We would rather they make the decision at that point than have them working with our customers.

It's hard to be on the inside and be able to say what is weird because it is just the way we are. For example, this one team had what they called 'Power Hour', so at 8 or 9 o'clock they would all put on these weird hats that they'd made and just have fun because it wasn't as busy during that time of the evening. You know, these things happen organically. I'm sure I'll see something weird today.

Our culture is our compass

ZAPPOS CULTURE
OUR BIGGEST ASSET

Zappos culture　　© 2011 Zappos.com, Inc

We talk about our culture constantly as we know that it's the number one thing that we have to protect. It allows for everything else that we do that's great; it allows that stuff to happen. So, as a management team, we talk about how we're going to make the new hire process better, how we're going to make the incubation process better, how we are going to make the Progression Plan better. How are we going to make sure that we continue to hire the right people? What types of little events can we run to help continue to keep people engaged and excited about what we do? How do we take it to the next level? How do we make it an even better place to work? How do we provide better service? I don't know if there's ever going to be one magic answer but we know what our value system is, we know that it's our compass to help us, to guide us in the future as we grow, we know that it all comes back to our culture, so that is what we focus on.

Do you speak Zappos?

Our culture is so strong that we could put together our own dictionary of Zappos-invented words. There are all sorts of random words that we use that are part of our culture. For example, we have 'zuddles' in the call centre. A zuddle is like a huddle, a team might huddle to talk about a specific customer issue, but we call that a zuddle. You can earn 'zollars', which are Zappos dollars that you earn for great work and you can redeem in a company store. 'Wow' is our big one, of course.

Blending high tech and high touch

There is an interesting generational change in that some of the younger customers are more into self-help rather than dealing with a person. I think that is because many young customers don't want to have to call a company because they are afraid of what's going to happen if they do. In that respect, we have to be able to take the online experience and make sure that whatever channel the customer prefers to interact with, we're providing the tools for them to get the assistance that they need without any frustration. **The customer experience is a holistic thing** and so our service is going to be constantly evolving in line with our customers' needs. Let's say if customers want to do live chat or Skype in their call and talk about a product, well, if those are the things that customers are going to want to do then that's what we're going to provide. We've decided on specific things about what we want the company to be about and then we work really, really, really hard to protect those things and to make them better.

 To hear more about the Zappos core values, click here: http://about.zappos.com/our-unique-culture/ zappos-core-values

Bold lessons

Decide your purpose and everything else will follow

When Tony Hsieh and his colleagues decided that their core purpose was to deliver the ultimate in service, the other decisions that they had been wrestling with became much easier. Get out of drop shipping, build our own warehouses, have onshore call centres. And even though these decisions were more costly alternatives, they created the foundation for the tremendous success that Zappos has enjoyed.

Create superheroes

Like the Geek Squad, Zappos understands that ordinary people can do extraordinary things if you will only allow them. Creating a culture that liberates employees to be themselves and do their best work by removing so many of the controls and processes that restrict is one of the bold things that these companies do. Zappos encourages 'random acts of kindness', which allow employees to take the initiative to do things that create goodwill with customers and colleagues.

Create cult-like cultures

It sounds slightly uncomfortable to say that many of the bold brands are cult-like in their desire for complete commitment and buy-in to their cultures and values. Of course, the cultures are by definition positive and people focused, so there are none of the negative connotations associated with the term. The stronger and more distinctive your culture, the more of a cult it becomes and the more likely you are to find that the employee hiring process becomes more self-selective through word of mouth. Zappos even has a 'rite of initiation', which is to offer new hires at the successful completion of their training a significant sum of money to leave the company.

Sprechen sie brand?

Just as national cultures have their own language and cults have their own jargon, so bold brands have their own words too. Language has a way of putting emphasis on those things we consider to be important. The Inuit Eskimos have 12 words for snow because it is pretty important for them. Our bold brands like Zappos and the Geek Squad invent terms to describe those things that are important to them too. This also has the benefit of creating 'insiders', which once again serves to emphasize the distinctive difference of the brand.

High tech and high touch

Research by organizations like RightNow and Convergys has found that the younger generations prefer self-help and automated technology to speaking to a person for routine transactions. How does a brand like Zappos which has made its name through service, preserve its differentiation? Through thinking about the various channels as an integrated and seamless experience where the values and tone of voice of the brand shine through irrespective of the channel being used at any one time.

Encourage the use of social media

Zappos, like O2 and The Geek Squad, is a brand that connects with its customers and so is a major user of social media like Twitter. Employees are encouraged to monitor Twitter and tweet themselves, so there is this constant dialogue going on between the brand and its customer community. It's a great way of keeping connected to your customers and in touch with the changing needs of the world and of exponentially increasing word-of-mouth recommendation.

Tony Hsieh has 1.7 million followers on his Twitter page.

You can read Tony's tweets for yourself; click on:
https://twitter.com/zappos

Zappos shows how you can use the power of human contact to create an extraordinary experience even in the remote and potentially impersonal area of online shopping. Our next bold brand brings the same approach to the often impersonal world of banking. Like Zappos, Umpqua Bank has created a unique retail experience, and like Zappos, it encourages its employees to engage in random acts of kindness...

Chapter Ten
Umpqua Bank

How many banks promise that your visit to their branch will be 'the best thing you did all day'? That's what Umpqua Bank, the self-styled 'greatest bank in the world', passionately believes; it thinks banking should be like a great retail experience and even calls its branches 'stores' to highlight that belief.

South Umpqua State Bank started in 1953 as a small community bank in south Oregon. Ray Davis took over as president in 1994 when the bank had assets of $140 million and employed 60 people. Under Ray's leadership, the bank grew to more than 180 stores, 2,500 people and over $12 billion in assets. Media outlets like *Fast Company*, *Business Week* and the *New York Times* have repeatedly recognized Umpqua as one of the 'coolest' places to work. In 2007 Ray wrote the story of Umpqua in his book *Leading for Growth*. For the past three years, *Fortune* magazine has included Umpqua on its best companies to work for list, including number 13 in 2008.

Umpqua has positioned itself very successfully as an integral part of the community and more than just a bank. It encourages its people to work in the community and creates store formats that provide a place where customers can come to spend time, not just bank. It has even taken its store promise out on to the street through its innovative 'handshake marketing', which promises 'Something wonderful will happen to you today.' Its culture is infectious and new employees and acquired businesses have been described as being 'Umpquatized'.

The name 'Umpqua' means 'raging waters' in Native American dialect: an apt description of the turbulence that hit the financial sector in 2008 and 2009. But Umpqua's culture helped it through these difficult years and once again poised Umpqua for growth.

So, welcome to the world's greatest bank...

Umpqua store

Bold practices

Umpqua Bank

- Every single employee attends a 'motivational moments' session every day.
- The bank's 'handshake marketing' programme allows employees to perform random acts of kindness such as buying a meal for complete strangers or buying coffee for the people behind them in the queue at the coffee shop.
- The branches are called 'stores' and the bank advertises for new hires in the retail press.
- Employees are trained in customer service by Ritz-Carlton.
- Employees can spend as long as it takes to satisfy a customer.
- Any employee can call the president, Ray Davis, on any issue.
- Every employee has to answer the phone with 'Welcome to the world's greatest bank' – people who don't want to do it, don't join the bank.
- They mystery shop at branches of banks they are thinking of buying to check the culture and customer-facing operations. The bank has successfully 'Umpquatized' 23 other banks since 1994.

Ray Davis – the game changer

Thank you for calling the world's greatest bank. This is Ray Davis... I came on as president and CEO of South Umpqua State Bank in 1994 with a motion picture playing in my head about what a bank could be.

The story started 15 years ago when I first joined the bank. It was just a sleepy community bank with six little branches in southern Oregon. It was like any other small-town bank and so the $64,000 question was 'How do we differentiate our company from the others? Why would you do business with my bank when you've got to drive by two or three competitors to get to it?' It didn't take us very long to figure out that we couldn't out-muscle the big guys – they had more branches than we did. It made no sense to try to differentiate ourselves with products – in banking they're pretty much a commodity. So, how do you do it?

Differentiating the bank

We quickly came to the view that the delivery of products could be different and we could perhaps differentiate ourselves from our competitors by putting together a delivery system that was unique to the industry. And that's where it all started.

The decision was based on 90 per cent gut and intuition and 10 per cent on what little information we had in those days. I looked around the marketplace and it was clear that nobody was doing anything significantly different. Everyone was copying the next guy and I thought there had to be an opportunity because of that. I had a motion picture playing in my head at that time. I visualized creating a retail brand in a small market and then expanding it by building a store network. From that day on we were in retailing – not banking.

I can remember going to our board of directors and explaining to them that everything that they knew about banking would change. We were going to turn everything inside out. Some of the people who had been with the bank for many years might not like the change and might decide to leave, and that was okay. They needed to get used to the fact that **change is not a four-letter word**, and change was going to become a regular feature in the organization.

When we first started on this journey, our investors were pretty leery about what was going on because it had never been tried before; even **our competitors thought I'd lost my mind**. I mean, this is supposed to be a bank! What they didn't understand, though, was that their very suspicion of what we were doing was playing into our hands, because we were trying to differentiate ourselves from them. So their reaction was validating exactly what we thought was right. We grew rapidly from that point on.

Umpqua store   © 2011 Umpqua Bank

Where do you start?

We started by stripping all the back-room operations from our stores so that the only thing our people did was to focus 100 per cent on the customer experience.

You can dress up a branch to look like a store, but if you are operating to the same procedures that you were before the change, you've wasted your money. So what we did is not only to change the entire appearance of our stores, but we completely changed the way that they operated and the kind of people that we put in our stores. When we recruit new associates to come and work for us, we don't advertise in the banking section of the newspaper. We advertise in the retail section. And while we teach them to understand the complexities of banking products and services, we also send them to train with the Ritz-Carlton to learn about delivering service that knocks your socks off.

We sent our people out on field trips to the nearest city and asked them to go into retailers or high-class hotels with little clipboards and pay attention to their senses. We asked them to make notes. What did they see? What did they hear? What did they smell? What did they touch? What were the things that were unique or different? Now, these were companies that we felt were successfully differentiating themselves from their competition and what we were trying to determine was, what was the secret of their success? We felt we could take those little gems of excellence and alter them so they would fit within a financial institution, which would differentiate us, because banks in general don't think that way.

One of the examples we used was The Gap. When you walk in, they greet you: they say, 'Hello, welcome to The Gap.' The sales people are walking around looking to help customers, they'll help you size the clothes you want, they fold up the products, they'll take you to the cashier, they'll check you out, and, at the end of the day, they balance their cash. When our people came back and told me that, I said 'That's all we should be doing in our stores.' Why would we do anything else?

Empowering people

One word that comes to mind every time I think about our culture is 'empowerment'. We hire decision makers. We give them a pretty big playing field to operate in. We incentivize them to make decisions. We hold them accountable. Understand that in our stores we do not have commercial banking lenders or loan officers. We're in the risk business, but if you really stop and think about it, in the greater scheme of things, the risks that can happen within a store are really quite small. For example, when a customer is upset, the issues usually revolve around smaller things: you charged me a fee and you shouldn't have; or my statement is late – something of that nature. All of our associates have the authority to make a decision right there and then on what they think is the right thing to do. They are trained to make those kinds of decisions and they do; they don't pick up the phone; they don't ask for permission; they have authority to make it happen. It's about managing risk and, that type of risk, as far as I'm concerned, is minimal compared with the benefit gained from empowering your people.

Your culture is an asset

We have been listed as one of *Fortune*'s best companies to work for far three years in a row and yet we've integrated 23 different banks in the last nine years into this company. What I tell people is that **the single greatest asset we possess is our culture**, and yet the area with the greatest amount of risk within our company is our culture, because if we grow for the sake of growth and we forsake the culture, then we're just going to become another large institution and bureaucracy will rule, which we refuse to let happen.

To have a strong culture, first you have to drive down decision making to the local level. I think that's critical. Our company doesn't have loan committees, for example. We make decisions locally so that we can respond faster to people in our local community.

Number two, you have to be involved in the community. For example, we have a programme called 'Connect' where we ask all of our associates – and we've got about 2,500 of them – to volunteer 40 hours a year of their time to non-profit organizations that focus on youth and education. They have to do their 40 hours during business hours and we pay them. Last year the company volunteered 31,000 hours in the communities that we serve.

We are very focused on our earnings and how well we do. We have a responsibility to our shareholders to do well but **there's no reason why profit and purpose can't go hand in hand**. I believe if people do the right thing the numbers will follow and the community will benefit.

It took us a while to show investors that there really was a value to creating this kind of culture. Most financial analysts have a lot of trouble putting a percentage or a dollar sign on culture. They can't quantify it. When you have a strong culture and things are going very well, a lot of people outside the company don't notice it. When trading conditions are difficult, your culture can be what saves you from tragedy. For Umpqua, the culture in the best of times was propelling us much faster than we could have gone otherwise and, when things did get tough during the recession, we continued to perform very nicely.

Measuring the experience

I think that **if you're going to centre your corporation on customer experience, you have to be able to measure it**. Everybody can say they create results, right? And yet nobody can prove it! So we actually measure the service that we provide in every department and every store within the operation. Just as financial metrics are based on return on assets, we have our own formula for the customer experience, which is called return on quality. Our people are measured as a team and as individuals on how well they perform on that metric. Of course, there are great incentives for those who do very well, and for those who don't there is coaching; and for those that don't respond to that, then there's a good chance that they won't stay long with the institution.

I think financial institutions have a serious issue that's approaching them very quickly and that is the value of the real estate that they're sitting on; in other words, the branches. The generations of today are so technologically adapted they don't need to walk into a branch to do their banking. So the test is, how are these branches going to stay relevant? Why would someone bother to go into them when it is more convenient to bank online or transact through some other channel like the mobile phone? What we set out to do 15 years ago was to increase the relevance of our store network so that people would want to go there. For example, most people when they walk into a bank branch do so to cash a cheque or make a deposit. What we want customers to think here is, 'I think I'll go to Umpqua and have a coffee while I do some shopping online, and while I'm there, I might cash a cheque or make a deposit' – a significant difference.

When you put customer experience in a design where it can flourish, you have something incredible. So there's a lot of science behind the design of our stores.

How do people walk into the store? What are the traffic patterns? How do you present the products and services to the customer in the most helpful way? Once again, we borrow ideas from the best retailers and adapt them to our banking environment.

Creating a seamless multi-channel experience

The challenge is to make sure that the same culture, the same feeling that the customer gets from walking into our store is also felt on the web. It must be felt in our call centres. It must be delivered through every channel.

We have created a division in our company which we've entitled 'Creative Strategies' and they're responsible for helping us to enhance the delivery system and that includes aligning the customer experience across the web, the store, whatever the channel may be, and to make sure that the unique feeling of Umpqua is delivered to the customer.

Innovation permeates our organization at all levels. We try to create new ways for our customers to enjoy themselves in our stores online, and even in our contact centre, with the latest technology or with traditional products and services. To me, that's the most important driver of our organic growth. The second route to growth, of course, is through acquisitions. The reason that we've been so successful with acquisitions is because we've created a very unique culture which aligns our people with the Umpqua strategy and brand.

I have found with the banks that we've brought into our company that you don't have to grow up within our culture to embrace it and be successful. The fact that our culture is stronger today than when we started after absorbing 23 other brands is quite an accomplishment. I think it speaks to the universal truths that our culture is built upon. I can't tell you how many times I've had people from target acquisitions come up to me and say, 'Mr Davis, let me make sure I understand this. Are you saying we get to adopt the Umpqua brand experience and enjoy all these things you're telling us about? Is that part of becoming part of this bank?' And I say, 'Of course it is, yes.' Their next question is, 'When can we start?'

Bold decisions

I think one of the boldest things we did was to create a bank store because that was unheard of in 1995. It was uniquely different and, yes, there were some risks associated with it, but I'll be honest with you, I don't think the risk was that great. I mean, if it didn't work, then we still had a great branch, right? I think we stumbled on something that just made a hell of a lot of sense and we took advantage of it.

The other bold decision we made was to keep the brand name Umpqua Bank. I dare you to say it fast three times; you'll get tongue tied! My first inclination was to change the name to a traditional bank name – 'Oregon National', you know, something boring like that. But I was talking to a young retail consultant – because we don't hire bank consultants – and she said, 'You know, Ray, we've talked about your desire to differentiate the bank and I'll give you a bit of free advice – never change the name of the bank because the name Umpqua differentiates you to begin with.' It's actually fun, getting out there and trying to help people learn how to pronounce it. Umpqua is a Native American name. It means 'raging waters'. I guess it sums up nicely what the financial services sector has been experiencing.

To hear more from Ray Davis, click here:
http://video.foxbusiness.com/v/3894340/
bank-ceo-will-pay-back-tarp-by-2010

Lani Hayward – the creative strategist

Thank you for calling the world's greatest bank. This is Lani Hayward... I am executive vice president of Creative Strategies, responsible for overseeing the customer experience, the brand and marketplace communications.

Creative Strategies is responsible for overseeing the customer experience, the brand and any public channel that our brand is expressed through. So our focus is on making sure that we are continually evolving and remaining relevant for the customer.

Our titles say exactly what we do

We try to make our job titles express exactly what we do. We're not just about marketing here; we are creatively and strategically looking at the company's brand assets. So it is not just implementing a promotion or an advertising campaign; our role is very holistic, it touches every area of this bank. When we think about the customer experience it isn't just about posters or brochures, or whatever you might have in a normal marketing department; it has to do with people, it has to do with how we operate in the bank, it has to do with sight, sound, taste, anything you can sense – in our stores, online and on the street.

The positive tension lies between being consistent and on-brand and also being creative. Ray is out there saying, 'Go do it, take it on, make decisions, be crazy.' And then there is me back here saying: 'We need to make sure that we are still looking like Umpqua and feeling like Umpqua, both from a cultural standpoint as well as through the channels.'

The Umpqua brand promise

Our brand promise is to 'make your stop at an Umpqua bank the best thing you did all day'. That promise is backed up by this big sign on the wall that says 'Welcome to the world's greatest bank.' So, between the brand promise and knowing we have to be the world's greatest bank, it's a huge ask of our associates. It drives everyone to create special moments.

Umpqua is known first and foremost for offering a different environment: stores that do not look or feel like a bank. We then evolved from retail stores into what I would call a community centre. These are places where people come to use the space. They have meetings here, they participate in events here; it's become so much more than a bank. But 50 per cent or more of the experience comes through the Umpqua culture and our people: how they hold themselves, how they help customers, how they describe the company itself. And that is the difference, those two things together: brand and culture together create the experience.

Handshake marketing

There's one thing we don't believe in: **we don't believe in traditional advertising**. You can ask any advertiser in the world, 'Do you believe that advertising works?' and they will say, 'Well, I am not sure but it's the best tool I've got in my toolkit.' But we all know there is too much of it; everybody is just screaming as loud as they can, and it's really, really hard to break through. So, about six years ago we started something called 'handshake marketing'. The notion was this: we have this very distinct brand, you can feel it when you walk into our stores, literally; you sense what this entity is all about, because you feel it. But the question is, how do you capture it and communicate it? I can't do it through an ad, I can't do it through direct mail; so what does that leave? And handshake marketing came out of that notion.

An example of handshake marketing is demonstrating 'random acts of kindness'. So a manager of a store might decide to ask the café down the street to select two lunch tables every day and ask the Maître d' there to give the customers a specially prepared receipt that says, 'Your meal is on us – Joe Smith, manager, Umpqua Bank'. You know that person is going to tell at least 10 other people what happened. It is being randomly selected to have 'something wonderful happen to you that day', which is our brand promise and allowing word of mouth to get that message out. I guarantee there are dozens of Umpqua associates standing somewhere today in a coffee line paying for the two people behind them. They don't say anything half the time; they just let the barista say, 'Oh, these are taken care of by Umpqua Bank today.' It is just the little things that any of our people can do any time.

Another example of handshake marketing is we entered the California market for the first time several years ago and half of the population thought we're owned by a band of Indians and were gobbling up small banks. They really didn't know who we are and what we were about. We decided to run some ads talking about our values, but we also created a branded ice-cream truck that went around playing great music and handing out free ice cream. It created an opportunity to talk with people as it drove through neighbourhoods and business parks. It was probably the best thing we could have done to introduce who we are and in a way that was very human.

Random acts of kindness

Occasionally we will have mass random acts of kindness initiatives and measure success by how many people were involved. But **mainly we don't measure; it is gut instinct**. We just know that if you do something nice for somebody, by and large most people are going to think well of you and they might go and tell somebody else. What has that cost me? It cost me $1.50 for a coffee, $15 for a bouquet of flowers or $30 for a lunch. Now, that kind of investment allows me to internally create a simple contagious process that allows random acts to occur, and externally it drives natural word of mouth. Occasionally we do try and put some markers down to measure it, but it's mainly gut instinct, and we've seen over time that it pays off.

Get in the flow of social media

We love the emergence of social media opportunity because it fits so well with our non-traditional marketing and word-of-mouth approach; it just helps us be

Ice cream   © 2011 Umpqua Bank

exponential about it. The biggest thing about social media sites like Twitter is that **the conversation is going on out there about your company regardless of whether you participate in it or not**. So we decided to participate. I remember one occasion when somebody tweeted, 'Umpqua stinks because they charged me a fee for something.' It was a very short but very aggressive tweet. Our contact centre saw it and tweeted back and said, 'Hey, sounds like you're having some issues, why don't you give me a call?' Well, he did, they talked, and then five minutes later he went back online to Twitter and wrote: 'Umpqua is the best, I love them' to hundreds of his followers.

We started something several years ago called 'Local space', which was a sort of MySpace of small businesses. It was about connecting small businesses to one another to not only use each other's resources but to gain insights from each other, foster networking and that type of thing. The internet is about community. As a community bank, this channel holds great untapped potential.

In 1994 Ray's vision changed the way people banked and allowed a different strategy for the industry. We really did shake things up. Banks began to understand that you didn't have to be severe and have buildings with pillars and marble; that they really could create a different kind of experience for customers; that we all sell products and services and therefore we could act more like retailers than bankers. What we did was rock the boat of traditional banking and it made a fundamental shift in the industry. We want to do that same thing online, and so while we continue to evolve the store environment, we have great focus on creating a digital revolution in banking.

How do you create an online experience that is so good that it might be 'the best thing you did that day'? We believe there are benefits, rewards and true value that a bank can bring into their customers' lives on a daily basis. That is what we are driving towards. There is a lot of very cool, very engaging stuff coming down the line. Imagine you are walking down the street by Joe's Coffee Shop and your cellphone pings; it says, 'Use your Umpqua debit card and Joe will give you $2 off.' You get immediate gratification and constant connection with the community, the merchant and your bank. These are the types of things that we are looking at.

If a company has vision and knows what it wants to achieve and then does the hard work of listening to make sure that it stays focused every single day, great things happen. Your vision moves from being a project, to how you live and breathe; and everyone, especially at the top, has to remain really, really focused on that. I've always believed that **culture and brand are the same, and you cannot have one without the other**. That is the magic.

To see Umpqua's vision of banking, click here:
http://www.youtube.com/watch?v=zmVDR6k8LTY

Barbara Baker – the culture enhancer

Thank you for calling the world's greatest bank. This is Barbara Baker... I am executive vice president for Cultural Enhancement, a position I have held since 2002.

I'd heard that Umpqua was looking for their first human resources executive, and that led me to meet Ray Davis. And it just seemed like the job I had been working towards for my whole life: improving my human resource skills, helping with mergers and acquisitions. It was the perfect job for me.

When I started here there were 325 people, and the bank had just hit one billion in assets. Ray told me, 'I want to grow and build a community bank that will always have the rich traditions of Umpqua Bank. This bank is built on giving extraordinary customer service and I want to keep that, and perpetuate that tradition, but I also want to build a bank that is capable of substantial growth.'

He told me that we have a four-legged stool: We set out to give our customers, our employees, our shareholders and our community a delightful and unexpected experience. So I said, 'Okay, what is my role in keeping that stool stable?' The answer is creating a great employee experience, because if you do that for employees they will pass it on to the customers and the community.

Creating a great employee experience

We're always making the connection back to the culture, and the experience we want for employees and customers, and I'll tell you why. There are many companies that, as they got bigger, took for granted their culture and assumed that it would naturally continue, and often it didn't. If you're not working on it every single day you'll lose it. So rather than calling ourselves 'Human Resources' we are called 'Culture Enhancement'. Just by saying our name, 'Culture Enhancement', every single person in my team is reminded of the job we do. It stays top of mind and you cannot help but think about it every single day.

We weave cultural messages into everything we do, whether it's our training, our sales campaigns or our benefits. We don't forget our culture or our non-negotiables. Let's say you take a computer class at the World's Greatest Bank University. Our trainers will always say, when they cover the learning objectives, 'If you learn this skill you're going to be able to do this for the customer and give them a delightful experience.'

People are not going to be drawn to you unless you have a great reputation. So we have carefully crafted ours through our branding, our messaging, our advertising and through our recognition programmes. We've been on *Fortune* magazine's list of the 100 Best Companies to Work For three years in a row. And over the past 15 years we've been nominated 13 times as one of the Best Companies to Work

For in Oregon. Our culture continues to bloom, as does the reputation. As a result we believe we're a destination employer and so we have the pick of the best people. When we're recruiting we look at two key competencies. Number one, do you have the skills to do the job? Secondly, will you fit the culture? We've developed behavioural interview questions that we believe screen very effectively. All applicants of Umpqua Bank have to go through four interviews and it has to be 'four thumbs up' for them to be hired. The most important question we want to answer is 'Do they have the passion to work for the world's greatest bank?'

Thank you for calling the world's greatest bank

You know, there are some people who say, 'I don't want to answer the phone with "Thank you for calling the world's greatest bank".' Well, then this isn't the right place for you. And that's okay, because we'll find somebody who thinks that it is. There was this young man who recently graduated from college and was going to be a commercial lender, and hoped to make good money. He said, 'I serve the most prestigious customers of this bank and I just think it's really childish to say, "Thanks for calling the world's greatest bank" when one of my customers calls.' So I said, 'Well, first of all, there's no job in the bank that's more important than any other job in the bank. Ray Davis answers the phone and thanks people for calling the world's greatest bank. It's a non-negotiable.' So he left.

Making mergers and acquisitions work

We use the same philosophy when we are carrying out due diligence for an acquisition. When we are looking at potential partners one of the first things we do is we visit their branches. They don't know who we are, but we go to their locations and see what they look like. We ask them about their products and services to see how they handle unusual questions. We think that **cultural fit is just as important as strategic fit and should form part of the due diligence**.

Once you have done the deal you have to be extremely sensitive to what they have contributed or invested in their institution. You cannot change everything overnight and say, 'We're going to do it the Umpqua way.' Rather, we go in and say, 'One of the reasons we targeted you is we like what we see, and everything that you've contributed to this bank is now going to become part of our history too.' Early in the transition everyone goes through our culture orientation. We embed Umpqua managers in the acquired stores and departments, so that we're there on the premises influencing and supporting the transition. For example, when we assumed Rainier Pacific Bank recently, we took 11 of our sharpest managers and allocated them to the new stores. They were there every day on the job, showing employees the Umpqua way, introducing them to what we call 'motivational moments', showing them how we serve the customer, teaching them about our products, our policies and procedures, and our credit quality standards, but also how we deliver all of this in a unique way. The most amazing part is seeing how quickly it works.

Motivational moments

'Motivational moments' is something that we all do every day in every department, in every store. Unless you're on a call you absolutely cannot get off, we all drop what we're doing and go out to the lobby. From Ray Davis to back-office file clerks, we all take a turn, and do something motivational. It was my turn yesterday. You have to get your inspiration from something and mine was a television show I watch on the Cooking Channel where they bring on four chefs and they have to make a meal out of whatever they're given. So yesterday I divided the group into four teams and I gave them eight words and the words were things like advancement, career, World's Greatest Bank University, success, fun, apple and so on. I said, 'Okay, here's your assignment, you have five minutes to write a new pitch for me that I'm going to send out to our associates, telling them why they should attend classes at the World's Greatest Bank University.' After a few minutes, all the groups stood up and gave their pitch and it was hysterical, and everyone had fun and got a great start to the day. As it turned out, our external PR firm had just walked in for a meeting, so I made them the judges and the winning team got a basket filled with candy bars and cookies.

We do a lot of German Oktoberfest festivals here in Oregon in the fall, and one of the things that's popular at these events is doing the 'chicken dance'. So we'll start playing music and we'll all do the chicken dance. One day an associate came in with his boom box and played the Rolling Stones' 'Start Me Up' and we all sang along and got motivated. It's just something fun, and it brings everybody together, from all levels, not just managers, not just associates: everybody standing together doing something really fun.

A unique language and culture

I hear words here that I've rarely heard used at any other company I've worked for. You will hear the word empowerment a lot. You will hear people say, 'I'm empowered to give that customer a bouquet of flowers, because they weren't happy with the service.' People talk about being 'Umpquatized', meaning they have embraced our culture. If you ask people to describe the culture they'll say that it's all about respect, so respect is used quite a bit too.

One of the things we do constantly to keep the culture strong is hold contests and reward and recognition programmes. For example, one contest was writing an essay of 1,000 words or less on 'What does the power of the culture mean to you?' All of these essays will go into our *Fortune* magazine submission for The Best Places to Work, and also feature in our 'Pride' book that we hand out to every employee.

Each department sets its service standards, and once a month you are scored by all the other departments and stores on how you did against those service standards. These return-on-quality scores add up, and at the end of the year the top five teams get a Celebration of Excellence award, which is our equivalent of the Academy Awards. In fact, the gold statue awardees receive comes from the same place that the Academy Awards statues are made. Even though it's a very friendly competition you don't want to be on the bottom! Our team strives to be in the top ten every month.

Associates offer feedback, saying things like 'I've never worked with a payroll department that made payroll fun. Every time I call there the person is so friendly and they give me great advice.' The return-on-quality system gives your peers and all the stores and departments a chance to tell you how well you're doing.

We do things that are very different. I don't know of any other employer that pays their people to use mass transit, for example. We pay 100 per cent of your transportation costs if you're taking the bus, the ferry or some other form of public transportation, because we want to support the environment as well as offer a benefit to our associates. We're one of the only companies I know of that has a medical plan that is free to employees. Also, a lot of young people breaking into the banking industry for the first time don't have the professional clothing to work in a bank. We dress up here, we look nice, so we also give an interest-free loan to associates to buy suits and ties and dresses. We are constantly aware that that we are trying to help people get ahead, so if we can help with some of those necessities and allow our people to balance their personal and professional life, we'll do it. If you treat employees right, they're going to pass it on in the form of great customer service and help the bank grow in our communities – and that is what keeps our four-legged stool stable.

Umpqua people:
http://www.youtube.com/watch?v=cM76XvCNTJM

JoEllen Nieman – the customer champion

Thank you for calling the world's greatest bank. This is JoEllen Nieman... I am responsible for Umpqua's contact centres and our customer service team.

One of the things that makes us so successful is that our employees are very happy with their jobs and it comes across over the phone. I had an outside company come in and evaluate the contact centre that I oversee and they told us they have never seen a company where the morale in the call centre was this high; they just couldn't believe it and, you know, I had given them free rein to talk to anybody.

We hold a lot of internal contests in the contact centre, whether sales or service related. Basically these contests are designed to focus our people on those things that are important, but it's also a fun way to reward them for doing a great job. We have weekly winners, we'll have an overall winner of the contest and we even have a team winner. There's a variety of different ways people can win. So that promotes excitement in the contact centre; it promotes teamwork; and it promotes competition – friendly competition, between each employee, and that's what keeps the morale up.

Call centre metrics

We measure the same things as other banking call centres: calls per hour, unavailable time, redirected calls, etc. We monitor these and our people have performance standards but I think the trick is to find the right balance between making the target so high they can't achieve it or so low that it's a walk in the park. For example, we manage calls per hour; **we're not really concerned about how long our people are on the phones** but I do pay attention to what our average talk time is and I have actually lowered our calls per hour target because calls are becoming more complex.

Their goal, for incentive purposes, is 13–18 calls per hour and I put a cap on it because I don't want our people being quick and getting customers off the phone. There's a fine line between good customer service and rushing the call. I don't care if it takes them 45 minutes, they must take care of the customer.

Our associates are empowered to help customers as they call in. It doesn't mean we give the bank away, but it means that we're empowered to help find solutions for any problems or issues that they may have. One example was that one of our agents had a customer call in from vacation. Their car had broken down and they called us because they didn't know what to do as nobody would take their cheque because they were from another state. They didn't have any credit cards with them or any way to access money to get their car fixed. So, after our associate had properly identified the customer, she got their authorization to debit their account, went down to one of the stores, withdrew the money from their account, took it to Wal-Mart and sent a Moneygram to an office which happened to be located only a block or two away from where the car was being fixed. I don't think that other organizations would allow an associate to leave the phones, draw the money and wire the Moneygram so the customer could get their car fixed and get home.

To outsource or not?

We have debated whether to outsource our contact centre but we just don't feel that we would ever be able to give the same type of customer service by outsourcing it. It doesn't matter if we outsourced it in the United States or halfway across the world: the Umpqua culture is something that you have to live and breathe every day. If you outsource, the agents don't have a connection to you and just can't deliver the type of customer service that we can in-house.

We have a social media team who monitor Twitter and blogs and respond with helpful hints or they'll proactively talk about events that the bank is planning. They look for tweets people write about Umpqua. There have been times where someone has said, 'We're looking for a bank, what do you know about Umpqua?' We'll pick the comment up and invite the person to stop by one of our local stores and have a cup of coffee. We will give them a description of our stores and introduce them to a local store associate. The team has surprised people by doing this and has obtained new business.

The evolution of the contact centre

One of the things that I feel we have done well is that we took this contact centre from being a service call centre to a sales and service contact centre. All of my associates look for opportunities to sell additional products to our existing customers. This was a real big turning point for Umpqua because in the past we were just totally service and people that are in the back office don't usually sell – in fact they're often there because they don't want to sell.

I did a lot of communicating so the associates got over the anxiety of 'I'm going to have to sell.' Actually we don't really call it sales; we call it 'educating the customer', because that's really what it is. We don't want to sell a customer anything that would not benefit them and so we really stress to the associates that they need to look for opportunities that would enhance the relationship and be of benefit to the customer. We've just introduced a software programme which pulls up the customer's information and tells you everything they have with you, so at a glance the associate can tell if there is a product that might interest the customer. So, for example, you don't want to talk to 50,000 customers a month about taking a credit card when most of them already have one and the others may not even qualify; you need to be selective about who you even talk to, and that's where our software enhances the contact centre experience.

The initial goal that we set was fairly low – 12 sales a month – and I thought that there would be anxiety to meet that goal. To my surprise, right out of the gate they started nailing the target; it was awesome.

Talk to Ray

Every associate in the bank can pick up the phone and talk to Ray Davis if they want to. He has associate town hall meetings in different locations every year and sometimes multiple times in certain areas. You can ask him any question that's on your mind and he'll answer it openly and honestly right on the spot. One of the things he tells people is that you have a right to an answer; you might not always like his answer but you will always get one. I think that's what makes Umpqua associates so happy to work here. They feel that they're heard and that they can make a difference; their input is important.

Every associate will hand out their business cards to people that they meet and say, 'Hey, if you're ever interested in changing careers, come and see Umpqua Bank.' We don't hand them out lightly, though, because we are looking for people that would really give outstanding customer service. The main thing I look for in associates is somebody that can incorporate the way we feel and think, who wants to help the customers, who wants to do an outstanding job, who will love working here. These are the important things – we can teach them banking.

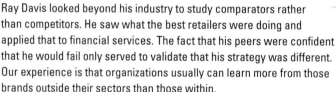

Bold lessons

Look outside your industry

Ray Davis looked beyond his industry to study comparators rather than competitors. He saw what the best retailers were doing and applied that to financial services. The fact that his peers were confident that he would fail only served to validate that his strategy was different. Our experience is that organizations usually can learn more from those brands outside their sectors than those within.

Be the brand

The fact that Ray answers his phone 'Thank you for calling the world's greatest bank' says something about his vision but also his willingness to 'walk the talk' and demonstrate his brand promise personally. All too often, executives distance themselves from the marketing promises their organizations make because they feel that providing service is the job of the front-line employees, not the executives.

Innovative marketing

Umpqua's 'handshake marketing' is a great example of how you can use innovative, inexpensive ways of getting your brand out there. It also involves employees, which ensures that they are part of the marketing mix too.

Create a branded customer experience

There is only one Umpqua: the look and feel of the stores, the technology used, the way that employees deal with you. All of these things combine together to create a distinctive customer experience that shouts 'Umpqua'. That is the essence of what we call a 'branded customer experience', one that is as unique to the brand as a fingerprint is to a person. And like a fingerprint, a branded customer experience is hard to replicate without it looking false.

Embrace digital but don't get distracted by it

Umpqua, like other brands we studied, understands the power of the internet and social media and uses these as a seamless channel for communicating with customers without becoming distracted by them. Monitoring and responding to tweets, creating business communities and integrating mobile technology are all important aspects – but first and foremost is service in the store.

Bold HR practices

Once again, Umpqua is a brand that understands the importance of the employee experience and works hard to create a culture that supports the service strategy. Empowering employees to do whatever it takes to satisfy customers, encouraging 'random acts of kindness', and daily 'motivational moments' are all examples of a fundamental belief in the power of people to differentiate a brand.

From running advertisements in the retail, rather than financial, press to sending people for training to Ritz-Carlton are examples of HR practices mirroring the strategy.

The number-one reason that so many mergers and acquisitions fail to achieve the objectives initially determined for the deal is because of the lack of due diligence around aligning strategies and cultures. Umpqua uses the power of its brand not just in communicating with the marketplace but also to communicate its values to those employees it absorbs.

What's in a name?

Like other bold companies, Umpqua believes in the power of language. By using titles that describe the output required – Cultural Enhancement, for example – people are reminded on a daily basis what they are there to do.

For more on Umpqua visit:
http://www.umpquabank.com/UmpquaBankHistory/
Home.aspx

Umpqua created a unique culture – almost cult-like – because it recognized that the only way to differentiate in a relatively commoditized area like banking was through the experience its people could deliver. Our next bold brand, TNT Express, similarly realized that the only way to differentiate in its commoditized market, logistics, was to transform the way it engaged its people and make them its heroes.

Chapter Eleven
TNT Express

The TNT Group can trace its roots back to 1752 but the current Express division was originally founded in Australia in 1946 as Thomas Nationwide Transport. TNT has grown over the years through mergers and acquisitions, demergers and sell-offs into a highly successful global business focused on express and post delivery. Headquartered in the Netherlands, TNT serves around 200 countries and employs over 160,000 people. It earned over €10.4 billion in revenues in 2009, with an estimated profit of over €280 million. It operates fleets of trucks, vans and planes and is thus in an industry sector which is a major contributor to emissions globally. Despite this, TNT managed to top the Dow Jones Sustainability Index for three years running.

When we wrote our book *Uncommon Practice: People Who Deliver a Great Brand Experience*, we included large organizations like Tesco, Virgin and Harrah's. Even so, people would sometimes say after speeches we have given, 'Well, that is all very well for entrepreneurial companies with a charismatic founder but it won't work in a large, complex corporate.' Companies don't get much larger or complex than TNT and so one of the reasons we love this story is that it shows how, when a management team share a common vision and then work together to achieve it, large companies can be just as bold as start-ups.

Bold practices

TNT Express

- TNT is an active partner in the World Food Programme, sending food to 90 million people worldwide through its 'Moving The World' programme.

- It invests in best-in-class vehicles in each of its markets, despite the obvious expense, rather than run down an ageing fleet.

- It operates a 'Lives matter most' road safety policy at the core of its business, which means it will end contracts with any road operator who has not ensured safety of drivers at all times.

- It uses a candid camera approach to researching its own and competitors' approaches to customer experience, to confront themselves with critical issues.
- It pioneered a 'human network' approach to culture building in Chinese operations using state-of-the-art software.
- The management team personally conducted 34 road-show presentations across China to communicate their new strategy.

Sure we can   © 2011 TNT Express

Marie-Christine Lombard – group managing director

Marie-Christine Lombard has been group managing director of TNT Express and a member of the TNT board of management since January 2004.

Sure we can

'Sure we can' is our brand promise. It stems from an attitude that is evident in TNT's people and our long history of being a pioneer either in the express world in Australia where we started, or now in Europe where we are a pioneer fighting against postal monopolies. It is true that TNT Mail is also a postal operator, but we are also the first postal operator that has been fully privatized and that has opened its market to competition. So we display a pioneer culture that stands against monopolies in general; we believe in free and open markets. When you are fighting against people who feel that they own the market and that nothing can take it away, **you develop an attitude of 'Well, we'll find a way.'** There are no problems, there are only solutions. And this attitude influences the type of people we're recruiting. We are a natural fit for people who want to go outside the box, who want to think differently, who want to serve customers rather than push them in the direction that they don't necessarily need or want simply because it benefits the company.

We run global networks, and when you run a network it's obviously very technical. But there is a flexible mindset about the way we listen to our customers. If they come with an idea, we don't reject it because it doesn't fit our network. We say, 'Okay, how can we make that happen for you, let's think about what we can do differently,' and that's why we say, 'Sure we can.'

'Sure we can' also drives how we think about corporate responsibility but it's much more than just sustainability. We focus on four stakeholder groups: our employees, the environment, our stakeholders at large – meaning suppliers, customers, subcontractors – and last but not least the world in which we operate. We have programmes in place to help improve performance in each one of these.

Lives matter

Take employees, for example, and even the employees of our subcontractors. In our emerging markets we are faced with more fatalities as a result of road accidents than in the mature markets. We do not just sit back and say, 'Well, that is the geography we are operating in.' Rather, we are active in explaining to the Indian government, for instance, that they have to invest in infrastructure, because most of the problems with road fatalities in India are linked to this, as well as to a general lack of safe driving practices. We have different training programmes for drivers, especially subcontractor drivers, in which we educate them on proper road conduct. We will not renew a contract with a subcontractor that has had a road fatality where the contractor driver is responsible and the contractor can't prove that they have made their employees aware of the basic road safety that we are proposing. We do the same in China, and we do the same in Brazil – in all the countries where we see there is a need. 'Lives matter most' is our mantra.

The environment matters

Turning to the environment, our aim is to improve the carbon efficiency of our operations – meaning to be CO2 neutral within five years. So we are in the process of measuring efficiently what we are emitting at the moment, and then we will replace our aircraft fleet, our truck fleet and subcontractor truck fleets in a way that we can achieve the objective of becoming carbon neutral. Our other environmental objective, which is air quality and which is linked to the CO2 footprint, is to increase the percentage of our vehicles that have soot filters. We have specific procurement policies to buy the best-in-class vehicles available in the market. We recoup the additional cost that we spend on being more environmentally friendly by being smarter: having shorter, more efficient routes use less fuel. And if you burn less fuel, you save on fuel costs, which helps us invest in more sophisticated vehicles and aircraft. These in turn require less fuel, less frequent servicing, less costly maintenance. **People think it's by keeping old stuff running that you increase profitability, but that's not true.**

And that takes us to another very important stakeholder – the world itself. We try to help by supporting the UN World Food Programme and the 'Moving the World' programme that we run. We make our trucks and aircraft available to transport food to needy areas at no cost when they are not required for our business. When there is a major disaster, such as an earthquake or tsunami, we will ship the logistics support, diggers, etc to the disaster zone as our contribution to the effort.

Customers matter

Of course, our customers are our final stakeholder group. Customer satisfaction is very important to us and so we measure that, but more importantly we measure loyalty. Take the high-tech industry in China, for example, where we have a recognized industry-first transport solution. This came from listening to our customers and the customers of our customers. We talked to the wholesalers and the retailers to understand where they experienced problems: too much inventory or late orders, etc. From this understanding we came back with a solution to meet their needs. So **'Sure we can' is more about how we operate than a tag line – which is as it should be.**

Michael Drake – the strategist; regional managing director North Asia

Michael Drake runs TNT Express North Asia, which covers six businesses including China International.

When I look into the future, specifically mainland China, I see a trend towards a desire for better service even if, at the moment, people aren't necessarily willing to pay for it. And if you put that insight together with history, we know that as countries evolve, customers will demand more and more and become more acutely aware of what they can get. Our brand in Asia, China included, is not as strong as our competitors because we have a different strategy – we don't advertise on TV or promote ourselves externally as much as our competition – so I realized that **we could become marginalized in this huge market unless we became famous for something**. So we embarked on a direction to become the market leader for customer experience. And it became for me a viable direction because, first, there is no recognized leader in our business for their customer experience and, second, customers will increase their demand for higher levels of service and experience as the market evolves. It has many organizational benefits because I believe that you can drive out cost if you start looking at your processes around the customer experience as well as the chance to drive premium pricing. Third, I think it has a huge benefit for employees because they enjoy working in an environment that is focused and has high energy.

Learning from comparators

I've been in Asia for 17 years, China for four. Two years ago you used to stand in line for about an hour in Customs whenever you'd come into the country. Now, if you come today, I can almost guarantee you won't be more than a few minutes in line. One of the things that they did, that I find extremely interesting, is that at every customs officer's desk there is a little keypad with four little buttons: a happy face at one end and a button with a sad face at the other end. At the end of the transaction, when the customs officer has processed you, these things light up and you can feed back immediately, happy or not with the service. And so I thought that if Chinese Customs can be innovative and improve their customer experience then we have no excuse.

In China, consistency and reliability are huge differentiators: because they are not readily available. You can get brilliant service one day and horrible service the next and we know that **variation is the thing that kills your service reputation**.

But, you know the first question I thought about was not so much if the market was ready for it, but what came across my mind was, are we as a company ready to deliver it? Iman Stratenus, our country manager of China will tell you more about the detail but we have shifted our culture over the last few years and, in fact, our whole organizational focus has gone from, what was a pretty short-term P&L type of drive to a much more customer-experience culture and all the things that go with that. We engaged the whole company answering questions such as what kind of culture they thought we had and what kind they thought we needed. And then, what shift was needed. And we've used some very innovative technologies for organizational mapping to help us.

The virtuous cycle

My own philosophy on how we make money is a kind of a linear process, which means if you employ the right people and then engage them they will deliver the right kind of services in the right way to our customers, and if you do that, you'll grow the business, and in a network business like ours, that will make you money as you drive scale, which means you can invest back in the people. In that way you have a very virtuous cycle.

I'll finish with a story that sums up for me what we have achieved around our culture. Every year we have an annual conference and we award prizes for achievements in people, service, growth, profits. We name the three finalists at lunchtime and then the big winner is announced in the evening. One of the finalists last year was a guy called Fred, who runs one of the sales teams; another finalist was called Alex, who runs a different channel; and then there was a third finalist. We had the three finalists up on stage and there was a big drum roll before the winner was announced. Everyone in the room was going crazy for their particular favourite. Bearing in mind that Fred or Alex could win, I looked up and I saw Fred screaming support for Alex to win and in that moment, I realized we'd come a long, long way.

Research conducted in 2010 has shown us to have achieved a market-leading position in customer satisfaction in China. Together with our above-market revenue gains and an impressive profit improvement over the last few years, this gives me every confidence our strategy is working. Our future is bright and along with my thousands of work colleagues we are very excited about it.

To hear more from Michael, click here:
http://www.youtube.com/watch?v=0R781PLW4Vs

Iman Stratenus – the visionary; managing director China

Iman is a lawyer by training and worked for McKinsey on various TNT projects. He joined TNT full time working as an assistant to the group CEO Peter Bakker before becoming country manager for Vietnam.

It was about the time that TNT announced its partnership with the World Food Programme that I thought, 'Why not join them, it's a very interesting company.'

What can we become famous for?

We were bold in that we went beyond the path that traditionally TNT takes, which is to say, 'Let's focus on this traffic lane, or focus on that vertical market.' That's where we usually start. What we did here is to ask bigger questions: 'What is the vision that we have for China, what are the values that we are going to inculcate, what's the culture that we want to create and what will be our differentiating strategy?' When Michael and I arrived here, TNT was trying to be everything to everyone. We had very little money for marketing and so we started to narrow our focus, saying, '**Well, what can we actually become famous for here**?' If you look at how other companies position themselves, you will see our competitors are very strong and say, 'We are big, we have lots of infrastructure, we have big teams, big trucks, big resources ready to go the extra mile for you.' An area not covered, however, was around the actual experience anyone provided. So we asked the question, 'Why don't we differentiate on that?' So we worked on our vision, our differentiating platform and then we started to work on how to bring customer experience into the business because, although we saw that it would differentiate us, it is not a simple strategy to explain, it's very much more difficult than saying, 'We're going to be the cost leader.'

China has so much to be proud of and we have the confidence to do things that are different, even bold perhaps. We may be considered a developing economy, but the intellectual level of the people that work here is certainly at the level of the people in Europe. The fact is that we have a far larger percentage of university graduates in our business than any of our equivalent businesses in Europe. So I take the view that if I can understand it, everyone can understand it. That has, I think, worked quite well for us. We have tried to simplify the concepts to get the message across and we've done some very unusual experiential research to give our people real feedback. The first thing we did was to use a candid camera approach to film ourselves and our competitors serving customers. And then we showed the film at a conference attended by our top 250 people. I tell you, it was absolutely shocking. The way that people behaved, the way people were dressed, the information that they gave or the lack of it, the way they were so rude to customers. We were totally shocked by the process but the one good thing was that of the four companies that we researched (our three competitors and ourselves), we were actually not the worst. So we said, 'Guys, right, we are at par with the rest but this is where we can make our mark.'

Changing the culture

We had quite a command-and-control culture three years ago, yet if you want to deliver great customer experience, there is no such thing as a manual for that. We can work on effective processes, yet the way people implement those processes actually makes the difference, and so we needed to have more empowerment. So we said, 'Okay, well, that means **we need a culture that is led by values**.' We conducted workshops around the country to define the values and we came up with six. Then we said, 'Well, how do we make those values come alive?' and

Culture trip   © 2011 TNT Express

the answer was that storytelling is the way to do that. Just like kids learn values from fairy tales, adults learn behaviours and values from telling stories, and the best way actually is if you tell your own story. So we designed a three-phase culture trip whereby my team and I conducted 34 sessions around the country. We had a two-hour programme during which we shared six stories, one for each of the values, and then for about an hour and a half we asked the local teams to tell their own stories about these values.

The first round was led by the country management team, the second round, which was a slight variation but still with very much the same focus, was led by the regional management teams, and now we're going one step further and we're going to bring customers into these culture trips.

Old ways, new technology

The next thing we needed to do was to get the message through to every person in the company. **We decided to merge traditional Chinese thinking about relationships with modern technology** to help us. We came across a company who have developed a survey tool and software that create a picture of the human network. You fill in a 12–15-minute survey that determines who you are connected to, in terms of who you admire, who's your friend, where did you get your information from, who gives you energy, and so on. The software maps the informal network inside your company and then you know who the people are that you need to be working with to change the culture of your company.

For example, Alex Xiang is extremely well-connected, partly because of his job, partly because of who he is. Now, we have put Alex into a crucial job where he can influence and get the message out. Now, let's say there's someone that we know is quite sceptical of what we're trying to do, we can put him or her closer to some of these influencers. So **we're taking a much less rigid approach around the hierarchy of the company and are leaning much more towards informal networks**.

One of the results of this approach is that our employee turnover has dropped from 35 per cent three years ago to less than 10 per cent now and it is zero per cent amongst the influencers we identified. That means that our people have become a lot more experienced, a lot more in tune with what we are trying to do as a company and that just makes a difference. If someone has been doing something for two years, there's a big difference compared with someone who's been doing it for three or four months, right? It makes people motivated to stay and have a career inside TNT. If you take customer satisfaction, we've seen improvement every single year, and this year we've seen improvement every month. In terms of customer loyalty we are currently running at about 75 per cent and the outcome is that through the recession we have not lowered our prices, whereas our competitors have, and our loyalty levels have actually improved, as have our earnings.

Challenging the myths

One of the key successes is that we've localized the company entirely, so I'm the last Westerner in TNT Express China. My whole management team is Chinese. I worked out very quickly that there is no truth to the myth that Chinese don't like to take responsibility. What they don't want is to get their heads chopped off if they make a mistake. So the first time someone makes a mistake, it's a fantastic opportunity to say, 'Okay, maybe that was your mistake but now it's our solution,' and you fix it together. That's a major improvement, because then it becomes an environment where people can say, 'I can take some risks here, I can be a bit bold here.' And that automatically creates an energy that is fantastic.

Alex Xiang – the champion

Alex started his career working with Kodak before joining TNT in 2007. He currently works as a branch general manager.

I think the way TNT approaches the market is quite different from our key competitors. We focus more on our employees, not just investing in hardware like operations and vehicles. In China, when you're doing business, the most important thing is to build a relationship with customers. If you can build a very good relationship you may get the business, no matter how big your competitor's infrastructure is.

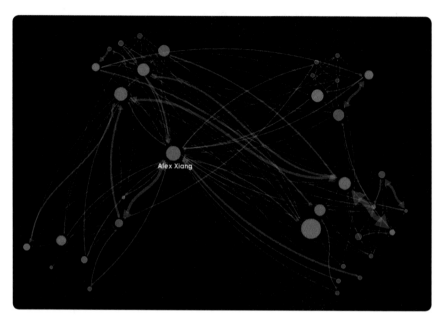

Human Network   © 2011 TNT Express

Guanxi

We have an ancient concept in China called *guanxi*, which means a person's network of relationships. It's very useful. Once you build up a relationship with the decision makers of many customers, it becomes much easier for us to get business. It also works internally too because if I know the head office, regional functional managers and their teams well, it becomes easy for me to get their support and cascade our ideas and information down to the front-line teams. It also enables me to get feedback from our teams so that we can adjust our strategy and our selling approaches to become more efficient and attractive to customers. Even under the quite tough economic conditions that we have seen in the last year or so, our revenue growth and profits are even better than the previous year. And if we look at the market share of TNT China, we have greatly improved our position in the industry. So it's really a powerful concept.

Creating the conditions for success

Generally speaking the leadership in TNT China is not just about measuring the final results. We also put a lot of focus on the process that people are using to get the results. So it is less about acting as managers and more about leading our teams to achieve the results. We put a lot of effort into coaching and working with our teams to create the conditions to get the final results. So we're not just focused on the numbers.

I think the key success factor of TNT China will continue to be our people. We will keep them highly motivated and recruit professional people in all functions. We will continue building our team and building our culture. We are focusing on developing our people with a customer-oriented mindset, with customer experience as our primary objective. Of course the infrastructure is still very important but our investments will be focused on the key, higher-value-adding areas, unlike our competitors.

Chris Goossens – the advisor; global customer experience director

Chris joined the company in 1988 in sales in Belgium. She was promoted to the board in 2004 and has been heading the customer experience function ever since.

Our customer experience strategy was driven by the fact that TNT has a growth strategy. We researched the markets very intently in terms of customer requirements, in terms of competitive landscape, in terms of how customers that were using both competitors and TNT rated us against the attributes that they felt were most important. And from that we realized very quickly that there are actually few

TNT people

barriers to enter our industry and no real opportunity to differentiate in terms of products, in terms of networks, in terms of infrastructure. To be in this field as an integrator and to be able to compete successfully you have to have your network in place. But more importantly, what we found is that as well as the basic functional requirements, **customers have a lot of emotional requirements that we hadn't addressed before**. And when we were looking at ways to differentiate that was where we chose to focus.

Creating a branded customer experience

From a mindset perspective, it didn't require us to change tremendously: it required us to provide the tools and the information to people to really deliver a differentiated experience. We followed up the initial research with customer focus groups and became more and more clear that, at the touch-point level, we were already doing something slightly differently from the rest of the competitors; we just hadn't captured what that was or formalized it as our strategy. So our customer experience unit was set up to ensure that we capitalized on that point of differentiation. We developed a global strategy that was a combination of network capability and delivering a truly branded experience.

The prevailing wisdom in the industry is that the delivery driver has to be fast, he has to be efficient, he has to deliver on time – all of which is true. One of our key competitors has been the leader in driver experience for at least 100 years, ever since they started. The founder said, 'Our drivers of today are the ambassadors for the customers of the future.' They had the right perception of the value from a superior customer experience a very, very long time ago. But they did not fully capitalize on it, instead mostly focusing on efficiency and productivity, so the experience part became secondary to that. **What we challenged in the industry is the belief that focusing on customer experience leads to increased cost.** We have proven that, on the contrary, because you empower your people to take immediate decisions within reason and within frameworks, you actually reduce time to market significantly; you improve the customer experience and loyalty; and you reduce cost of not doing things right first time. But it may mean that you take a bit longer to pick something up at the customer premise. You spend a bit more time with the customer at collection and delivery point, rather than going for the industrial engineering approach which prevails in the industry.

Challenging industry beliefs

Another myth in the industry is that if your customer service centres are based close to the customer you will service him better. Actually, our customer service people are centralized at country level yet they create terrific intimacy because they have better tools with better information. The feedback from customers on our service performance is that we have excelled every single year. And yet that was a clear myth that lived in the industry for some while: you have to be physically close to your customer base to be able to service them in a personal way. That is absolutely not the case. If you provide the right information to your people, anyone can help a customer and make them feel like they are truly known to the organization and are very important. It's the tools that you use that enable that, not where people are located, and it's also how you manage the teams and how you drive performance, and that to me is the most important part of customer service if you want to be able to deliver a differentiated experience. We believed that measuring our people on delighting customers was going to lead to the right behaviour, and that is exactly what has happened. We have invested quite significantly in new locations for our people, in tools, in equipment, in training, in competencies; yet we have actually reduced the cost of customer service as a percentage of turnover by 0.3 per cent, despite all the investments.

Simplify your strategy

As we saw the first signs of the recession, what we all agreed on was that in a growth scenario you focus both on retention and on bringing in new business, either through acquisition or through organic growth, but **in times of a recession what is absolutely paramount is to focus even more on your existing customers**, to make sure they don't defect. So the recession actually confirmed and reinforced our commitment to customer experience as our differentiation strategy.

In January 2009, Peter Bakker, the CEO of the TNT group, communicated what we were going to do as an organization to help us get through the recession. He outlined six priorities – we call them the six C's. The first is 'Customers' because you will not survive in a recession if you don't stay very close to your customers, anticipate their changing needs and respond to them. The second is 'Care'. Care for customers, but also care for employees, who are not going to feel comfortable in a recession which leads to job losses; so you have to be able to instil the third C, which is 'Confidence' that this company knows what it's doing: we're there to protect both our customers and, equally important, our employees, and they are entitled to be confident that the company they work for has the capability of steering them through difficult times. 'Climate' remained a very important element of the TNT strategy. Simply put, our industry is one of the polluters, so we believe that we also have to be one of the problem solvers. This means really going for green fleets and innovative solutions to reduce CO_2 emissions. 'Communication' was going to be more important than ever before to stay close to customers, but also close to employees, so we've never communicated as much from the top down, and from bottom up, as we have done in this last year; and we've done that through innovative webcasting formats, web chats, etc. 'Cash' is the C for the investors;

what they look for in times of recession are the companies that will still produce good cash flow and therefore a solid investment platform. So what we did extremely effectively was to focus the whole organization around these six priorities and the initiatives that were developed to support them.

As a result of our focus, our customer churn was even lower than in the growth years and we have been able to bring in more new business to compensate for lost volumes as a result of the downturn. That is despite the fact that there has been a real challenge in terms of pricing in the industry where, up to a certain point, we had to follow the trend because our customers were equally under pressure in terms of cost. But what we also noticed was that when we said to customers, 'If you wish us to reduce our rates, what is it you would like TNT not to deliver to you any more?' those price reductions became far less significant than customers initially asked for; and secondly, when we did lose customers on price, they tended to come back six months later for our service. So **what the recession did for TNT was to expose our true value proposition for customers**, which is quite a nice by-product of the downturn, wouldn't you say?

Bold lessons

Bold leadership and strategy

Peter Bakker's six Cs strategy was a very simple, understandable yet powerful way of navigating 160,000 people through the recession. It balanced the needs of the customers, employees and shareholders and maintained focus on the fundamentals that differentiate TNT. Peter shares the same virtuous circle philosophy that many other bold leaders do.

Connecting your people to a higher purpose

Tens of thousands of TNT colleagues took to the streets in cities across the globe to 'Walk the World' in show of their support for the World Food Programme and the fight against hunger. The walks, moving around the globe like a relay race, put hunger in the spotlight and raised enough money to feed 14,000 schoolchildren. TNT operates in 200 countries, many of them poor, yet that doesn't stop their employees from raising money to help people less fortunate than themselves. The fact is that by connecting people to a higher purpose, providing this is sincere and not corporate social responsibility spin, it has the effect of making everyone feel better.

TNT also utilizes its fleet to ship supplies and earth-moving equipment like JCB diggers to disaster zones around the world.

http://www.youtube.com/watch?v=KPgKUhgVkOI

Zagging when everyone else is zigging

When TNT Express China reviewed the market it became obvious that they were playing catch up, so they decided to play a different game and differentiate through the customer experience. If you can't win the game, change the rules. Marty Neumeier, author of *Zag*, believes this ability to spot the gaps when everyone else is skiing into the trees is the number-one driver of performance brands.

Challenge traditional thinking but build on traditional skills

TNT Express decided to challenge the belief that managers and employees in China were low grade and a commodity to be used. Instead they fell back on the traditional skill of relationship building in China to help them support their customer strategy. But they brought it bang up to date with the very latest social networking software.

To find our more about Lantern software, click here:
www.reyagroup.com

Embrace and respect local culture

All too often, companies believe that their way is the only right way and ride roughshod over the cultures and markets that their companies move into. History is littered with brands that failed to adapt their approach to new markets. The secret is to stay true to your vision and strategy but be prepared to be flexible about the way in which you achieve them through creating an internal culture that aligns your people with your customers.

To find out more about TNT, click here:
http://group.tnt.com/aboutus/index.aspx

TNT proves the essential importance of 'soft' factors such as brand building, service and culture in a 'hard' world of logistics. Our next bold brand is in an even harder world, literally. A world of hard hats, rugged machines and tough conditions. JCB makes the diggers that TNT often ships to disaster areas. There's nothing soft about JCB, you might think. Until you read their story and realize that this 'product of hard work' is born of a company built on vision, values and beliefs.

Chapter Twelve
JCB

It holds the diesel land-speed record of 350 mph; it entertains people around the world with its dancing diggers show; its replica toys are popular Christmas and birthday presents; its vintage machines are collected by enthusiasts and its name and bright yellow colour has become a byword for digging and excavation machines throughout the world. Joseph Cyril Bamford could hardly have envisaged the global success of the family-owned business he founded in 1945 (his initials gave the company its name). From a small garage in Uttoxeter, Staffordshire, UK, making agricultural trailers, JCB has grown into a company employing 7,000 highly skilled people in 18 manufacturing plants around the world.

JCB's first innovation was the Backhoe loader, which combined a tractor with a front-loading shovel and a hydraulically operated digger arm at the back end. It transformed the construction industry and JCB remains the world leader in Backhoe sales. Joseph Cyril Bamford used the French term *'jamais content'* (never content) to describe his attitude to work and that philosophy continues to drive the business as a mantra today. The new ecologically efficient Dieselmax engine and the world diesel land-speed record are among the most recent examples of that. Since 1975, the firm has been run by his son, Sir Anthony, who has overseen its growth from a British-based business into a truly global brand which is unique in the manufacturing sector. The firm prides itself on its customer centricity as well as its belief in another of its founder's mantras – 'a sense of urgency'. JCB is also zealous in promoting the cause of manufacturing and engineering.

 JCB website: www.jcb.com

Bold practices

JCB

- Won the diesel land-speed record with Dieselmax.
- Established the JCB Academy – a state school with an emphasis on engineering.
- Employs local people to run local plants; does not impose British management.
- Created the world's most efficient Backhoe loader and diesel engine.
- Donates its diggers to support disaster relief.

JCB Backhoe   © 2011 JCB

Sir Anthony Bamford – chairman

Sir Anthony Bamford is the chairman of JCB, which was founded by his father in 1945, the same year that Sir Anthony was born. As well as being dedicated to the JCB business, he is also a passionate advocate of manufacturing in Great Britain.

Our whole company is an engineering company. We're a private, family-owned manufacturing company that doesn't need to worry about what the Stock Exchange thinks about us. This means we can take a long-term view on the things that really matter: customers and products.

We talk about products all the time. We talk about making sure that our product is the most efficient it can be for our customers. We depend totally on customers. Many of them around the world are family-owned small businesses that we've been dealing with, in many cases, since the 1960s or even the 1950s. Quite often I'll meet the owner of a business and find his grandfather used to deal with my father years ago. Keeping them happy is paramount. I mean, to lose a customer is a very, very serious thing. It's hard enough to get a customer... so to lose them is really terrible.

Keep close to your customers and listen to the smallest things

Every single day, I and many of our senior people are meeting customers. We encourage customers from all round the world to come to our plants. We use the plants, more than anything, to reassure the customer that we're putting something extra into the product. But we learn so much from the customers too. It's a two-way traffic and I learn new things every day. Often small things, like the wiper blades ought to be two or three centimeters longer or the fuel filler cap is in the wrong place. You might think they're little things but they're very important to me because they're important to the customer.

Focus on what means most to your customers

We focus on our customers' total operating cost of a machine over, say, a three- or five-year period. Total operating cost means the initial purchase price, what a customer can sell it on for at the end of that period and how much they have to spend on it during that period. We give very good value for money. We are not the cheapest nor are we necessarily the most expensive. But our sell-on value in most instances is substantially more than our competitors. Also, we have a strong relationship with our dealers – we only sell through dealers – and our dealers are people we have been in business with, in many instances, since the mid-1950s. So it's a long-term relationship and they know that the back-up to their customer is there, because their customer is our customer.

Build your brand through exceptional service

I have a saying – 'The first machine is sold by a salesman and the second one is sold by the service back-up' – which resonates around the business here. It's what happens after the initial machine is sold that is so important to the brand.

I think a brand with nothing behind it is a pretty hollow thing. But I must say that I didn't realize until about 15 years ago the real value of our brand. I knew of the value of our products obviously but I just didn't realize how valuable our brand was. Good products, good service and a strong reputation for customer care built our brand over many years, almost without us even realizing it at the time. Now we are fully aware of its importance to us. Something like the world land-speed record is about pushing the brand even further... there's a sort of halo effect that comes from that which strengthens our reputation around the world.

Sell the 'sizzle' and the substance – the land-speed record to promote diesel engines

We'd been looking at making diesel engines for a long time. Emissions legislation was getting tougher and the suppliers we were using were not ahead of the curve in our view. They weren't reinvesting in new designs. So we decided to make our own diesel engines. We used two or three world experts to help us: an English company called Ricardo Engineering who are world experts on diesel engines and a company in Austria called AVL. We set pretty tough objectives, particularly on emissions, on fuel efficiency, economy, noise and the adaptability to use the engine around the world and to meet future legislation. So it's got a four-valve head, cut-away pistons, it's super-efficient, and has a very strong bottom end because it's designed for heavy work. It will do 10,000 hours before any form of overhaul is needed and, if you bear in mind that the product probably does 1,000 hours a year, that's 10 years' life before you need to put a spanner to the engine.

I thought, 'How do I promote this engine in a way that makes it more than just a mundane digger engine?' Well, I'm interested in motor racing and as a child I used to collect world speed records of people like Malcolm Campbell who were *Boys Own*-type characters, people that I used to look up to. I asked Dr Tim Leverton, who was responsible for the engine development, to do a bit of checking to see what the land-speed record was. And we found out it was 280 mph or close to that. I asked him, 'Could we design a vehicle to beat the land-speed record and, if so, what horse power could we get out of our engine to achieve that?' This is an engine which normally produces between 70 and 140 horsepower. Ricardo worked with us on this and we initially got the power up to 350–400 brake horsepower per engine. We then decided that the vehicle needed two engines to beat the record. We had a whole team of people, mainly Formula One people. We had an aerodynamicist who designed the Bloodhound missile. Andy Green – who is actually the fastest man on earth – agreed to come along and be our driver. He's a Wing Commander in the Royal Air Force and broke the speed record of 700 mph with a vehicle called Thrust. So we were looking at something which was half the speed. We worked with the engine more and finally, got it up to 750 horsepower. So we had two engines totaling 1,500 horsepower, took this beautiful-looking machine to

Bonneville, which is near Salt Lake City, and broke the record by a very big margin – 350 mph compared with the previous record of 280 mph. It was a great rallying call within JCB, it gave us an enormous amount of airtime round the world in all sorts of strange places. It's part of what I call selling the 'sizzle'. It's not just selling a digger. You're selling something apart from that. And it's enabled us to go and sell engines to all sorts of people that probably wouldn't consider us otherwise.

Dieselmax land-speed record:
http://www.youtube.com/watch?v=y80HKtAIeqE

Going global but acting like a local business

We're a global company. We manufacture in the Americas, in China and also in India, which is a very important marketplace for us. We have been there since 1979, employ a lot of people there and enjoy a substantial market share. JCB is Indian as far as India is concerned because every component on the machine that's sold there is made there. And all the people in the JCB India business, now approaching 3,000, including the management, are Indian. There are probably only three or four Brits there and they'd be specialists. Wherever we have businesses we try to have nationals throughout the business. We don't impose British

The Dieselmax team   © 2011 JCB

Dieselmax – the record breaker   © 2011 JCB

management. Wherever we are, we're part of the community, we're involved in charities and we try to be a good neighbour in each area where we have plants. And in some parts of the world, we've adopted villages. In Brazil, we're putting money into a soap-making factory. We're employing people who were completely out of work and at poverty level. We have 11 plants in Britain and each one is community based, so we're employing local people and are part of the community here too.

The vital importance of manufacturing

I simply cannot understand how any country can survive in the long term without a strong manufacturing base. Britain can't live off tourism; we don't have the climate to do that. We can't depend on the service industry. The City has done a fabulous job as a financial services centre. But we can't rely on that either, it can disappear overnight. We need to manufacture to create wealth and employment for the country. There are still areas where we have expertise in manufacturing – such as the sort of products we make. Our plants in Britain make state-of-the-art diesel engines, state-of-the-art gearboxes and axles. These are products which require skilful engineers to design and manufacture them. If we had more engineers, there'd be more people thinking up new things to make. There'd be more entrepreneurs coming through. Manufacturing and engineering, to me, are the key. We have to have a long-term industrial strategy. It needs to be quite simple and have all-party agreement, covering investment, taxation, the knowledge base, etc. There needs to be more investment in the educational side. And, in my view, it starts a lot earlier than university age. The whole thought of making a car or designing a bicycle must be engendered in young people a lot earlier than when they're 18.

The JCB Academy – investing in the future

We feel that we can play our part. We've sponsored an academy which will be completely engineering based. The academy is also supported by other strong engineering-based brands – Toyota, Bombardier, Network Rail and Rolls-Royce.

It's a former Arkwright cotton mill which was lying derelict for many years and has been renovated very sympathetically. It is one of the most environmentally friendly schools as well. It has an Archimedes Screw turbine that generates the majority of the electricity used by the academy. When the students first walked into the building, it looked new, felt new, but it's actually an old building that's been restored. Its starting point was rooted in the industrial revolution and it's got a new lease of life in the modern industrial era, which seems very fitting.

The pupils will come to us at 14 and leave at 18. They'll be doing a lot of practical work, and we hope that when they leave they'll go to university to study engineering. And that will stand them in very good stead for getting a job when they leave. We'll inspire them, because, actually, engineering is fun. They'll be fully involved in creating products, which is exciting. I mean, this is the thing about engineering; it's a creative thing to do.

The JCB Academy (Sir Anthony Bamford, far right)   © 2011 JCB

John Kavanagh – director of communications

John Kavanagh joined JCB in 2008 after a career in sales, marketing and corporate communications with Corus.

JCB sets out to create products that customers want to buy from us. Once they've bought, we want them to continue to buy from us in the future. It's all about the future sustainability of our business and our customers' businesses.

The focus is on providing sustainable solutions

At the most basic level, what our Backhoe loader did was gave someone the opportunity to run and sustain his own business. So, as long as he was able to raise finance for the machine, it became his business. He was digging ditches for the council one day, mucking out a neighbour's yard another day and that's how their business evolves. An owner-operator becomes a businessman, able to earn a livelihood for him and his family based on a very versatile, multifunctional machine from JCB that can do any number of jobs.

But as our business has grown, we have developed more sophisticated solutions to complex problems across all kinds of sectors: construction, agriculture, defence, industrial and waste. The big solution that we have helped develop for the defence industry is mobility. Once the troops get to forward lines, how do you dig them in and how do you sustain them there? The problem had always been that a Backhoe loader had to be carried on a low loader which then travelled at 20 mph, possibly through hostile territory. We have created a high-mobility Backhoe that can actually run under its own power at 60 mph using the Fastrac technology we pioneered in our agricultural tractors. It's a very highly regarded solution in the defence world because it gets the job done more quickly and far more efficiently.

The customer experience is the centre of everything JCB does

The JCB customer experience comes first. We are quite prescriptive about it because it's the charter by which everyone at JCB, including the dealers, in fact especially the dealers, need to live. Otherwise the customer's experience of our product will not be as we would wish it – and believe me, our standards are very high indeed. It starts with the belief, which was set out by Joseph Cyril Bamford himself many years ago, about how customers can get along without us, but we can't get along without them. Then it's about acting with a sense of urgency. There

Military backhoe

© 2011 JCB

is a quote from the founder that you'll find on the walls of many offices here at JCB. When he was asked what it took to succeed, he said it was the very same thing as when he started back in 1945, which was a sense of urgency about getting things done. And that's the ethos that still runs through the organization.

Proving the JCB story in difficult times

The recession was a very difficult time for the organization. It was a very difficult time for our chairman, Sir Anthony Bamford, in particular, because he knew that tough times called for tough decisions. He was very concerned about the significant social impact it would have on JCB people. And we were all frustrated about the absence of a nationwide short-time-working policy in this country. Our competitors in mainland European countries, where short-time working was implemented, were able to retain valuable skills in readiness for the upturn – that option simply wasn't available to us.

Good companies communicate all the time, not just when things are going well. So in the unenviable situation we found ourselves in during the recession, we explained to our guys how difficult the economic situation was and why we had to take tough decisions. At no point during the downturn, which lasted about 18 months, could anyone say, 'I don't know what's going on.' We got all our employees together on a regular basis to explain and communicate, and make clear that the tough measures being taken were about securing the long-term future of JCB beyond the downturn.

An agreement struck with the GMB trade union in late 2008 resulted in our own version of short-time working; a landmark decision which involved our guys going from a 39-hour week to a 34-hour week; the quid pro quo being that they were actually saving jobs. I think it was a classic example of JCB agility in response to a particular situation. These guys took quite a sizeable pay cut to do this, for the good of the company and for the good of each other ultimately. They deserve a huge amount of credit for this. Now, here we are in late 2010, when the public sector's about to go into pay-freeze mode and we've just agreed a three-and-a-half-year pay deal with the workforce. And we're actively recruiting again. I'm not saying we're out of the woods yet, there are still a lot of economic concerns out there. But in terms of the downturn itself, we were ahead of the game in seeing it coming, ahead of the game in terms of how we responded to it and, as a result, now ahead of the game in terms of how well placed we are for the recovery.

JCB Finance is a good example of playing to your strengths during tough times. Our customers were most concerned about cash flow during the course of the recession. We were able to use our joint-venture finance company to underline to customers that the trustworthy, reliable, reputable JCB you know as a manufacturer is also there to support you on plant finance. When they did a 40th anniversary supplement for one of the trade magazines recently, there were some great testimonials in there from key customers around the country saying, 'JCB was there to help us.' That felt really good!

The JCB charter

It's about moving heaven and earth for the customer, doing whatever it takes, being never content about what you do for the customer. When customers think of JCB, they should be thinking that JCB people are positive, friendly, enthusiastic, knowledgeable, helpful, passionate, honest and versatile. If we do all of that we should have customers for life. It's about nurturing them through the life cycle of their investment, right from the purchasing decision through to product replacement. If we don't take our eyes off them, they'll stay loyal to us. That's the JCB customer experience. That's what we've signed up to and need to live up to in everything we do, be it in product development, engineering, sales, marketing, the dancing digger displays, whatever – it's all based around surprising and delighting the customer.

A Product of Hard Work

I. THE REALITY

Mr JCB used to say: "Our customers can get along without us. We can't get along without them." And we should constantly remind ourselves of this fact. When a customer has a demand, we must act with a sense of urgency to make sure they are delighted.

2. MOVING HEAVEN & EARTH

We must do everything possible to make it a pleasure for customers to deal with us. We should be renowned for providing legendary customer service. Happy customers tell others and there is nothing more powerful than word-of-mouth.

3. SURPRISE & DELIGHT

We must not be satisfied with simply meeting our customers' expectations. We must aim to exceed them every time and remember when we do, it soon becomes the norm. The customer should always be pleasantly surprised by our responsiveness to their needs.

4. WHATEVER IT TAKES

We must never let a customer down - whatever it takes. A customer complaint should cause ructions throughout JCB. Customer complaints to dealers or directly to JCB must be dealt with immediately and the customer kept informed at all times. We need to make certain of a 100% satisfactory outcome.

5. NEVER CONTENT

We must constantly question the way we do business - never content. Always listening and finding better ways to satisfy the customer.

6. QUALITY QUALITY QUALITY

JCB must deliver world class quality - every time. Quality not just over the entire range of products that carry the JCB name, but in all aspects of doing business. From our suppliers to the services we offer and ultimately the way we deal with our customers. This quality must be consistently good, so that customers then know what to expect and indeed should demand.

7. HARD WORKING, TALENTED PEOPLE

We must only employ the most exceptionally talented people. Equally important, they need, through their attitude and behaviour, to be able to deliver JCB's vision and brand values.

8. TEAMWORK

We must all work together to create a culture of delivering outstanding customer satisfaction. There can be no 'us and them' attitude anywhere. We must pull together to solve problems as quickly and as easily as possible. The customer must always come first.

9. THE JCB DIFFERENCE

When customers think of JCB, they should instantly think of people that are positive, friendly, enthusiastic, knowledgeable, passionate, helpful, honest, versatile, hard working, innovative and dynamic. Never arrogant, never rude; treat the customer just like you would expect to be treated yourself.

10. CUSTOMERS FOR LIFE

Customers should be treated with the type of care reserved for someone special. They need constant nurturing every step of the way, throughout the lifecycle of their investment - their machine. We shouldn't take our eye off them for a moment, constantly checking to see how they are getting on and not waiting for them to call us. Only then will our customers remain loyal.

Alan Blake - Chief Executive Officer

The JCB Customer Experience

www.jcb.com

The JCB charter

© 2011 JCB

Sustainable innovation is an area we've really concentrated on in the last few years – looking ahead to the next decade and beyond. The more efficient our machines are, the less carbon they're using, which means better fuel consumption. This lowers the overall operating cost because our machines are tools used to do business. So then it becomes a win–win. We look at three areas: first, our operation, which is the manufacturing process, the transport, upstream with our suppliers – so our suppliers also have efficient, green businesses. Secondly, our product philosophy is about efficient design – this involves every aspect of the machine and how it's used. Finally, there is the social aspect, which revolves around the communities that we're involved in, the communities where our employees live and work and also the communities where our customers and our machines work. And the Bamford family have been very proactive in offering support in the wake of recent calamities that have happened around the world – particularly earthquakes and tsunamis. A lot of our machines have been sent straight out to help in the relief efforts.

Agility is key to delivering the brand

In companies I've worked for previously, you've got to go through layers of clay if ever you want to make a decision. But here you can make one phone call to our chairman and decisions are made instantly. After the Haiti earthquake, JCB Inc in Savannah, USA sent machines directly to the disaster area as soon as possible after the tragedy. They were ready within 36 hours at the factory and sent in straightaway by the US Army.

This demonstrates our 'sense of urgency' but also the agility and lateral thinking within the organization.

Another example is the work we did with the American Red Cross on a fundraiser for Haiti after the earthquake. Our people said, 'We're on the east coast of America. We'll drive our new, more fuel-efficient Backhoe model onto the beach, pick up some sand in the bucket and drive over to the west coast. After 26 days, they arrived in Santa Monica in California, drove onto the beach and deposited the sand from the east coast on Santa Monica beach. In doing so, they made a lot of money for charity. One hell of a road trip!

A Product of Hard Work

I. THE REALITY

Mr JCB used to say: "Our customers can get along without us. We can't get along without them." And we should constantly remind ourselves of this fact. When a customer has a demand, we must act with a sense of urgency to make sure they are delighted.

2. MOVING HEAVEN & EARTH

We must do everything possible to make it a pleasure for customers to deal with us. We should be renowned for providing legendary customer service. Happy customers tell others and there is nothing more powerful than word-of-mouth.

3. SURPRISE & DELIGHT

We must not be satisfied with simply meeting our customers' expectations. We must aim to exceed them every time and remember when we do, it soon becomes the norm. The customer should always be pleasantly surprised by our responsiveness to their needs.

4. WHATEVER IT TAKES

We must never let a customer down - whatever it takes. A customer complaint should cause ructions throughout JCB. Customer complaints to dealers or directly to JCB must be dealt with immediately and the customer kept informed at all times. We need to make certain of a 100% satisfactory outcome.

5. NEVER CONTENT

We must constantly question the way we do business - never content. Always listening and finding better ways to satisfy the customer.

6. QUALITY QUALITY QUALITY

JCB must deliver world class quality - every time. Quality not just over the entire range of products that carry the JCB name, but in all aspects of doing business. From our suppliers to the services we offer and ultimately the way we deal with our customers. This quality must be consistently good, so that customers then know what to expect and indeed should demand.

7. HARD WORKING, TALENTED PEOPLE

We must only employ the most exceptionally talented people. Equally important, they need, through their attitude and behaviour, to be able to deliver JCB's vision and brand values.

8. TEAMWORK

We must all work together to create a culture of delivering outstanding customer satisfaction. There can be no 'us and them' attitude anywhere. We must pull together to solve problems as quickly and as easily as possible. The customer must always come first.

9. THE JCB DIFFERENCE

When customers think of JCB, they should instantly think of people that are positive, friendly, enthusiastic, knowledgeable, passionate, helpful, honest, versatile, hard working, innovative and dynamic. Never arrogant, never rude; treat the customer just like you would expect to be treated yourself.

I0. CUSTOMERS FOR LIFE

Customers should be treated with the type of care reserved for someone special. They need constant nurturing every step of the way, throughout the lifecycle of their investment - their machine. We shouldn't take our eye off them for a moment, constantly checking to see how they are getting on and not waiting for them to call us. Only then will our customers remain loyal.

Alan Blake - Chief Executive Officer

The JCB Customer Experience

www.jcb.com

The JCB charter

Matt McClurg – global marketing director

Matt McClurg is responsible for coordinating all of JCB's marketing globally, ensuring it is of the same consistently high standard everywhere.

Sustainable innovation is a core value of the brand

Sustainable innovation is in our DNA. Since we first created the Backhoe, which transformed the construction industry, we've also launched Loadalls, or Telehandlers as they are known in the construction industry, which quickly became our second best-selling product behind the Backhoe.

The agricultural roots of the firm are still very strong. Our first tractors were launched in 1990. And the whole concept of our tractor was revolutionary. We had been watching how people queue behind a tractor moving from one field to another or from one farm to another. So the designers asked 'How can this tractor be more versatile and more productive, increasing its speed?' So we built the Fastrac with independent suspension so it could actually work at a higher speed in the field and introduced anti-lock braking so it was safer on the road. There was so much innovation in this tractor that it rattled the agricultural tractor industry.

Our key features on our machines include Live Link, a telematics GPS system that allows us to know where the machine is and how it's operating. We found that theft was a big issue with the smaller and mid-size machines so we also built immobilizer capability into the machines. As a result, we were the first company to get the Thatcham three-star rating, which means UK insurance companies will provide insurance to customers at a lower cost. So we're constantly looking at what the customers need and delivering a complete solution.

Ensuring the dealership experience is consistent with the JCB brand

We have 1,650 dealer depots around the world and the best back-up in the business. It's basically because we've selected our dealers very carefully – dealers that fit with our culture – so that they deliver the same JCB customer experience worldwide.

It's all about people and if we don't have the right people in our dealerships, they are not going to deliver the JCB experience to their customers in the way that we expect. We have full support training for the dealers. We offer technical training online and we have sales trainers that travel to dealerships around the world. When we launch new machines, we bring dealer salespeople in for product training. It's all about giving them the right tools to do the job.

Dancing Diggers © 2011 JCB

Demonstrating innovations through marketing

The main thing is to differentiate the way we offer the product to reflect the innovative pedigree of the company. We are recognized in the industry as being best in events; the whole dancing digger routine has its roots in JCB. We've got to keep thinking out of the box, not just to demonstrate the innovative features of our machines but to entertain people. If they go to trade shows, they want to glean knowledge but they also want to have an enjoyable day and a memorable experience. Our positioning is very much the BMW of the construction equipment industry. So we've got to make sure that all the customer-facing marketing communications are at the same high standard. We need to ensure the marketing people in different regions have passion, because this brand is all about passion. And the customers are really passionate about their machines – they're very proud of their machine fleets, especially if they've put their own name on it as well. So our marketing collateral reflects that passion – not just in ourselves but in our customers.

Dancing diggers:
http://www.youtube.com/watch?v=
uFBAzRc5vXE&feature=related

Sustainable innovation is an area we've really concentrated on in the last few years – looking ahead to the next decade and beyond. The more efficient our machines are, the less carbon they're using, which means better fuel consumption. This lowers the overall operating cost because our machines are tools used to do business. So then it becomes a win–win. We look at three areas: first, our operation, which is the manufacturing process, the transport, upstream with our suppliers – so our suppliers also have efficient, green businesses. Secondly, our product philosophy is about efficient design – this involves every aspect of the machine and how it's used. Finally, there is the social aspect, which revolves around the communities that we're involved in, the communities where our employees live and work and also the communities where our customers and our machines work. And the Bamford family have been very proactive in offering support in the wake of recent calamities that have happened around the world – particularly earthquakes and tsunamis. A lot of our machines have been sent straight out to help in the relief efforts.

Agility is key to delivering the brand

In companies I've worked for previously, you've got to go through layers of clay if ever you want to make a decision. But here you can make one phone call to our chairman and decisions are made instantly. After the Haiti earthquake, JCB Inc in Savannah, USA sent machines directly to the disaster area as soon as possible after the tragedy. They were ready within 36 hours at the factory and sent in straightaway by the US Army.

This demonstrates our 'sense of urgency' but also the agility and lateral thinking within the organization.

Another example is the work we did with the American Red Cross on a fundraiser for Haiti after the earthquake. Our people said, 'We're on the east coast of America. We'll drive our new, more fuel-efficient Backhoe model onto the beach, pick up some sand in the bucket and drive over to the west coast. After 26 days, they arrived in Santa Monica in California, drove onto the beach and deposited the sand from the east coast on Santa Monica beach. In doing so, they made a lot of money for charity. One hell of a road trip!

Tim Burnhope – group MD

Tim Burnhope is group managing director for product development and commercial operations. He joined from Caterpillar in 1999.

JCB has a passion to improve everything. We want to involve everybody in those improvements. We have a great team of people and a great team spirit. Everybody's always asking every day, 'What can we do better?'

We always set very, very ambitious targets. **We believe big targets lead to big results.** Our teams are used to that challenge, which comes right from the top. Sir Anthony Bamford gets involved with me in the product reviews and we encourage our teams to go further, to make changes and avoid compromise. We challenge our teams to come up with the best solution but at the right cost. And our approach works in that it helps to focus minds on getting everything right: quality, functionality, cost and so on.

Set simple goals

I set very tough goals and work hard to explain to my team why we've got to achieve those goals. I involve them very much in looking at the next three to five years. This conditions their minds to achieving much bigger goals in the future. I try to make the goals very clear and concise. The goals of the 10 areas that report to me are very clearly set out on a single page: the products we plan to introduce, the innovations we want, what we expect to sell, the market share, the volume, the number of parts we want to sell, the number of attachments, what we want from our marketing and PR activity, and so on. All very, very simple. I translate them into seven key goals and three business improvements, and at my weekly management meeting we all run through the figures so we know exactly where we are. This is really what drives the JCB business forward.

Be willing and able to change course quickly

We're not scared to change our plans if market conditions change or if customer needs are suddenly different. We encourage lots and lots of customers to visit our factories. When they're here, we ask customers not what they want from a product but 'How can we help you make your business better?' They'll say, 'Oh, I need to consume less fuel,' or 'I need the machines to be more productive,' and we'll actually work on the things that they want and in many cases work with them as partners to achieve these goals.

In some businesses, the organization itself can be a constraint and can stifle innovation and product development. This is not the case at JCB. We're organized into 17 business units, each with its own management team. We are always challenging the directors of each business unit to run it like their own business. This makes them very entrepreneurial, largely because the bureaucratic element has been stripped away. Our chairman's very good at getting us to benchmark ourselves with different organizations; not just construction or engineering companies. This helps to drive the innovation agenda. We visit lots of companies to exchange ideas. And quite often it's the small ideas that stimulate the innovation. For example, everybody's talking about sustainability right now. So we really want to engage with our customers on a journey around fuel efficiency. The one thing they understand is, if they use less fuel, they'll be happy. And it's up to us to help them to improve their businesses.

Our new Eco range of backhoes will save our customers over £800 for every 1,000 hours of work they do. A typical Backhoe in European markets would do 2,000 hours a year. So this would be a saving of over £1,600 in one year. So if a customer has one of these machines for three years, that's £5,000 or so. That's around 50 barrels of fuel they'd save, with no loss in productivity.

Listen to the wisdom of your elders and stay close to the pulse of the market

Our senior team of chairman, deputy chairman and CEO are almost like 'elders' within the JCB organization in that they let us get on with the drive and ambition in running the business but are on hand with the wise words. So when we were selling lots of machines in 2007, they would take you aside and say, 'Just remember. Your very best year is often followed by a few bad years.' I'll never forget that. And they were right. It's very easy to think that the markets will continue to grow but they don't. They never do.

What makes JCB different from its competitors is this: we're always the first to sense a change in market conditions and we're always quick to respond to changes. Whereas a lot of other manufacturers look at machine sales to distributors, we look more closely at customer activity in terms of retails and machine utilization. Retail sales started to fall in early 2008, so while competitors carried on building machines which ended up sitting in their dealers' stockyards, we decided to cut back on production straight away. Most of our suppliers said we reacted about six months earlier than the competitors. Just as well we did, because as history now shows, things got a lot worse very quickly. Doing what we did, as early as we did, protected our business and our dealers' businesses. So listening to what the market is saying and reacting quickly are very important. That's the JCB way.

The thing I love about working for JCB is that **I firmly believe when we come to work every day, we can do something that helps change the world**. And that might seem quite corny but if we can make a new Backhoe that is 16 per cent more efficient, that will have a bearing on thousands and thousands of customers who feel better because they're using less fuel. That's a great feeling.'

Kevin Balls of J C Balls & Sons – the lifelong customer

J C Balls are family-owned plant hire and excavation contractors based in Derbyshire, UK. Kevin and his brother Chris now run the business, which their father started in 1963 and for which their own children now work.

We've been involved with JCB since my father started business in 1963 and bought his first JCB. Their products are among the best on the market but it's the service and the backup which are second to none. Our company has grown from strength to strength through the JCB product and the JCB people. They like to come and talk to *us* about how *we* feel about JCB. They like to treat everybody as a family.

We're plant hire and excavation contractors. We're on 24-hour call-out with machines and lorries. We work seven days a week, 52 weeks a year. We even get called out on Christmas Day, and that is one of the reasons why we have JCB – because of the product itself, the reliability and the back-up that we get with it. JCB and the JCB dealers understand how we work. If we have a call-out in the middle of the night and the product breaks down and we can't fix it ourselves, we ring our local dealer and, within an hour, there's somebody there to repair it.

If they're well maintained, a JCB will run up to eight to ten years. That's around 10,000 hours of work. Then we will sell it on. I now know there are machines that we've sold to Cyprus or South Africa that are still working up to 20,000 to 25,000 hours. The resale value is exceptional. And that is another reason why we stick with the product.

I collect vintage machines as well. I've got a 1954 JCB Mark 1 that was the 103rd built and is still in full working order. You could still take it out and do a day's work with it. That just says how good the product is. And it's the same with the modern machine today as with the machine from 1954.

When they're bringing out a new product they talk to the customers who run them. They ask us to send drivers up to talk to JCB to see how the operators feel about what improvements they can make with the machines. That's good because the operator needs to feel happy sat in the machine. And that, to be fair, has gone on since 1963.

When my father started there was a gentleman called Bill Hirst who was one of Mr Bamford's first welders. Bill still keeps in contact with our family. He's retired now but he calls in to see us. When they first built JCBs they used to put a welder's number on them to show who welded the part so that if anything broke, they knew who'd welded it. One day I took Bill into the shed to show him the 1954 JCB Mark 1 that I'd restored and he said, 'There you are, Kevin, that's my welding number on that from 1954.'

You still get the same feeling of pride and care with the people who work for JCB now as Bill all those years ago.

Bill Hirst and his welder's number from 1954   © 2011 JCB

The need for speed

Joseph Cyril Bamford's creed 'a sense of urgency' is one which
all our bold organizations heed. In JCB's case, this sense of urgency,
the appreciation that you have to act quickly and with determination,
has propelled the firm from a small garage in Staffordshire to a worldwide
brand. A visit to its global headquarters in Rocester, Staffordshire,
reinforces the perception given by the interviewees in this book that it is
people who are possessed with this sense of urgency who get things
done. This is manifested in much of what JCB has done, whether it's
building faster tractors, Backhoes that can travel at 60 mph into combat
zones for the military, the swift response to human crises such as the Haiti
earthquake, or the breaking of the diesel land-speed record. Bill Bernbach,
the legendary advertising man, once said 'In this real world, the good do
not drive out the bad, the energetic drive out the lazy.' JCB would agree.

Restlessness in pursuit of better

A mantra at JCB is '*jamais content*' – a favourite phrase of the founder.
It captures well the spirit of relentlessness in pursuit of improvements that
characterizes the business. Regardless of function in the business,

everyone is challenged to think how they can be better tomorrow than today. This is not something which can be forced on to a culture and is therefore a key characteristic that the company looks for in its people.

Little things count a lot

Related to the above learning is the attention to detail and the understanding that it is the little things that matter to people and which they remember as much as the big things – whether it is Sir Anthony Bamford adjusting the fuel cap in response to a customer's feedback or the story of the welder's number that Kevin Balls shared. It is these small touches that show the sincerity of purpose in the organization. You can't fake the small stuff.

An agile organization

Tim Burnhope points out that a lot of traditional corporates are constrained by their very organizational structures. Some businesses have even had a head of organigrams whose job is to trace and set in stone the hierarchy of the business. JCB needs agility in the organization if they are to act with a sense of urgency and swiftness of response to customers. By establishing individual and entrepreneurial business units to design and produce the various product lines but then filter those to the public through a common sales and marketing channel, they achieve agility and consistency. And of course, the fact that the chairman and the leaders of the business make themselves available to give swift decisions as well as empowering people to take legitimate risks ensures a culture that is agile.

Continuous measurement

All our bold companies have a purpose beyond profit as their principal motivation, but this does not make them sloppy or inefficient. In fact, JCB is a great example of continually focusing on and reviewing the key metrics the business needs to set in order to reach its targets. As you would expect from an engineering company, they are constantly evaluating against data in real time but the data is as much predictive as it is outcome based. Tim Burnhope sets targets and goals and reviews those measures every week. Great companies measure what matters relentlessly.

True customer focus

Perhaps above all what stands out in the JCB story is the complete line of sight on the customer that the organization has. Sir Anthony shares an obsession about winning and retaining customers with the leaders of our other bold businesses. The fact that everybody is operating with the end customer in mind makes decisions easier and gives real focus to their work. It is also, as

Tim Burnhope shares at the end of his interview, a source of real pride for the people in the business.

The power of the brand

JCB also shows that you can differentiate anything, even diggers. You can create a powerful brand providing you focus on what the customer values and then concentrate all of your efforts on delivering that value better than anyone else. And if you do that your brand becomes the byword for quality in the category.

For more on JCB see: http://www.jcb.com/

At the heart of JCB is a restless pursuit of creating better products and a refusal to compromise on quality. It's something they have in common with another distinctive British brand, albeit one that is considerably younger and in a completely different market: innocent drinks.

Chapter Thirteen
innocent

Few brands have captured the imagination and created such an infectious enthusiasm among their customers as innocent drinks in the UK. Founded in 1999 by three friends in their late twenties, the combination of the natural goodness of its product and the quirky humour of its packaging created a demand both for smoothies and for companies to use language in a more engaging way.

Famously, the company started after the three founders booked a stall at a music festival and bought £500 worth of fruit to make and sell their smoothies. They asked drinkers to throw their empty cups into one of two bins marked 'yes' and 'no' in response to the question, 'Should we give up our day jobs to make smoothies?' By the end of the day, the 'yes' bin was overflowing.

Now headquartered in Fruit Towers, West London, innocent sells an estimated 2 million smoothies every day. Its revenues in 2009 were estimated at £128 million and the brand is sold in the UK, Ireland, Holland, Germany, France, Austria and Belgium.

In April 2010, Coca-Cola, who had acquired an 18 per cent stake in innocent in 2009, increased its holding to 58 per cent for an estimated £65 million. The deal raised eyebrows in some quarters and led to predictable speculation about 'innocent selling its soul'. But innocent operates with almost total autonomy within the Coca-Cola business and, as these interviews reveal, remains passionately independent in spirit and committed to its cause of getting good food into the widest number of people possible.

Bold practices

innocent

- Ten per cent of all profits are given to charity through the innocent foundation.
- Investment in FORTUNE: a state-of-the-art forecasting system to ensure year-round fruit supply from properly accredited sources.
- They source fruit from Rainforest Alliance farmers, which costs them 30 per cent more than if they bought from conventional sources.

- Despite being a private company, every year they hold an AGM ('A Grown-up Meeting'), where consumers are invited to Fruit Towers to learn about innocent's results and plans.
- Host 'Fruitstock', a summer festival.
- Created first recyclable plastic packaging.
- Golden Bottle Awards to reward staff every year.
- Banana phone answers all enquiries.
- Every employee has a 'fruit name' – a jocular title that reflects their work or role.
- Tour guides will take consumers around the office whenever they 'pop in'.
- Every Christmas, customers are invited to hand knit little woollen hats for the smoothie bottles. Thousands of different little hats are made, adding uniqueness to the product and generating income for charity.

Woollen hats   © 2011 innocent

Richard Reed – chief squeezer

Richard Reed co-founded innocent drinks with two friends, Jon Wright and Adam Balon, in 1999.

We came into the market thinking, 'We would love there to be something we could have on a daily basis that's completely natural, that's really good for us and tastes delicious.' That was the beginning, to make it easy for people to do themselves some good and to make it enjoyable. So the original idea of getting fruit, crushing it, putting it into bottles so people could grab one on the way into work in the morning was just a simple solution to what we ourselves, as three 26-year-olds living in London, needed and wanted. We didn't think as manufacturers or as producers or as investors. We didn't think about what was the most profitable, we didn't think about what was the easiest or most convenient. We thought: 'Given that we're drinking these each day, what do we want them to be made from?'

The importance of being natural

The whole business can be summed up in one word: 'natural'. We didn't invent smoothies but we were the first people in the UK to bring out a completely natural smoothie made from fruit, not concentrate, one that doesn't have any preservatives, flavourings or additives. It allowed us to differentiate in a way that was extremely relevant to the consumer.

When we started out, there was a brand that made smoothies from concentrate; it wasn't that it was bad, it just wasn't that good. We thought, 'Well, we can beat the product, because they're making it from this gloop, whereas we're going to make ours from fresh fruit.' And we looked at the brand; it was called PJ's for 'Pete and Johnny's' but there was no Pete, there was no Johnny; it was just a manufactured identity that sounded a bit like Ben and Jerry's. We thought that was strange as well. We wanted to be absolutely transparent and authentic. Those things now are clichés but I realize that **what has created a huge amount of value in innocent has been our congruency**, the fact that the way we appear is congruent with the products we make and the way we act as a group of people.

The famous smoothie
© 2011 innocent

If at first you don't succeed...

But innocent is a business that nearly didn't happen. We'd been working on the business idea in the evenings and at weekends. We didn't have the confidence to give up our day jobs because we didn't have any evidence that people would buy our products at the right price. So we came up with the idea of selling them at a music festival. We bought £500 worth of fruit, turned it into our favourite recipe and set up this little stall. We had originally written out a massive three-page market research questionnaire that we were going to get people to fill out after they'd bought the smoothies: age, sex, rank it on a scale of 1 to 8, how did it make you feel, etc – classic market research questions. Then a couple of friends said, 'Well, don't you really just need to know whether they like them or not? Why don't you just stick up a sign that says, "Should we give up our day jobs?" and a bin that says "yes" and a bin that says "no".' So we did and at the end of that weekend the 'yes' bin was full. I went into work on Monday morning and resigned.

But we had absolutely misunderstood the difference between making it once at a market stall versus making it day in day out on a commercial scale to sell to shops. It sounds embarrassing to say that, but we were just three 26-year-olds full of the excitement of doing it.

We got turned down by every single possible source of funding. We went in and saw one guy and he said, 'You scored zero out of 5 in the investors' handbook. You're too young, you're all friends, you haven't appointed a clear leader' – we said we'd do it together as the three of us – 'You've got no experience of setting up a business before or indeed working in the food and drink industry, you're going up against the world's biggest food and drinks companies. It's a dreadful investment opportunity.'

We tried banks, venture capitalists and private investors; they all said 'no'. We were about to throw in the towel. Then a friend talked about this theory that says everyone knows Kevin Bacon, the actor, via six degrees of separation. He said we must know someone who knows someone who knows someone who's rich. So we sent out an e-mail, partly as a joke, partly because we had nothing to lose, with the subject line 'Does anyone know anyone rich?' We got two responses back, one of which was from Maurice Pinta, who sometimes made investments.

Maurice said he thought it was a crazy idea but he believed in us as a team. He would put in £50k and he'd get the other £200k from six other friends. We went back three weeks later and he told us that his six friends, for the first time in 20 years of investing together, had all turned him down. He then put in the extra £200k himself. He's since said, 'I put that money in out of obligation, and I thought I was going to lose it.' So even he thought it was slightly bonkers, but now he says it's the best investment he's ever made. I guess the reality is we just didn't stop and we also got lucky. I think those are the two things you need to be successful. Well, not quite. First, you've got to start!

Stick to your strategy

What did we do differently from everyone else? First, we said 'natural' and everyone else said 'processed'. Secondly, we said 'fresh' and everyone else said 'from concentrate'. We were absolutely intransigent on those points; that's why it took us so long to get to market. Potential suppliers said, 'Look, we can make a smoothie for you guys, no worries, we're going to use this flavouring because that will give you much better profitability, and you need to make it shelf stable otherwise you're going to run into wastage issues.' We said, 'No, no, we want real fruit.' They said, 'Well, you don't understand, that's not how it works.' But we said, 'We're called innocent, our whole thing's about being natural, so if you take that away from us, we don't actually have a business idea.'

We were just aware that we couldn't win through muscle, we couldn't win through advertising spend, **we could only win through having a better product**, so if we didn't have a better product, our strategy was gone.

Eventually we found a Welsh guy who'd grown up in Jamaica as an orange farmer, moved back to Cardiff and imported oranges to make freshly squeezed orange juice. He still didn't think it was going to work because our fruit (bananas, etc) is much harder to work with than oranges. But essentially he said the same thing as Maurice: 'I think you're wrong but I'll agree to take a chance with you.' So then we could invest in little bits of kit to make smoothies within his manufacturing site rather than having to build a manufacturing site ourselves. That would have been a disaster, because we would have been spending all our time building factories rather than developing products and communicating with consumers.

An innocent tone of voice

We didn't have any money to spend on advertising but we wanted to communicate. I remembered hearing media salespeople talking about how targeted their magazine or newspaper was to this particular consumer base and I remember thinking, 'Well, at least I know 100 per cent of people reading the side of our packs are going to be innocent consumers, that's an opportunity.'

So we wrote stuff on the side of our packaging. We wanted to be ourselves so we wrote in our stupid sense of humour. I think the single most value-creating thing we've done is in our ingredient panel. It says 'Six crushed strawberries', when everyone else would put '19 per cent strawberry puree'. Six strawberries is the language of the kitchen, not the language of the manufacturing facility. It got to the heart of what we were all about in a way that was impactful given the context.

The Real Thing about the Coke deal

We had a business plan that said we'd raise the original money to get started and at some point we'd go back for a second round of funding to extend the business. The main reason for raising the cash was to fund international growth and also to put money behind our new innovations. Funnily enough, we started fundraising the day Lehmans went under in September 2008, a terrible time to start raising funds. We got eight offers. There were three we took through to the second round and Coke was our favourite. They said: 'We love the brand, we love the philosophy, we don't want to get involved but we'd like to help you.' Great. They'd put the cash in, leave us to get on with it, but help when we asked. And they've been absolutely true to their word. In the first year after the deal we had three two-hour meetings with them, so that's as hands-off as you can get. They don't do chilled juice, they do cans of ambient long-life product; we're making bottles of short-shelf-life chilled product. They don't do what we do, so they're happy to leave us alone.

We had 280 complaints out of four million customers, and of the 280 who complained, I'd say the majority were anti-Coke people rather than innocent consumers. We got more grief when we started selling our kids' smoothies through McDonald's. Someone said, 'It's like finding out your uncle is a paedophile.' Our mission is about getting healthy food and drink into as many people and places as we can. So a kid can have a smoothie in their Happy Meal for no extra money, which gives them a portion of fruit instead of a fizzy drink. That's exactly what we *should* be doing.

Staying true to your brand is not cheap

Being bold costs us all the time – in little, medium and big ways. We place an emphasis on procuring fruit from farms that have high social and environmental standards. That's a nice little soundbite but it means that the pineapples we get from Rainforest Alliance farms cost 30 per cent more than conventionally grown pineapples. That's a big deal. I can't show you that it translates into sales. It sure as hell doesn't translate into better profits but we feel like in the longer term it's where we want to be as a brand.

Giving 10 per cent of our profits to charity, that costs us. We spent four years developing the world's first recycled plastic bottle. Have we got the money back from that? God, no. Do I think it's creating long-term brand value? Yes. I think the value is caught up in the relationship between the brand and the consumer, the brand and the retailers and the brand and the employees, and it's congruent. The spreadsheets don't show that. But I think that **spreadsheets only reflect the past, not the future**.

It all keeps coming back to the mission. I guess we're just deeply in love with the idea that when food is natural and tasty and healthy and sustainably sourced, amazing things happen. I like the fact that we use all the tools of marketing, all the tricks of the trade to get people to buy more, because it's coming from a sincere place. The more you eat, the healthier you get.

Dan Germain – guardian angel

Dan has been head of creative for almost 11 years. He joined innocent through, in his own words, 'blind nepotism', having studied geography with Richard Reed at university.

Packaging was our first medium for talking to people. I think purely because there was a gap, physically, on the back of the label and there was nothing left to put there. Once we had put the barcode, the ingredients and the legal stuff on, there was a gap. We looked at what other people did and most of it was pretty dull. They either redescribed the product, using more words than were necessary, or had a picture of a serving suggestion, like cornflakes in a bowl with a spoon. Very helpful. So we decided to utilize it in a way that has now become a bit of a trademark, I guess, by writing dumb stuff on the back of the label. I found I could do that quite well and Richard (Reed) used to do that as well, so we worked a lot together. And we still do. We still share ideas. He would be my creative partner, I guess, if we were an agency.

The freedom to have fun

I think we had the luxury in the early days of thinking, 'Well, nobody's going to read this,' so we wrote some quite stupid things. And it seems that encouraged contact and we realized that by writing stupid things, people were more likely to get in touch. I was also doing quite a lot of responding to consumer contact, responding to e-mails and letters when I wasn't doing deliveries in a van or trying to sell drinks, or doing a bit of everything as you do in those early days. I had this wide range of exposure to our wholesalers, to the shopkeepers and to the people who were buying the drinks, and I think that helped generate the stuff we wrote.

We had a pretty plain website to begin with. After nine months or a year we said, 'Right, we have got to make this interesting to match all the other things we're doing: such as the writing on the labels or going out dressed up in stupid outfits to give away drinks to people.' That was when we started transferring what was written on the labels to other places.

So **we began to think about what innocent sounds like** or what message we need to tell people and what is the best way of us delivering that message. Richard's background in advertising meant that he had a structure in place for thinking, 'This is how you work out what you want to say to people and where you need to say it.' I didn't have any of that structure. He knew *where* and I knew *what* we were going to say. So it kind of worked well together.

When it came to making a TV advert a few years later, we were ready. We'd been talking about doing TV for years. We're about getting as much good stuff to as many people as possible and TV is one great way of doing that. We kept having to stop ourselves in the early days because we were only on sale in about 10 shops (and we had no money). When we were in enough shops to justify TV advertising, we did something that I guess was relatively interesting. First, we went to an agency who were really good. They gave us an idea that we thought was funny. We made the advert. But when we got the advert back, we watched it and it just felt too much like an advert, it didn't feel 'innocent'.

We didn't have much time and so the challenge was put to me: could I make an advert in the next week? Then we could see if it was better than the one we had got and we could stick it on the telly. So I went to a park, Gunnersbury Park, on a Saturday, with my friend Ed, who is a bit handy with a camcorder, and we made an advert. Me, him and a bloke called Henry. We did a little stop-motion animation thing. And that was our first TV advert. It was great. It worked really well because it kept things simple, it was honest, there were no tricks. It really was made by three blokes in a park, the Saturday before it was on telly. So it was authentically innocent.

To see innocent's first ad, click:
http://www.youtube.com/
watch?v=2eOi87AwDSA

Growing the team, naturally

It took me about a year and a half to find someone specifically to come and write with me. I interviewed all sorts of people – copywriters, people who had written for the TV, writers of all types – and in the end it was someone who was already working here, a lady called Ceri. I just realized, she's been making me laugh for a couple of years – just around the office. And when I read stuff she had written, I thought, 'It's really good, maybe she should do it.' And she's been brilliant.

I look for people who can make me laugh and are really honest. They don't have to be like me, they don't have to share the same views and feelings that I do. There is now someone in Copenhagen, someone in Hamburg and someone in Paris. I don't speak their language, I don't know if they're funny in their mother tongues. I interviewed them but I also just talked to them a lot and realized, 'Well, I could be comfortable working with you and I think you would be interesting to other people, you'd make other people laugh. So, therefore, you could do this job.'

Originally, my job was sitting there writing the stuff and giving it to someone to print or make into something. Now there are 20 or 30 or 50 people somewhere in the world doing things for innocent, producing a TV ad or designing bits for packaging and I just have to make sure I'm right there with them at the beginning and in the middle and at the end, saying, 'That's good – what about doing it like this – what about thinking about doing it like that... what about changing that?' You know, just being the chief interferer. I have probably used up all the good ideas I am ever going to have about smoothies in the last 11 years. My job now is to make sure other people continue to have those great ideas.

A bold future

If five years ago someone had said to me, 'What is it going to be like when you are a £100 million brand and there's 250 of you?' I'd have said, 'I have no idea, it sounds quite scary.' Now I think, 'Well, it's been all right so far; wouldn't it be quite nice to be a billion dollar brand or a billion pound brand and employ 10,000 people?' Maybe *that* would be fun. Imagine the electricity of ideas going round somewhere like that. For innocent to become something like that is a great ambition. Maybe we will get there... maybe we will just stay as we are. But it would be a shame, having got this far, to say, 'Remember that our tone means that we can only ever be small and cute and lovable.' I'd like to think we can aim for more than that. We could be bigger; we could do more dramatic things.

Steve Spall – paranormal greengrocer

Steve Spall is accountable for the teams that run innocent's operations, from sourcing fruit, making smoothies and logistics to sustainability, IT and the Fruit Towers facilities.

We have got a nice cheesy title for our long-term vision, which is Sustainable Cheaper Operations Reliable Every Time (SCORE). Will J (Will Jefferies, innocent's packaging buyer) came up with that title. That's everything we need to do to get Europe's tastiest, healthy stuff made and distributed simply, reliably, sustainably, and competitively on cost and service.

We work with a small set of close business partners – whether suppliers of processed fruit, our blending partner or our co-packers – with whom we have long-term relationships. We expect them to be the most competitive in the marketplace on quality, cost and service. In return, we put a lot of time and effort into helping them stay ahead.

innocent's distinctive van

The five steps to success

We talk about everything in fives here (five values, five pieces of fruit and veg a day, etc). So we have five aspects to our work. One is building the capabilities for growth. We want to double the size of our business: that's new products we want to launch and new volumes we want to achieve. So we've got to put in place the capabilities for that growth, which means, for example, having enough manufacturers and enough machines in their different sites.

The second is building flexibility in the network to manage when demand is lower as well as when it's higher. So our fully outsourced operation must be able to cope with changes in demand and changes in availability of produce.

We've come up with an idea we call RALF, which stands for Resilient, Agile, Lean and Flexible. It's how we want our network to be. That means building a partnership among all our outsourced partners where they trust each other as well as us, so they are happy to be able to support each other, recognizing that they are good at different things.

The third thing is to understand the best ways to make products without unnecessary cost. We're under a lot of cost pressure right now because we source so many of our raw ingredients from dollar and euro economies, where the fruit grows that we need for really good quality products.

We have to understand the different locations around the world where we can source fruits, the different kinds of fruits that we can use in each of our recipes (because only a few varieties work well without sugar or flavourings) and what consumers expect each recipe to do. What do they expect strawberry and banana to do? What do they expect mango and passion fruit to do? What do they expect kiwi, apple and lime to do? Do they want one to be refreshing, one to be comforting, one to be very exotic?

Then we can get that optimum balance of different fruits in there, in order to be what consumers want, but cope with the fact that sometimes certain fruits might be really difficult to get hold of because, for instance, of a climatic issue in the country that we source them from. So if we can get more varieties of mango that work, let's say, from different parts of the world, we're better able to do a great job in our mango and passion fruit smoothie and we can move sourcing around if there are times when the crop's not available.

Our forecasting process is important for that. We have a state-of-the-art tool we call FORTUNE. It is really leading edge in terms of the ability to have one set of numbers – whether you are from commercial and are looking at sales or margin, or in manufacturing and want to know how many products you're going to make in March in a year's time or how much fruit you're going to have to buy the season after next – we've got a level of forecasting and a provision of information on a shared basis which is second to nothing I have seen externally.

For us, it's really important because obviously fruit is seasonal and you need to be able to make commitments in time for the harvest that will last for the next 12 months. So you need to know perhaps 18 months ahead what you expect to require in the way of strawberries, raspberries or boysenberries. We don't just buy a standard spec for many fruits – we work pretty hard with different farmers and processors to get a particular spec that means our smoothies still taste great without any sugar or flavourings added – so we have to get the quantities right.

Having great forecasts not only enables you to make sure you stay in supply for your customers and don't have a lot of waste on a short-shelf-life product like ours, but also helps you to get your contracts right and not end up with a whole bunch of fruit you can't use or scrabbling around trying to find more fruit.

The fourth area is around sustainability – it's an underpinning principle throughout our business that we will do as little damage to the planet as we can, while making our smoothies as delicious as possible. Jess (Sansom) will tell you all about that.

The fifth area is around people. How do we ensure that people want to continue to work in the operations part of innocent over the long term? As we grow in complexity and size, we want to pass more routine activities to our suppliers and create roles for our people that are broader, such as contract management, change management or technical management. So we can keep the same-size team but still generate opportunities for people to develop.

One of the things that's important for me here is working with a group of people that you actually want to spend your time with – people who are like-minded. I guess sometimes when people come in here they are a bit confused by the casual look and think that it means that it's just a kind of party zone. But the reality is it's a place where people are very ambitious and very driven. They want to do business in a fair and equitable way but also they want to win and make money. It's rare that people like that all come together in a single organization.

Jessica Sansom – head tree hugger

Jessica Sansom is head of sustainability for innocent drinks. She joined in 2007 after working for many years in the sustainability field for both private companies and governmental organizations internationally.

The sustainability role is to ensure we do business in a more enlightened fashion. Our ultimate goal is to move towards what could be described as sustainable capitalism. It's an ambitious goal and maybe you never really 'get there'. But we put

in place the principles and the methods of doing business that will ensure that we have a more positive environmental and social impact.

On a day-to-day basis that needs to be embedded into the entire operation of the business, from buying fruit at farms across the world, getting them pressed or pulped or juiced, bringing them through the supply chain, getting it into our products, selling our products into different retailers for sale, even down to what kind of packaging we give our consumers to dispose of once they've finished the product. It's my job to work across the business to make sure that we've got the right decision-making processes, information and structures to achieve a more sustainable result. It might be as simple as increasing the recycled content or the recyclability of our packaging. Or it might be as complex as our project to bring smallholder African farmers into our trade network. That project is about establishing a commercial trading relationship with these farmers that aids their development. To alleviate poverty in those communities requires a highly different kind of trading relationship from a standard purchase contract.

I think we're very lucky within innocent that the employees are highly predisposed towards implementing sustainability. **We recruit based on the values of innocent** and one of those five values is to be responsible. So you've got a group of people who are already very aware of what the issues are and willing to do the work that's required.

Sustainability and commerce are intertwined

Sustainability has to be entrenched within the commercial nature of our business. When we do something which is for sustainability, it's not just about doing the right thing; it also has to be the right thing for the business into the future. We keep asking ourselves, 'Are there cost savings we can realize out of improved sustainability practices? Are there different markets we can access out of improved sustainability attributes? Is there greater diversification or security in the supply of fruit to our business because of sustainability?' I think that's absolutely essential, because if you don't have a business reason, then as soon as the times get a little bit tougher, sustainability goals will drop off the pad and all the work that you've done is wasted. So the challenge is to always **build it into the business model**.

We buy what I call the 'ugly' fruit: the fruit that might not look good enough to go on the supermarket shelf for a fresh buyer, but it tastes exactly the same, and saves the fruit from being wasted. However, this is a much smaller segment of the market for our growers. So we have to work hard to get them engaged because the direct commercial benefit to them is not as great as with other segments. We're not such a big company that we can say, 'Jump!' and they ask, 'How high?' We say, 'We'd like you to jump,' and they ask, 'Well, why?' They need a lot more information from us to be able to understand why it is we're pushing for a certain activity to happen and for them to buy into it and get on board. But the benefit of that is if people truly buy into it you're much more likely to have a long-lasting and more sustainable – in the real sense of the word – solution.

Working with the wider world

We purchase some of the strawberries for our products from a region in Spain which has considerable water stress, because of growth in the agricultural sector and housing developments in that area. It borders the Doñana National Park, which is globally important wetlands – there are six million migratory birds that pass through there every year, there's also a number of endangered species like the Iberian lynx living there. If the water is not available for those wetlands, then the ecosystems start to break down and the biodiversity is lost, the migratory birds have nowhere to go, and so on. WWF brought the problem to our attention and asked if we could work with our strawberry growers to address the levels of water usage in the agricultural production. So we're developing a programme to identify exactly how much water is being used in those regions, what constitutes best practice and then start to disseminate that best practice amongst the growers in that area.

The entrepreneurial nature of the company means that we have a lot of flexibility to be able to find the right approach – both for the business and for sustainability – whereas in a much larger or more established organization you often find that it just takes longer to achieve change because the process of bringing everybody on board and changing business structures is a lot less flexible. That's given me the most satisfaction within innocent: that huge appetite to achieve a really positive goal and then the flexibility to be able to say, 'Right, well, yup... if that's what we need to do to get there, then we can do that and we can change the way that we do our business.'

Joe McEwan – juice figalow

Joe McEwan is the consumer projects lead and people's champion for innocent drinks. He joined innocent after university, where he had a memorable encounter with the brand.

I was sharing a house at university with a nice chap called Ian. His mum had written a poem to innocent about how much her son liked their smoothies. She didn't ask for anything, she just thought they were a nice company and wanted to let them know. A few days later a delivery of fridge-chilled drinks arrived on our doorstep with a handwritten note on top that said, 'Your mum writes a lovely poem. I hope you enjoy these smoothies.' I was just blown away, really. Nowadays, you're never sure whether an e-mail you send to a company is even going to get read, let alone acknowledged in such a personal way. This is a company run by human beings, I thought, somewhere that values the personal touch, and somewhere I'd enjoy working.

Being a champion for the brand and a champion for the customer

After university, whilst struggling to find a job that really grabbed me, I listened to some wise words from my mum – as everybody should – and went to the innocent website to look for vacancies. They were looking for a new people's champion. The role would basically involve responding to people who got in touch with the business in a really personal way; writing creative responses to their e-mails and making sure that the words people had sent into us were listened to, spread around the business and, as much as possible, acted on. It sounded so much more than standard customer services, so I sent in an application and a long covering letter talking about my passion for the brand. Luckily, that covering letter and my CV, and, more than anything else I think, the genuine enthusiasm I had for the brand, got me the job. I think what I've learnt most about innocent is that this company stays alive and its values stay alive, despite the fact that we've grown, because we continue to hire people that have that level of passion for the brand.

Hold the banana phone...

Half my time here is spent being a people's champion – talking to drinkers on the banana phone, sorting them out when they've had a problem, answering a general enquiry or, as is so often the case with innocent, just chatting to people when they call up and want to hear a joke, ask if the banana phone is real, or tell us what they like, what they don't like and so on. It's about being on hand to give people a personalized response as quickly as possible – but it's more than just speedy responses. The quality of the response is really important too. It's great to get a quick response, but it's no good getting a quick response if that response has obviously been rushed, so it's a balancing act between speed and quality. It's just a case of chatting to people like you'd want to be spoken to, I guess, and treating the contact – as corny as it sounds – more like a pen-pal experience than a standard customer service experience. Taking the time out of your day to show someone around Fruit Towers, if they pop in, or handwriting a letter to someone – those are the things that, hopefully, set us apart from many other brands. **We've got a team of about 30 tour guides** now, all of whom are people that work here who have volunteered to help out, and they show visitors around our office. The tours are a great way for people here to have direct contact with our drinkers, and help to keep our feet on the ground.

Know exactly what each of your customers wants

The other key part of being a people's champion is to collate all the feedback we get. The system that we use to record and get back to consumers enables us to categorize the type of enquiry, complaint or praise that we receive to quite a fine level of detail. We can then recognize trends and use what we've learnt to steer business decisions, which ensures our claim of being a consumer-led business isn't a hollow one. Making a banana-free smoothie is a great example of the kind of thing I'm talking about. Hundreds of people wrote in requesting that we make a smoothie without bananas. We listened, made a note of their comments, and then pestered the relevant areas of the business to make a banana-free smoothie because our drinkers were crying out for it. After much perfecting in the kitchen, we finally made one – our kiwi, apple and lime recipe was the first smoothie we'd ever made that was completely banana free. To accompany the launch we sent out an e-mail to all the people that had originally written to us asking us to make it. We said something along the lines of 'Just thought you'd like to know that we've made what you asked for' and asked them to respond with their address. We then sent out a handwritten card and voucher for them to try the new recipe. The feedback from that card and voucher was so positive. I remember someone saying, 'In this age of machinery, it's just so encouraging to see a company still valuing the personal touch.' So we try and do as many of these send-outs as we can. It's so important for businesses to use this kind of activity alongside large-scale marketing. Yes, big-money adverts draw people in and make them go 'Wow!' for 30 seconds. But it is just as important to put out those little things, those small touches, that perhaps only touch a few hundred people but that touch those people in such a strong way that the person is talking about it with their friends and family for days. **If you can give someone a great, truly personal experience, they'll tell lots of people about it.**

Invite your customers in to your business – innocent's 'A Grown-up Meeting'

I work on various other consumer-focused initiatives, like organizing this year's AGM. It's a very innocent take on your usual AGM. We call it 'A Grown-up Meeting'. Basically, we invite a hundred of our consumers into the office for the day for a bit of a chat. They hear from the founders how the last year has been – the stuff we've done well, the stuff we've learnt from; they get to taste new products and decide what our next veg-pot recipe should be; they visit exploration stations around the building and have a go at making a smoothie in the kitchen, or visit the fruit team, or chat about our sustainability initiatives, and there's always plenty of tea and cake. It's a really interactive day, and all very informal.

The innocent AGM   © 2011 innocent

The most important part of the day for people is probably the Q&A session with Rich, Adam and Jon where they just ask, very openly, any questions they might have about what we do. We film all the Q&A answers and put them up on our website so that people who weren't able to make it to the meeting can still engage with the event. The AGM isn't something that generates vast amounts of PR, it's a thing that we do because it keeps us close to the people that buy our stuff, and keeps us true to that ideal of staying small as we get big. It's as important an event internally as it is for the consumers that come. The guys here love having the opportunity to chat to consumers and there's always a real buzz in the office in the week after.

AGM 2010:
http://www.youtube.com/watch?v=_
M5vFojkcNU&feature=related

Karen Callaghan – chief grower

Karen is head of the people team at innocent. She joined after a career in HR with Standard Chartered Bank.

When I joined, it surprised me how much appetite there was to professionalize the business but in a way that still retained what we were about and totally in line with our values.

Take hiring, for example. We have always sweated every new hire. It really matters to us that we bring in great people who are not only going to do a cracking job but will really add something to the team and make the company stronger. We make sure that the people who are going to work most closely with an individual get involved with the recruitment process. That can add hours and hours to the process but we think it's worth it.

Hire for fit

People ask me what the ideal innocent person is, if there is such a thing. The simplest way to answer that is to use the values. We have five of them: natural, entrepreneurial, commercial, responsible and generous. We recruit people who we think resonate with those values. So we have a series of questions or challenges that we'll set people specifically to test the extent to which they are, for example, entrepreneurial or commercial. Some of those questions might seem pretty strange. For example, we ask people to work out how many cups of coffee they think are drunk in any one day in London. We're testing your ability to deal with ambiguity, a lack of information and like to see you can do your sums too: all part of our values of entrepreneurialism and commercialism.

Measure what matters

From a commercial point of view, we love our data; we are all over the numbers and very transparent about that performance of the business. So every single week on Monday morning, everybody in the business gets together or is on the end of a phone and we talk about our numbers and what's going on across the teams. I love that transparency. Oh, and we do an exercise together, to get ourselves warmed up for the week.

Another example of transparency was during the financial crisis of 2008, when we had to make people redundant, letting 20 plus people go. That was really tough, probably one of the hardest things we have had to do, but it was values led in how we chose to deal with it. We were unusually transparent, we got all the UK-based people together to talk about why and what we needed to do and then we broke off into teams and we talked about it some more, taking people's questions. Every morning for three days I got up in front of the company and we talked about where we were in the process. We gave people as much support in terms of going on to find other things as they needed. And even though it was obviously tough for those affected, we got great feedback about the process. We had to kick it off on a Monday and by the Friday when we had our Christmas party pretty much everybody who was affected still came along, which was a surprise – a nice one.

Reward what matters

We consciously try to recognize people who have lived the values, for example through our annual Golden Bottle Awards, kind of like mini-Oscars. We have Best Male, Best Female, Best Newcomer, Best International Artist and Best Direction (which is our best leader). So every year we ask people to nominate those people who have particularly demonstrated the values. A small team of people from across the company then shortlist and decide on the winners. Then we film people who've nominated the shortlisted people and it is announced at the Christmas party. It's a great touch, a bit of a highlight of the year.

There's another lovely little touch when people leave. They get a golden bottle which has their name on it and then on the side it's got an ingredients list and a bit of blurb that is pertinent to them. Their team develop it with a bit of help from the creative guys. It's brilliant. It distils that person: what they brought to the team, their quirks, the funny stuff. People absolutely love it, and it's not unusual for people to shed a tear.

Bold lessons

Never compromise your strategy

The first lesson we learn from the innocent story is the importance of sticking to your strategy. Strategy involves choice and choices have consequences – for good or bad. The clearer you are about your strategy, the clearer you are about the choices you have to make and, in a sense, the easier it is to run your business. Richard and his co-founders were faced with a number of easy choices they could have made early on in the life of innocent. They could have compromised their '100 per cent fresh fruit' product strategy, it would have been cheaper and easier. But they realized that if they did that, then they would have no differentiator as a business and they would have betrayed the key principle upon which they set up the business. 'Nothing but nothing but fruit' has become a consumer proposition as well as a core business strategy.

Keep your eye on the figures

Being strategically bold does not mean being commercially reckless. Anyone who enters Fruit Towers, as Steve Spall points out in his interview, could be forgiven for thinking that the place is run like a playground. But the relaxed vibe belies steeliness in the discipline and determination of the business. Like other successful companies that we have written about, such as Tesco or Carphone Warehouse, the company interrogates its sales and operational figures every week, enabling it to take early action to capitalize on or improve business performance. innocent's forecasting and planning tool utilizes state-of-the-art software to ensure that there is real rigour to ordering raw material.

Language is a medium for engagement

Perhaps the most obvious legacy that innocent has given to marketers is the celebration of language as a way of expressing personality, engaging consumers and encouraging dialogue. As we have long argued, business is the most human of pursuits and language is the attribute that most distinguishes us as humans. Business unfortunately often reduces language to a series of impersonal phrases, littered by jargon which alienates consumers. The natural, unfeigned approach that innocent took to its language not only encouraged people to buy their smoothies but also to become advocates of the brand. The key to their success, though, is that it was 'natural', authentic to them. Every brand needs to find its own authentic voice and not try (as some tone-of-voice briefs we have seen given to agencies) merely to 'do an innocent'.

Language helps to emphasize the uniqueness of the brand

SCORE, RALF, FORTUNE, AGM: all of these acronyms serve to create a language that is unique to innocent, not only through tone of voice but also through the meaning they have for people on the inside of innocent. Don't confuse these acronyms with industry jargon which may be indecipherable to the layman but which is generic to the trade. Bold brands have words which are all their own and serve to reinforce the difference of the organization.

Never underestimate the little things

Many business people are obsessed with 'the big idea', the 'big, hairy audacious goal'; they want 'game changers' and are constantly poring over strategy reports to find ways of making 'paradigm shifts'. But even more important than these, the big things are the little day-to-day things that make an enormous difference to consumers and employees, that earn their advocacy and loyalty, cost little but reap financial rewards and demonstrate your authenticity. The personal notes that innocent write to their consumers might seem quaintly irrelevant to sharp-suited bean counters but encourage a dialogue with consumers which leads to product innovation, service improvements and employee loyalty. The story of innocent is crammed with a thousand daily kindnesses and at Fruit Towers you will find on the walls letters, anecdotes and pictures spontaneously sent in by consumers that tell of their love for the brand.

Sustainability is a core business purpose

Jess Sansom's role at innocent is not 'greenwashing' but a key part of the company's operations and is commercially grounded. This is part of a growing trend among businesses – as Jim Leap of WWF mentions in his interview in the next chapter. In innocent's case, this is partly driven by their mission to get good food into the widest number of people but it is also a natural characteristic of the kind of people who are attracted to working for the company. Alignment between their personal beliefs and the company's operating practices is how sustainability becomes rooted in the culture.

Sweat the recruitment process

Personal beliefs and attitudes are vital to the maintenance of the culture and thus the success of innocent. That is why they 'sweat the recruitment' process, in Karen Callaghan's words. Ensuring that new hires – especially senior ones – have been interviewed by the broadest range of colleagues, including the people they will be managing, means that they have a better chance of keeping innocent a high-performing and special culture.

Dramatize the brand

The banana phone, the cow van, the guided tours of Fruit Towers are all ways of creating an experience that makes the brand tangible in the eyes of consumers. It is easy for competitors to copy the smoothie. It is much more difficult for them to copy the experience and, if they do, as Robert Stephens of the Geek Squad points out, they are just shown up to be imitators.

Always keep the main thing the main thing

This is a mantra of Richard Reed's and essentially means that you need to keep in mind the core purpose of your business at all times, communicate it, make your choices according to it and resolutely defend your actions in the light of it. This way you maintain personal and commercial integrity. The way in which innocent has responded both to Coca-Cola's overtures to buy into the business and to the criticism it has received from some quarters for accepting its offer is a testament to that. Like Sir Terry Leahy, who is relentless in his communication about the importance of Tesco's customer in their business decisions, so innocent are relentless and resolute about communicating their core purpose. The Coca-Cola deal, Richard and the rest of his company explain, has been done to help achieve the 'main thing' to get good food into the widest number of people. And nothing but nothing will distract them from that goal.

Sustainability is a key issue for innocent, as it is for many other of our bold brands, and it is the cause that lies at the very heart of our last brand, WWF.

Chapter Fourteen
WWF

Few brands can claim they want to save the world but that is WWF's aim. Their ambition is to ensure a world where man and nature live in harmony. That means nothing less than helping governments, businesses and communities around the world to confront the most challenging threats to the survival of life on this planet.

WWF began life in 1961 as the World Wildlife Fund. It was inspired by the work of Sir Julian Huxley, a renowned biologist and an adviser to UNESCO. He had been appalled by the degradation of the habitat he had witnessed in East Africa, warning that much of the region's wildlife would disappear within 20 years. His words struck a chord with businessman Victor Stolan, who argued for an international organization to raise funds for conservation. They gathered together a group of scientists and communications experts that based its operations in Switzerland. There they produced the Morges Manifesto, essentially the founding document of WWF; it read 'We must save the world's wildlife – An international declaration'.

WWF is now one of the world's largest and most respected independent conservation organizations. Its Panda logo is famous throughout the world. It has more than five million supporters throughout five continents, and projects actively running in more than 100 countries. And since 1985 the organization has invested well over US$8 billion in more than 12,000 projects. All these projects and activities play a part in the campaign to stop the accelerating degradation of earth's natural environment, and to help humans live in greater harmony with nature.

WWF prides itself on being fact and science based and on bringing groups of stakeholders together in a spirit of common purpose, to solve the world's biggest problems. However, the Panda can show its claws when it wants to, as the World Wrestling Federation found out when WWF took them on in a major legal battle to stop their use of the WWF trademark and won.

The challenges facing WWF are huge; and the people who work for the organization today are as dedicated, determined and, as these interviews show, as inspired by their belief in the WWF mission as its founders. WWF embodies, probably more than any other brand, the boldest trait – that of taking a seemingly impossible challenge and committing to achieving it.

Bold practices

WWF

- Earth Hour – one of the largest mass-participation events in the world, which happens every year.
- Refuses or is prepared to accept the loss of funding from donors rather than have their policies compromised.
- Deliberately focuses on the most difficult challenges and often in the most remote and challenging places.
- Helped create and fund programmes for eco-labels certifying seafood and other products, such as those by the Marine Stewardship Council (MSC) and the Forest Stewardship Council (FSC), which help consumers around the world make sustainable choices when shopping and dining.
- Brought together 13 heads of state in Africa to develop a sustainability plan for the Congo Basin.
- Brought together the Brazilian government and the World Bank to secure the future of parklands in the Amazon that are the size of France.
- Fought the World Wrestling Federation for the right to use the WWF trademark around the world – and won.

Jim Leap – director general

Jim Leap started working with WWF in 1989. He has been the director general of WWF International since 2005.

We have taken on the biggest challenge facing humanity today, which is how we live on this planet in a way it can sustain. We bring to that challenge a unique set of strengths: the strengths of local organizations that are established, trusted and influential in countries all over the world, joined together in a global network that can reach decision makers anywhere, whether in governments, in the private sector or in civil society.

Our mission is to help people find ways to live in harmony with nature. Our approach is guided by a strong commitment to being science based, to being focused on solutions and to working with others.

What 'people living in harmony with nature' means

If we're serious about finding ways for people to live in harmony with nature, we need to do two things. We need to be focused on conserving the earth's biodiversity and that means working in the most extraordinary places on earth, places like the Amazon, like the Congo Basin of Africa, like the coral triangle of the Pacific, like the Arctic: places that are unique and crucially important for the biodiversity that they hold. At the same time, we recognize that we have to find ways to lighten humanity's footprint on the planet, to reduce the overall pressure that we are putting on the planet's resources. That's of course addressing challenges like climate change but also the challenge of growing the food that we eat, the challenge of managing the world's fisheries and finding a way to use resources sustainably.

I'll give you three examples. We've now worked in the Amazon Basin for decades, but about 10 years ago we helped start a programme that took protection of the Amazon to an entirely different scale. We collaborated with the president of Brazil and with the World Bank and others to help Brazil create a network of parks, protected areas that could ensure the conservation of a large swathe of the Amazon. The government of Brazil has, through this programme, set its sight on protecting 60 million hectares, an area larger than France.

For the last 10 or 15 years, WWF has been leading sustainability in the management of the world's fisheries. In partnership with Unilever, the largest seller of frozen seafood in the world, we created the Marine Stewardship Council, certifying fisheries that are well managed. It provides a vehicle for rewarding fishermen who are taking good care of the ocean on which they depend. Today, more than 10 per cent of the world's fisheries are in the MSC system, more than half of all the whitefish fisheries in the world – supplying the fish you find in fish and chips, fishsticks, McDonald's fish sandwiches, etc – are in the MSC system. So it's become a powerful vehicle for bringing sustainability into the marketplace and creating a market reward for those who are doing it right.

A third example, and entirely different, is Earth Hour. Earth Hour was created in 2007 in just one city – Sydney, Australia. In 2010, in more than 4,000 cities and towns in 126 countries, literally hundreds of millions of people on one night, 27 March, at 8.30 pm turned out their lights to signal their concern about climate change. They created the largest demonstration on climate change ever and a powerful platform for expressing the public's demand for action.

Earth Hour 2010   © 2011 WWF

Sustainability: from CSR to CBI

Ten or 15 years ago, much corporate engagement with these issues really came out of corporate social responsibility, or CSR. Now, more and more companies see a commitment to sustainability as a core business interest, or CBI. They are acting for a variety of reasons: because of the concerns of their customers or their staff; because of the values of the company; because they think it is important to their social licence to operate; because they think it's important to future supplies of resources upon which they depend. Their reasons vary, but many of the biggest companies are serious about sustainability. Take the example of seafood. The largest retailers in the world – companies like Wal-Mart, Carrefour and Sainsbury's – are sourcing sustainable seafood. That sends a powerful signal to the marketplace that it is important for those in the fishing industry (including producers and fishermen) to move towards sustainable practices. So there has been a big shift in the private sector and there is huge promise in that.

Be audacious, determined and optimistic

WWF is an organization of people who are passionate about this cause, passionate about conserving the earth's biodiversity, passionate about finding a way for humanity to live in a way the planet can sustain. But also this is an optimistic organization. We find ways to solve problems that chart a course for sustainability. To do that, you have to be a pretty determined group. We are focused on how we engage others in that cause – whether it's hundreds of millions of people in an event like Earth Hour or communities and corporate partners in the cause of conserving the oceans. Because, in the end, if you look at the scale of the challenges we have taken on, this organization is tiny compared with those challenges and we only make a difference if we engage others. We can connect fishing communities in Indonesia with markets in Europe, North America and Japan. We can connect governments in Indonesia, in the Philippines and in Papua New Guinea to governments in the US and China whose fleets are catching their fish. That ability to make those connections is crucial to cracking some of these problems.

It's a cause which requires audacity.

Focus on a few key things

A crucial thing in this organization has been to say, as a network, we're going to focus on a relative handful of big things that we are really going to go after. **You have to pick things that are indisputably important and where you can make a difference**, game-changing opportunities where you can have a globally significant impact. But even then it is hard to make those kinds of choices for a networked organization which has offices all over the world, each of which, of course, has strong ideas about how best to make a difference.

The power of connections

But when we come together it is an extraordinary thing. When you can see colleagues who are working in the water with fishermen in Peru joining forces with colleagues in Indonesia and in Japan and in Germany to make a difference to those

Greg Armfield from WWF-UK in discussion with the local women's group in Thulo Syabru
© 2011 WWF

fishermen and also to the marine environment on which they depend, that's amazingly powerful. That's the kind of work that allows us to make changes that will last and will both improve livelihoods and take better care of the environment. That's what makes me proud: to see the full strength of this organization unleashed to make a difference that really matters.

Natasha Quist – regional director, WWF Central Africa Regional Programme

Natasha Quist is responsible for WWF's programmes in the Congo Basin. She joined WWF from Oxfam; before that she had worked for Walt Disney and Nike.

We're bold in our mission statement and we're also very bold in where we decide to work. We work in some of the most difficult areas. It would be easier to do conservation in countries that are closer to big cities. We're working in the heart of Africa in places that it's even difficult to get to. Places that nobody even knows of, places that it's difficult to work in, places that people don't necessarily want to fund. But we've made tough choices to focus on regions where we can make the most difference. We want to conserve nature for everyone and not just in the bits that are most visible. We are in the field working with communities, working on the ground in these places that are two, three, four days' drive away from any major city.

Conservation in the Congo – acting as a catalyst for change

One of the major projects we are working on is the upcoming Kinshasa Summit. We're trying to save the forests of the Congo Basin. When we talk about rainforests, people immediately think about the Amazon. Not so many people think about the Congo Basin, but it has the second largest tropical forest in the world. We've spent a lot of time and money encouraging and supporting the key governments in this region, 13 of them, to come together and say, 'Look, this is all of ours.' This isn't just one country, this is several countries' forest – the forest covers many millions of hectares. It started more than 10 years ago and they work almost like a secretariat now, with a plan on what they have committed to do. Yaounde is the capital of Cameroon, in which the initial heads of state summit took place. A second summit took place in Brazzaville and the third one will happen in Kinshasa. The name of the commission that they've put together is Comifac. So it now has its own secretariat, paid for by the governments, to help push forward their views, their vision and their objectives.

WWF has played a catalytic role. If you want to save rainforests, if you want to have conservation happen in this region, it's not about an international NGO coming in, it's about governments wanting and being able to make that change happen. WWF's ability to convene these meetings, to encourage and maybe support these governments working together has really been a key to making sure that we can conserve the Congo Basin's rainforest.

Conservation in the Congo © 2011 WWF

The power of the brand to attract the right talent

My most difficult task is making sure that we can get the right people in the right place, keep them motivated, keep them happy and make sure they have a career within WWF. Finding the right people to work for WWF here is complex and difficult; it takes a lot of time. We need a diverse group of people. We need people to work in the field, miles away from any major city. We need people who understand conservation. We need specialists in marine life, specialists in elephants, birds and other wildlife. But we also need professionals: financial managers, human resource managers, logisticians. We have to take people and equipment and satellite phones to all over a huge area of the Congo Basin. We need to have a strong technical team; we need a strong support team. But sometimes a technical person will have to be a support person and a leader and a manager. So it needs multifaceted people. The upside is, because of the brand name of WWF, many, many people are very, very motivated to work for an organization like us and sometimes motivation goes a very long way. When you have staff who have done very good jobs in the field, you have to make sure that we keep the learning and are able to cross-fertilize with other countries. We have exchange programmes with people who work in the Amazon, for instance. We also share knowledge and people and staff with Malaysia or with India.

I love being part of this massive network. WWF has a vision and a value system that I absolutely identify with. And I know how what I do here contributes to the network in general. So, you know, even though we are far away from maybe the core in Switzerland, I know and I take great pains to make sure that my staff know that even our smallest project makes a difference to our world.

Lasse Gustavsson – executive director, conservation, WWF International

Lasse joined WWF in Sweden from Greenpeace in 2003, eventually becoming its chief executive. In 2010 he was appointed executive director, conservation.

Bringing the Baltic together

Our Baltic programme is fantastic. We have been able to pull together nine different countries with very different political realities – Russia, Estonia, Lithuania, Germany, Denmark, Sweden and the other Baltic coastal countries – into one programme. The Baltic Sea is one of the most polluted seas on the planet. Fifteen per cent of the world's commercial shipping is in the Baltic. Most of it is oil going from Russia to Holland. It is one of the busiest sea straits on the planet. We've put together a comprehensive but simple programme. We work on fishing and on eutrophication – which is the overload of nutrients, basically agricultural pollution, nitrogen and phosphorus running into the ocean and creating toxic algal blooms. It is a big problem. But we have been able to put together a programme that has helped create the European governments' strategy for the Baltic Sea region. We organized it without a lot of funding. Basically we have two people who hold it together, in the nine WWF and partner organizations in the nine countries. It's a great example of WWF at its best.

Climate change is already happening

The Arctic is probably one of the most dramatic ecosystems we have right now. Climate change is beyond repair in the Arctic. So we will see ice melt, we will see new oceans that have been covered by ice for hundreds, maybe thousands, of years – this is irreversible. The climate change impact on the Arctic is happening already and we will not be able to reverse it. So the Arctic we will see is different from the Arctic that we have, and it is already different from the Arctic that we had. This is the first time ever that we face a big global ecosystem that is changing so fast and so dramatically that we have to get smart about adaptation strategies for species, ecosystems and cultures to cope with a changing climate in the Arctic. It is really about redesigning the Arctic. What can be saved? What can be used? What needs to be protected and conserved and how?

We have grey whales in the Mediterranean this year – the first time, I think, in a couple of hundred years. The only way that I can understand how the grey whales actually came there is that they're swimming through oceans in the north that didn't exist two years ago. It is truly dramatic.

The power of science allied to the power of communication

I think that more than anything we are a convener of processes in the Arctic but we are also there to lay out the facts together with the scientific community, saying, 'This is what it's like – this is happening and this is real.' We have a communications capacity that the scientific community doesn't have: to reach out to decision makers to make things happen. We have been working in shipping, fishing, oil and gas: in fact, all the industries that are now just waiting to exploit the new opportunities offered by the Arctic. We are in dialogue with them about where they can go, and more importantly, where they can't.

I don't think there's any organization that is better placed or better equipped to help the world come to grips with what I think is the biggest challenge of all: to fit the human ecological footprint into the carrying capacity of the planet. We are on our way to eight, nine, maybe 10 billion people. We will all want to eat and drink, have healthcare when we get sick and jobs and shelter and all that. This is a tall order. But we have ideas for the solutions to most of the problems and we are well received in most quarters. So I think on a daily basis we are improving the planet – not as fast as we want to and certainly most things remain to be done – but we are making a bigger difference than most.

Danielle Chidlow – director of brand strategy at WWF International

Danielle Chidlow was appointed director of brand strategy in 2008 after many years working in advertising and marketing.

We are a network organization made up of a large number of offices around the world. This means that we're incredibly diverse in terms of our culture, how we approach issues and how we tend to communicate. But for me it's WWF's iconic brand, and all that it stands for, that we all have in common. WWF has a well-known and powerful logo which has built enormous equity over the past 50 years. All that this logo signifies is what we hold dear, and what binds us together. My role, as the director of brand strategy at WWF International, is to ensure that all of us within WWF can agree and consistently articulate those characteristics that are at the very core of our organization.

One way of getting to the heart of WWF and identifying those characteristics that bind us together, is to ask a basic question: '**What is special and different about WWF?**' What sets us apart from other environmental organizations? As a network, we believe there are four key areas that set us apart. One is the idea that WWF is a 'connecting' organization – we connect together various decision makers (heads of state and governments), we connect with corporates, we connect with various partners and we connect with people – we have over five million members. In fact, I think we have the biggest membership of any environmental organization across the world. So, as a global organization we're operating across borders to engage anyone and everyone who can make a difference. But at the same time we're also working in the field at a local level, as part of civil society, which gives us an important legitimacy. So, essentially, we connect multiple stakeholders with our science, to drive forward our agenda.

Another area that sets WWF apart is the fact that we are a leading organization. WWF has forged unprecedented partnerships with governments, other NGOs and the private sector. We were the first environmental organization to engage with the private sector to bring about truly transformational change. We've also inspired so many people to take action. This isn't about saying 'We're the best' but it is about acknowledging the fact that WWF has fundamentally changed the playing field over the years. WWF is also a solutions-focused organization. We're not simply a campaigning organization that identifies the problems, but we work closely with others, in a constructive and positive way, to find solutions to the issues that we are tackling. And finally, we recognize the interconnection of issues. This is a rather clumsy phrase, but it means that we are not a single-issue organization. For example, we don't just focus on specific species, or just on climate change, or just on marine-related issues. We bring all those things together and recognize that they all work together in a very complex way and so, in order for us to solve the environmental problems that we face, we need to actually tackle them in an integrated, interconnected way. There are other organizations who could certainly claim to share one or two of these traits with us, but there isn't any other conservation organization that embodies all of them. Together, they are what make WWF unique and powerful.

The importance of shared brand values

Having a common understanding of what defines WWF, and what sets us apart from others, is incredibly important because, internally, it gives the people a sense of pride in the organization. It gives them a sense of who we are, why we are doing what we are doing, why we do it in the way that we do, and why that makes us special and different. In turn, this underpins all that WWF does and the way that WWF communicates externally. It is an essential first step in enabling our global and disparate network to speak with one powerful and authoritative voice.

WWF has an incredibly broad and ambitious mission. One of the big challenges that WWF faces is to make sure that people understand the scope of our work, and that we are tackling some of the most serious challenges facing our planet. This is really crucial if people are to appreciate the relevance and credibility of the organization – and ultimately support us! We make sure that it is either articulated word for word across all of the communications materials that we produce, or at least that the essence of it is communicated across everything that we do. So while we often talk about specific issues like palm oil or specific species such as tigers, we're always trying to make sure that we do so within the broader context of our mission. To help with this, as well as to help us achieve consistent decision making and a unified 'voice' for WWF, we have four brand values: knowledgeable, optimistic, determined and engaging. These work together as a toolkit to help guide us in ensuring WWF-appropriate actions and communications.

For example, when it comes to 'knowledgeable', it's important for us to emphasize our experience and expertise. We always try to communicate a sense of 'optimism'. Not that every story is a happy one, but we are striving for solutions, and we aim to inspire others to do the same. 'Determined' is an important value. It encapsulates the fact that there is a sense of urgency to what we do – not 'throw your hands up in the air and panic' urgency, but a steely determination to move forward and to achieve what we set out to do. 'Engaging' is an obvious one, but unless we engage people in a way that they are interested in and understand, and speak to them in a language that means something to them, we're not going to cut through. It's not about having an equal 25 per cent of each of those four brand values across every single thing that we do. We dial up and we dial down according to audiences and according to what we are trying to achieve.

None of these ideas or concepts was created externally and simply 'slapped onto the face' of WWF. They come from within and they reflect a truth that has emerged strongly from a fascinating and inspiring consultation process. I think there is a reason for that: it's because there is this sense of commonality to the people who work within WWF. It never ceases to amaze me how strongly our people agree with that sense of what makes WWF special and different, and with our brand values – which essentially hold them to certain standards in terms of their actions and everyday work. It speaks volumes that so many different people, with different projects of work, different cultural references and different ways of approaching things, are so united in delivering WWF's mission and are doing so in a way that brings us together and makes us stronger; it shows how bonded we are.

Expedition crew. Mountains of Tumucumaque National Park, Amapá, Brazil, 2005

© 2011 WWF

Eric Bohm – CEO, WWF Hong Kong

Eric Bohm has been in what he describes as 'this privileged position' of CEO of Hong Kong since July 2004; before which he spent his entire career in business, including with Sara Lee.

WWF sees the interconnectedness of the world: how what happens in one area of the world has a direct and fairly relevant impact on another part of the world. WWF stays in for the long haul and recognizes that there is not a simple solution to these problems.

Showing how everything is connected – the Coral Triangle

Take an initiative that we are running here in the Coral Triangle which deals with the issue of reef fish. Hong Kong is probably the world's largest consumer of reef fish on a per capita basis. It also is the major trade hub of the fish coming into the world market because the fish are flown into Hong Kong and then, of course, distributed into Southern China and basically around the world. So what we are trying to do is to influence the consumption pattern of the people of Hong Kong. But also to influence the organizational behaviour of the traders so that they are aware that they can't continually overexploit an asset and think it is infinite. If you protect the habitat, you protect *all* the species within that habitat.

Showing how each person has the power to make changes – Earth Hour

Another initiative that probably best exemplifies us – because it was really impact-ful on a global basis – is the Earth Hour project. Hong Kong was absolutely amazing. We were on the Kowloon side, looking at the Hong Kong island side, and all of a sudden these lights went off. Except for one company whose watches must have stopped because they turned off the lights half an hour later than everybody else and stuck out like a sore thumb for a while. What absolutely amazed me was it showed the impact of modern communication technology. The communication was done through YouTube and based on Twitter; we logged into groups of people who used these methods of communication. We can now communicate globally almost in an instant! That initiative helped us to address a constant theme that we're confronted with, which is 'What difference does it make if I stop doing something as an individual?' That is a major hurdle for us. 'Okay, so I eat one shark's fin – that's one shark – so what?' That is the public's perception – they are powerless individuals to be able to really make a change. So this type of campaign does make a change. It reinforces the sense of the collective impact of people's individual acts. It shows that we can communicate on a very broad scale in a very short space of time with a large number of people. It is a paramount issue in the public's perception – climate change – and it recognizes that the way we consume energy is a major contributing factor to climate change.

Keeping the vision in mind at all times

We have an Asia-Pacific strategy and WWF Hong Kong is just one of its leaders. When we get a little bit off the rails, all that happens is one or two of the leaders get up and say, 'Let's chat. Our business is conservation. Just never ever lose sight of that end goal.' And I think that's how you get it across in a federated organization. And you have to recognize that in a federated organization, there *are* going to be tensions, there *are* going to be complications but, at the end of the day, what you do is you've got to say to the teams, 'This is the end goal. Never lose sight of it. Never let go of that end goal,' and that what everybody does is important. We have an enviable global framework, a global structure to deliver probably the most difficult thing in branding, ie a value system – that's basically what we're delivering to people. 'Here are my values. This is what we believe in. This is what we want you to believe in and if you believe in it, you will change your behaviour. You will become conscious of your environmental impact and you will do something about it.' When you listen to these scientists talk – what enthusiasm, how they see the world, how they comprehend the world and how it operates, I just sit in awe and fascination.

Stick to your principles, even when it costs

We make it very clear to any organization or corporation who donates to WWF that they do not dictate the conservation policy. Have we ever made a decision to push the principle before the money? Yes, we have. One major donor wanted to put a liquefied natural gas (LNG) terminal on an island which was a designated fishery spawning area. We said, 'No.' We didn't attack the donor; we placed it in the context of an overall energy strategy. They were saying they had to put this LNG terminal in this location to reduce their pollution caused by coal-fired power stations. We said, 'Well, yes, we support the decision to move from coal to LNG, but you can't do this in isolation in this particular area because the region is a huge consumer and there is a huge increase in the demand for energy. You'll have to have an energy strategy for the entire region if you're going to deal with climate change and efficient energy production.' Well, they just stopped all their donations. We stuck to the issue that there were other alternatives to be offered even though we faced a tremendous amount of pressure to enter into an arrangement. We said,

'We've got to apply pressure on the government to see an alternate solution.' We actually took this campaign to the relevant energy ministry, saying, 'Look at this challenge on a regional basis for the longer term.' And we won. We could have lost – but you have to stick to the issue. You have to make those tough decisions from time to time. At the end of the day, I'm sorry, just because you donate to WWF doesn't mean that you dictate to us what our issues are.

David Nussbaum – CEO, WWF UK

David Nussbaum became the chief executive of WWF in the UK in 2007.

At the heart of what we stand for is the combination of people and nature that goes right back to our founding in 1961. Even then, our founders said, 'We are not just here as an organization to save whales and tigers and so on but we are ultimately concerned with the happiness and, indeed, survival of humans on the planet.'

Leading but not dominating

There are three things in our strategy – here in the UK – we focus on. The first is safeguarding the natural world, thinking about the special places and species that we particularly value and how we can safeguard those for the future. The second is tackling climate change. Climate change is a threat to the good work we have been doing for almost 50 years – climate change could undermine the positive achievements we've created over that time and is obviously a direct threat to the natural world being safeguarded. Thirdly, changing the way we live. That's because, if you look at the threats to the natural world, most of them come down to the impact humans are having on the planet. And so our one-planet future vision says, 'How can we have, on this one planet, a way of living that only consumes what one planet can provide for us humans and leave space for wildlife and wilderness?' Those three things take us everywhere from the forests of Borneo to the corridors of Whitehall and Westminster.

Let me give you an example of an issue we have been working on that is affecting climate change and where we are trying to change the way we live, in order to safeguard the natural world: aviation. The emissions into the atmosphere of carbon dioxide and other pollutants from aviation are a significant problem and growing very rapidly. If we're not careful, aviation would consume the whole of the allowable carbon that this country and, indeed, the world, will be able to emit in a few decades' time. So we thought, 'How do we tackle this?' We focused specifically on business flying. Of course, one approach is just to say, 'You shouldn't do it. You're being very bad and you should stop.' What we did, though, was to ask, 'How does business look at this? What would be attractive to them? How could we work with businesses?' So we identified that a lot of businesses wanted to fly less and yet they wanted to maintain connectivity. They wanted people to be and feel connected to each other, between organizations and teams and so on. We realized that one of the key things here is technology – modern technology and particularly videoconferencing – especially, perhaps, some of the really upmarket video-conferencing, for example Telepresence.

First, we issued a report called 'Travelling Light', which looked at how businesses wanted to and could reduce their travel and replace a big chunk of it with videoconferencing and other such technologies. Then we also thought, 'Well, we need to find a way for businesses to do something about this.' So we created what we called our 'One in Five' campaign, which is a challenge to businesses to reduce their flights by 20 per cent over five years. We have now got a whole range of companies, ranging from Marks & Spencer to Sky, signed up to reduce their flying. We've developed a positive approach which looks at the cost reductions, the carbon savings and the improvement on people's lives (ie not being away from home so much), that can be achieved. We're not taking an absolute position; we're not saying you shouldn't fly at all. We're looking at how it can be reduced and yet, how business can be enhanced through that. It's a good example of an evidence-based campaign combining facts and feelings, principles and passion, coming up with an attractive, pragmatic approach to alternatives to travel.

A world with a future

When you look at a picture of the world from space, what you see is, largely, blue, green and white. White clouds, blue sea and green land. That speaks to me of the variety, diversity and healthiness of the planet and the life on it. I am working for an organization which is seeking to conserve that picture for the future. We are trying to prevent the alternative: a grey future in which the whole planet is turned into just a system for supporting humans, where we've greyed out all the amazing variety of the natural world. I want to maintain that vision of an amazing place, this one planet we occupy.

Planet Earth

Bold lessons

Deliberately focus on the most difficult challenges – never think it's impossible

Bold missions tend by their very nature to be hard to achieve. It means that you must be absolutely determined to see them through regardless of what it will cost and how long it will take, if you seriously want to achieve them. WWF works in a world where governments change, corporate objectives move, people's interest waxes and wanes. WWF has deliberately decided to focus on major challenges ('game changers' in Jim Leap's words) and in the most difficult areas of the world, areas which people might not even be aware of. They have to remain extraordinarily focused and determined as a group of people to achieve their goals and not allow any setback to stop them.

Stay focused on the big picture – don't get distracted by 'internal' issues

A key to that determination is to focus on the higher purpose that unites you rather than any operational, cultural or day-to-day considerations. Geographical differences, arguments over resource allocation or programme priorities can all be settled by reminding everyone to keep the bigger picture in mind. That is the major role of the leaders in WWF and any company that wishes to be bold. Articulating a higher purpose that your people can buy into is leadership at its best.

Be bold in whom you ask to help – if they're the right people to help

WWF works best by connecting people with similar interests, by convening meetings of the powerful or influential and by engaging multiple stakeholders in issues that concern them. They act as a catalyst for change rather than the driver of change. They have found that if the problems are too big for one organization to solve alone, then the most effective strategy is to partner with others who have part of the solution. This might sound like an admission of weakness. In fact, it is a statement of ambition – because WWF is fearless in asking the most powerful people in the world to help make things happen. This is a lesson which the commercial world has started to learn and needs to practise more. This is a strategy that Sir Richard Branson has adopted with his Virgin Unite and 'Elders' initiatives.

Collaborating with people who might seem adversarial to your cause can be much more effective than confronting them. But it depends whether your starting point is to make a difference to people's lives or to your profit line. The learning for companies is to take a holistic view of the brand and the business and decide where they can get the best people to help them. Virgin Galactic has brought together a team of diverse skills from different companies. JCB is developing its academy with the help of other manufacturing businesses and innocent partnered with McDonald's to get more fruit into more kids.

Never compromise your principles

WWF repeatedly demonstrates the importance of sticking to your principles despite the costs that might incur. This can mean that it loses money from donors or potential donors that it disappoints or cannot accept. WWF holds its ground. It knows that if it is to achieve its mission – and that is all that counts – it cannot afford to compromise its principles for the sake of any one of its stakeholders, as Eric Bohm points out so clearly. The lesson for corporates here is that if you run a franchise operation, as many hotel companies and retailers do, you cannot afford to let them dictate what your brand should stand for or what the customer experience should be like. If you do, the brand will be reduced to the lowest common denominator.

The brand is built from within

The WWF brand attracts sponsors and donors, is respected by governments and policy makers and most importantly is a magnet for highly skilled and dedicated talent. This is because the brand has been built from within on a culture that is committed to a common mission, a core set of values and a way of approaching its work. Danielle Chidlow, the director of brand strategy, said that she could not believe how easy it was to get agreement to the brand values, but it says a great deal about the authenticity of the organization that such agreement was relatively easy to get and that the values are not saccharine but set standards by which they have to operate.

Sustainability is a core business interest

Jim Leap's observation is that corporations are changing their approach to sustainability from being essentially CSR (corporate social responsibility) to CBI (core business interest). This mirrors what we have found in other companies featured in this book. Whether it be JCB's revolutionary diesel engines, Virgin building aircraft entirely out of composites, innocent drinks working on practices in fruit farming, or Six Senses's 'intelligent luxury', sustainability has become an economic *and* environmental imperative. What these organizations are finding is that there is a natural synergy between economics, the customer experience and operational efficiency. When you get it right; everyone wins. Consumer pressure, governmental mandates and economic efficiency are driving this change, as well as the individual principles and concerns of the people who are now working for and running these businesses.

Prepare to be in it for the long haul

David Nussbaum's closing words paint a picture of a world whose beauty WWF wants to conserve for future generations. Fittingly, they echo Richard Branson's words at the beginning of this book. He talks about a future where space tourists will 'marvel at the beauty of our planet'. Both Virgin Galactic and WWF exemplify the most extreme example of a trait we see in other bold brands: they are not in it for short-term reward but long-term gain. They are seeking to change the way we think and act. In WWF's case it has a huge challenge to change our behaviour. Resources are scarcer than we think and will become scarcer still as the planet's population increases and its consumption rises. Biodiversity is under threat with consequences for our environment – natural and built – which are hard to foresee. Global warming is a fact – whether we believe it is wholly or partially manmade – and is already changing our world. Every one of us needs to think about the implications of our personal and our commercial behaviour. Earth Hour is a small way that each of us can make a difference, can register our concern that governments and businesses act with the ultimate higher purpose in mind – one which is simply but boldly expressed by WWF: to ensure a world in which man and nature live in harmony.

Earth Hour 2010, Canada
© 2011 WWF

Chapter Fifteen
How to be bold: practices, principles and people

Now more than ever before, businesses need to be bold: to defy conventional wisdom, to walk against the crowd, to try out new ways of doing things in the full glare of social media. Whether it is Virgin Galactic deciding to design a new spaceship because of customer feedback, Six Senses Resorts refusing to offer branded bottled water in their luxury hotels to reduce their carbon footprint, or TNT zigging when all its competitors were zagging, these brands are bold – bold in thought, but more importantly bold in action and bold in measuring their success in new ways.

Through extensive one-to-one interviews with leaders of these brands, we identified a wealth of actions and behaviours that encapsulated successful bold practice. After refining and testing our findings with each of the brands, we distilled the list down to just eight bold practices, each with their own specific actions.

They explain how these bold brands are behaving in the new millennium; how they turn bold ideas into bold practice and ultimately into experiences that turn employees and customers into their greatest fans.

At present, these practices are probably demonstrated by only a handful of organizations, but over the next few years we believe they will increasingly influence how businesses will need to operate, not only to compete but to survive.

Just as *Uncommon Practice* helped to shape some of the original thinking around the customer experience movement in 2001, so *Bold* practice will, we hope, guide organizations seeking to thrive in 2011 and beyond. Our bet is that only those companies who stand out because they stand up for something will be the ones that customers – and employees – around the world will want to engage with.

http://www.amazon.com/Uncommon-Practice-People-deliver-experience/dp/0273659367/ref=sr_1_1?s=books&ie=UTF8&qid=1281866661&sr=1-1

The bold practices: the what

Bold vision – keep the main thing the main thing

- Create a bold strategy or vision for the company.
- Be willing to trade short-term profit to achieve your long-term vision.
- Have a clearly defined brand/customer promise.
- Align the strategy, the brand and the customer experience so that they are inseparable.
- Boldly change/challenge traditional thinking in the industry.

These practices are all about having clarity and a line of sight in your organization. From innocent's insistence on 'keeping things natural' to Six Senses's lyrical 'innovative enlightening experiences that rejuvenate our guest's love of SLOWLIFE' to Azran Osman-Rani's strategy of 'one, two, three,' each of these brands has a clarity of vision that is communicated simply and powerfully throughout the organization.

Having communicated it, they then ensure that everything else is aligned with it. They start from this vision and work back, rather than starting from industry practice and working forward. In this way they challenge many of the beliefs that underpin the way that business works in many industries. Richard Branson has built a business empire on this practice.

Bold vision is also about taking a different approach to others, zagging while they zig. Marty Neumeier, in his brilliant book *Zag – The Number One Strategy of High-Performance Brands*, quotes *Harvard Business Review* research that showed that those companies whose customers believed had become more differentiated realized a stock gain of 4.8 per cent on the year whereas those that were considered less differentiated saw a loss of 4.3 per cent over the same period.

One leader that understands this is Steve Jobs. Some years ago Apple had lost its way, so he gave a game-changing presentation to his people on why Apple had to think differently. He told his people that the brand needed to be simple and clear and famous for something, it had to have 'soul', without which it couldn't grow. It had to streamline its products and above all it had to understand who its customers really were and how they were motivated. He then famously introduced the iconic 'Think different' campaign, featuring Freud, Ali, Monroe, Gandhi, with the words, 'You know if they had ever used a computer, it would have been a Mac.' Today Apple is the world's largest company in terms of market capitalization. That speech remains a defining moment in the turnaround of the Apple brand.

See the video that started Apple's turnaround here:
http://www.youtube.com/watch?v=vmG9jzCHtSQ

Bold leadership – demonstrate zealous leadership

- Develop a unique leadership style that dramatizes the culture.
- Communicate the vision and purpose powerfully and clearly.
- 'Walk the talk' when it comes to demonstrating the company values.
- Spend significant time with customers and employees talking about your vision.
- Rely first on gut instinct and intuition rather than on research and analysis.

Sir Richard Branson, Tony Hsieh, Angela Ahrendts: these leaders are their brands. They are very different people, but each in their own way, they are the embodiment of the brand. Sir Richard is passionate about changing industries, Tony is obsessive about service, and Angela walks, lives and breathes the Burberry brand.

It isn't necessary to be the founder or even the CEO, but if you want to be a bold brand, first and foremost you have to be a bold leader and that means embracing the brand and working zealously to deliver what it promises. Most importantly it means dramatizing the brand values through your own personal behaviour. Ray Davis answering the phone 'Welcome to the world's greatest bank' is but one small example.

Bold marketing – engage in infectious communication

- Clearly and honestly communicate the brand promise and values to customers.
- Actively involve customers in helping to create/improve/protect the brand.
- Use innovative viral marketing techniques to reach target customers.
- Foster active customer communities that support the brand.
- Achieve high levels of customer advocacy or 'fandom' to drive referral business.

From Zappos's 'powered by service' to the Geek Squad's slightly pithier 'We'll save your ass', these brands are honest in their communication and engaging in their tone. They use social media and their websites to create customer communities. innocent does this through the simple words they use on their packaging. Burberry uses 3D high-tech broadcasting of their runway shows; and Chilli Beans uses music and events to involve customers in the Chilli Bean world. Communities of 'fans' validate these brands; they help to reinforce them, inform them and sometimes even to forgive them when they get things wrong. The passion of Apple fans giving feedback enabled the brand to overcome teething troubles with its fourth-generation iPhone that could have sunk lesser brands.

Bold customer experience – dramatize the customer experience

- Deliver a customer experience that is consistent, intentional, differentiated and valuable.
- Make protecting and managing the brand a priority.
- Bring the brand promise alive for customers in dramatic ways.
- Focus the entire company on delivering a dramatic customer experience.
- Align marketing, operations and HR around the customer experience.

The more you can dramatize the customer experience, the more powerful and distinctive it becomes. The Geek Squad is famous for this. As Robert Stephens observes, 'Marketing is a tax that you pay for being unremarkable.' TNT Express China focused the whole company by recording the customer experience and playing this back to their people. JCB uses Dieselmax and its dancing diggers to bring their engineering alive for customers in a dramatic way. Burberry has bought back many of its franchises so that the experience can be made more consistent across the globe. Six Senses greets its guests and immediately asks them to remove their shoes to dramatize the concept of intelligent luxury. In all cases these brands operate from a common agenda, with marketing, operations and HR operating as one to dramatize the brand: what Shaun called 'Triad power' in his book with Joe Wheeler, *Managing the Customer Experience: Turning Customers into Advocates*.

http://www.amazon.com/Managing-Customer-Experience-customers-advocates/dp/0273661957

Bold innovation – be in pursuit of wow

- Constantly innovate in both large and small ways.
- Drive innovation from a deep understanding and insight about what target customers value.
- Ensure products, services and your people are distinctive and aligned with the brand promise.
- Use innovative technology and processes to support the delivery of a superior customer experience.
- Ensure your people demonstrate superior customer service skills and capabilities.

Virgin Galactic redesigned VSS Enterprise so that passengers would have the wow experience of weightlessness. Zappos understands that when you connect emotionally with customers through a wow moment they will never forget you.

JCB built a vehicle to break the land-speed record to demonstrate the technical superiority of their new diesel engines – boys of all ages say 'Wow!' when they see it. O2 gives priority access to its customers so that they can get close to their rugby or pop star heroes for that wow effect. Umpqua uses random acts of kindness by its people to deliver small wow moments in the community. Delivering a bold experience is about pushing the boundaries so that customers have an indelible memory of you.

Bold culture – create a cult-like culture

- Believe in and commit to a higher purpose.
- Align internal values with brand values.
- Create a distinctive culture and a brand DNA, and ensure it permeates the company.
- Reward people for delivering the promise to customers and share their stories widely.
- Develop unique phrases or language and use these to create the cult-like culture.

It is unfortunate that the word 'cult' has negative connotations, because it comes from the same root as 'culture'. The stronger the culture, the more cult-like it becomes and the more effective the brand. Apple and Harley-Davidson have long recognized the power of customers and employees who identify with the brand. In the case of the bold brands we are seeing this too but with an added dimension: not only are customers affiliated to the brand but also what the brand stands for, its higher purpose.

The bold companies use titles, names and language to create meaning for their people. 'Umpquatized', 'zuddles', 'Secret Weapon'. All these words and phrases serve to reinforce what is special and different about these brands and set them apart from the mediocrity of being 'average'. TNT Express even maps the culture using sophisticated software to ensure that they recruit brand champions with the influence and skills to cascade the message and protect the culture.

Bold HR – develop rites and rituals

- Create an employee experience that is as distinctive as the customer experience.
- Hire for attitude and fit with the culture.
- Ensure the reward systems reinforce the desired behaviours around serving customers.
- Use innovative and experiential training to help your people understand the brand promise.
- Do not tolerate people for long who fail to demonstrate the brand values.

Closely associated with the culture are the rites and rituals it adopts, which serve to keep the culture alive. These brands pay enormous attention to recruiting for fit with their cultures: what we call 'hiring for DNA rather than MBA'. Chilli Beans, Umpqua, Six Senses, BBH, Geek Squad, Zappos all invest significant time and resources in the hiring process. They use 'triangulation' by involving senior people, peers and direct reports all to form a view on the candidate and their fit. The Geek Squad sets a 'Mission Impossible' task to test for the skills an Agent would need. Umpqua's daily 'motivational moments' and Zappos's zany theme parties all create that sense of being special.

These brands have an intolerance of people who do not embrace the culture. Zappos tests for this by offering a cash incentive to leave. Umpqua insists that everyone answer the phone the same way. The Geek Squad uses its uniform to find Agents who are humble.

Bold measures – measure what matters

- Maintain a clear focus on target customers and what they value.
- Measure the complete customer experience, not just satisfaction.
- Regularly gather feedback from the front line of the organization on how the experience can be improved.
- Focus on employee and customer satisfaction, not just the bottom line.
- Measure the upstream indicators that drive economic results.

The bold brands may measure a number of things but they focus on a select few and those are the ones that are most closely aligned with their purpose.

Burberry measures 'the Burberry experience' by using mystery shoppers across all its stores. AirAsia X measures the amount of revenue from non-airline-related sources. TNT Express measures the retention of its brand champions. And O2 measures fandom – a bold word but exactly the right one to use in a world in which social media sites are encouraging the creation of 'fan of the brand' sites. Fandom is an extreme form of customer advocacy. It transcends mere 'I'd recommend this product.' Brand fans are passionate (and that is not too overused a word here) about their particular brand. They engage with it, write letters and send drawings and even gifts to it. They tattoo its logo on their bodies, doodle its logo on their books, wear the T-shirt and become Facebook fans, as four million Burberry customers have done. They buy whatever they can from it and can take it very personally if they meet someone who is critical of their preferred brand. They are fans first and foremost because the brand does something for them which they need and respect but they are fans above all because the brand has an attitude, a point of view, and a higher sense of purpose that align with their own.

Of course, none of these practices are worthwhile unless they lead to successful business outcomes. The most important outcomes for most of these organizations are increased revenues and sustainable profit. All these organizations are achieving superior financial performance. Even Umpqua Bank, which suffered as all banks did during the global financial crisis, was able to pay back in full the money it had been lent by the Federal Reserve under the US Troubled Asset Relief Program – one of the few banks so to do. Virgin Galactic, which has yet to take off, has already passed the revenue targets investors set for it. And WWF, albeit a not-for-profit organization, is the largest NGO in revenue terms of its kind.

The bold principles: the why

So that's *what* these organizations do, their bold practices. But *why* do they do it, other than for money? As we interviewed these executives and looked at their organizations, we gained a strong sense that the way they think has a huge impact on what they do. So merely following these bold practices won't necessarily make you a bold brand unless you also buy into the beliefs that underpin them. It struck us that there were a few beliefs that these brands shared that really seem to explain how and, more importantly, *why* they are different.

Purpose beyond profit – connect people to a cause

When we started the research for the book we were intentionally looking for brands that stood for something in people's minds – brands that were unique in their markets and perceived as adding value to customers' lives.

It is probably true to say that most organizations start off with a purpose – a vision or mission, an idea that drives them. However, it is also true that as many organizations get bigger, the sense of purpose gets lost – trodden down by financial metrics which begin to drive the organization instead.

As you read through each of the brand narratives it is apparent that these organizations go out of their way to hold on to that core purpose. This sense of purpose is not necessarily altruistic or about saving the planet, it is about the belief in something which transcends the business results but at the same time drives them. For BBH, the purpose is 'the work', producing the very best possible creative work which can change consumer and category expectations for its clients. For JCB, it is the belief in the importance of engineering and the sense of urgency and discontent that drives it to continually improve its products. For AirAsia X it is the desire for everyone to be able to experience the wonder of long-haul travel. For WWF it's about saving the planet, for the Geek Squad it's about 'saving your ass'.

This sense of purpose runs throughout these organizations. Their people are motivated to make a genuine and lasting difference to the particular world (market, country, product area) in which they live. It acts as a 'North Star' governing everything they do and enabling them often to make decisions rapidly and clearly because they have that internal 'moral' compass. It is their purpose that has been instrumental in driving their profits. As Sonu Shivdasani of Six Senses puts it, 'You need to stay true to your core purpose – it becomes the compass that guides you.'

It also attracts the right kind of people to keep the culture and the promise true. Recessionary pressures might be expected to create a labour market where people will be less discriminating about where they work. However, our experience and research show that, especially in developed markets, people are making choices about their jobs based on the values they believe in and the commitment and energy they want to put behind those values.

And of course, it meets a genuine need among customers for the provision of something genuine, of something that meets their emotional as well as functional needs, and of something that gives them a sense of belonging, of connection to a wider community of people who think and feel like they do. Increasingly, consumers are inclined to favour those brands they perceive as sharing their own values.

Holistic – it only works when it all works

The O2 brand promise, 'We're better, connected', and Ronan Dunne's imperative 'It only works when it all works' are perfect expressions of the way organizations need to think holistically. With an ever-sceptical, marketing-savvy and demanding customer, you have to ensure there is consistency across everything you do internally and externally.

There has long been a belief in business that, put at its simplest, growing your reputation and revenue (usually through sales and marketing) could be separated from protecting your assets and profit (usually through operations and finance). However, bold organizations believe that not only is there a clear causal link between what you communicate, how you operate and how you protect your earnings, they are in fact interdependent and you can't get any one right unless you get them all right. The Burberry and O2 stories are excellent examples of CEOs who are simultaneously customer centric and delivering business results.

But all the organizations recognize from the top down that their job is to ensure that links are made throughout to give everyone a 'clear line of sight' to the primary purpose of the organization and to act to stop anything getting in its way. This does not mean they always get everything right for everyone all the time but it does mean that they are relentlessly committed to it.

The 'yin' of the soft factors (marketing, people, customers, values, cultures) is inseparable from the 'yang' of hard factors (sales, inventory, expenditure, profits, etc). innocent is a notable example of this: it keeps a beady eye on the 'hard data' every week and its forecasting tool is state of the art but it never lets the hard data drive out the soft stuff. Rather it uses it to help understand how to improve the soft stuff and achieve its higher purpose of getting good food into the widest number of people.

Similarly, the yin at Burberry is the relentless attention to design and the customer experience, the yang is the constant focus on managing the brand consistently across the globe.

These brands don't believe that you have to trade off in certain classic areas. For example, many companies give the impression that you have to trade off a 'high-tech' experience against a 'high-touch' one, ie that if the experience is mostly enabled, delivered or concerning technology, then the element of personal and human interaction will have to suffer. First Direct, the highly successful direct banking arm of HSBC in the UK, showed that high tech and high touch are not only compatible but are essential bedfellows. They combined a very intuitive website with extremely friendly call centre agents.

Research has shown that increasingly consumers expect to be able to move seamlessly between channels and experience the brand holistically at each and every touch point. The brands in this book take this concept even further. Zappos, for example, is an entirely online experience but it is facilitated by people who go out of their way to ensure a highly personal interaction through specific acts, such as encouraging writing a thank you note to a customer or answering a tweet. Burberry has taken its iconic product, the trench coat, and made this the centre-piece of a high-touch store experience and a high-tech online experience.

Similarly, these brands demonstrate that you don't need to trade off price against quality of experience. AirAsia X – as with Virgin Atlantic before it – creates entertaining experiences that make flying with them fun as well as affordable. O2 with its Simplicity offer makes it ever more affordable to use personal communications and through its Priority proposition provides amazing entertainment experiences for its customers.

These companies all show that it is possible to make the customer experience enjoyable, entertaining and rewarding as well as inexpensive. They stand in contrast to Ryanair, a brand that is equally bold about its strategy and business model but with a difference: it appears that the lower the cost the poorer the customer experience has to be and if customers don't like it – well, tough, that is the price you pay for a cheap ticket. That is a dangerous path to tread because these bold brands all have fans, customers that have real affection for the brand and are willing to support it through thick and thin. In the absence of affection you are left only with low price as the draw and that means, as you grow larger, you may become increasingly vulnerable to smaller start-ups with lower costs and more innovative solutions. Just as in relationships, there is no true loyalty without love.

Relentless – 'sweat the small stuff'

These organizations are also possessed by a relentless commitment to improvement, to seeking a better way. Sometimes it can be game changing as in the case of Virgin Galactic's SpaceShipTwo, but often it is just the everyday focus on innovation in many small ways throughout the business; just so long as they make things better for customers and contribute towards achievement of the 'main thing'.

An important aspect of this relentlessness is that these organizations understand that 'little things have a big impact'. So they are often obsessed by detail and just endlessly curious about even the smallest aspect. Whether it is JCB's Sir Anthony Bamford personally adjusting the fuel cap on a Backhoe digger, or innocent's use of language in their packaging or the random acts of kindness delivered by Zappos and Umpqua. They are all manifestations of the fact that a small action can have a big impact. In fact, just as the devil is in the detail, so it is that consumers will often judge how authentic you are less by the big new product launch or mass communication campaign, but by the story they hear of personal kindness or by the attention to the tiniest touch point of your experience with them that other brands would not even be aware of. One small example: as we were interviewing Sonu Shivdasani for this book, he ordered and tasted six fruit cocktails from the resort bar to check on their consistency and quality.

Another key aspect of this relentlessness is the need for speed – what Joseph Cyril Bamford, in the remark that has since become JCB's corporate creed, called 'a sense of urgency'.

Time has never been a friend to the businessman but it is now openly hostile. Consumers want information and response to their requests now, new products have an increasingly limited window before being replaced or copied. In fact, they are often superseded or imitated while they are still in development. Think of the speed of replacement of handsets like the Apple iPhone. More people are more demanding of more products more of the time than at any other time in history. Technology and liberalization of markets have enabled them to get it. Competition is everywhere and accelerating the rate at which people can find and buy pretty much whatever they want whenever they want it. Business is moving so fast while businesses are, all too often, moving too slow.

The bold brands all demonstrate the restlessness that leads to moving as quickly as possible. As Nigel Bogle of BBH says, 'You have to be quick to embrace change.' But it is not just an economic imperative that has made them recognize the need to respond or anticipate changing needs and demands. Their sense of purpose also compels them constantly to pursue as speedily as they can the improvements and innovations that will make them the very best at what they do at any given time.

Authentic – you can't force it, fake it or fudge it

One of the most challenging lessons of the book is that you can't succeed unless you are genuine, true to yourself and absolutely honest with your customers. This is challenging for those people in business who believe that as long as you learn by rote the 10 tips for business success, follow the seven successful habits, or promote five corporate values on your website (usually the same ones your competitors promote as well), it'll be enough to get by. And as long as you say the right things to shareholders and customers in your annual report, advertising or PR, then, short of committing a criminal act, it doesn't much matter the extent to which you actually practise what you preach.

We have suggested 40 bold practices but slavishly adopting them will not make your company bold, just as inventing new words in your organization will not make your culture strong. These behaviours have to come from your beliefs.

Bold companies are run and largely staffed by people who care passionately about what they do because they see it as an extension of their own values and personality. Yes, you need to learn new skills, adopt new strategies, develop different business models and all the rest, but fundamentally you have to invest your true self in the business.

And that also means that you have to 'sweat the recruitment process' as all these businesses do. They ensure through multiple interviewing and the personal involvement of senior people in the process that they find people who genuinely care as much as they do. Zappos's innovative approach of offering $2,000 to people to leave at the end of their first week of training is a clever way of checking that they've recruited people who really do want to buy in to their culture. The people are important because without the right ones you can find yourself not only faking it (like the fictitious 'Pete' and 'Johnny' of PJ's smoothies) but also forcing it or fudging it.

By *forcing it*, we mean that sense of trying too hard to be something you're not. The Geek Squad has its competitors who try to take a similar approach but it doesn't require too much first-hand experience of them to know that the values come from the marketing department rather than the heart; more superficial than superhero.

By *fudging* it we mean those moments of 'on the one hand but on the other' that brands often fall into – promising you the earth in the headline copy only to caveat their offers in the small print. The example that Charles Wigley of BBH gave, of turning down a significant part of the work that was on offer from the Singapore Tourism Authority because they would not be able to do it well, is an example of honesty bringing its own rewards (they won the pitch). Take also the example of Kevin Balls of J C Balls & Sons, a long-term customer of JCB and whose individual welder's number was on Kevin's vintage digger, so that if something went wrong they could trace back not just to the company but to the person who had actually welded the part. There's a strong sense of pride in putting your reputation behind your work.

Joe Pine and Jim Gilmore in their book *Authenticity* make the point that customers can smell a fake a mile off. Consumers demand authenticity from their brands today and especially from the people who work for them.

And talk of smelling fakes takes us to the final belief.

Sustainability – CBI, not CSR

For some organizations sustainability has been one of those things that corporate PR has insisted be mentioned in the annual report to meet the expectations of shareholders. But increasingly, sustainability has moved from being a bit-player in the corporate social responsibility agenda and peripheral to the main business to being an integral core business interest, or CBI. Jim Leap, the director general of WWF, is probably one of the people most qualified to talk on this, working as he does with so many of the large multinationals such as Unilever. However, in this book, you can see from the other brands how sustainability has become crucial to the economics and purpose of the business. Jess Sanson at innocent talks eloquently of how it is embedded in the operations of the business, helping both to differentiate the brand and effect operational performance. Virgin Galactic has a mission to boldly go where no brand has before and put the world's computer servers into space so as to reduce one of the chief causes of global warming, but in so doing they have developed the most fuel-efficient and environmentally friendly aircraft on the planet. Six Senses has the courage of its convictions and is building zero-carbon resorts despite the increased up-front investment. It has an absolute focus on the customer experience but it will never compromise its core business interest of sustainability. As Sonu Shivdasani says, 'We've got two values, one is around our concern for the environment and the other is around the guest experience, but the environment comes first.'

But it is not just sustainability in the 'environmental' sense which has become a core business interest. Not all of these brands are big on environmental issues, although most are. But all of them are in it for the long haul and concerned about sustainability in the socioeconomic sense. JCB invests long term in the communities in which it manufactures, trades and serves. Its commitment to manufacturing is underpinned by a fervent belief of Sir Anthony Bamford that it sustains economies (both at a national and a local level). Six Senses, innocent and WWF are committed to practices that sustain livelihoods for their suppliers, partners or the communities that they work with. Umpqua sees its role as building and supporting communities – traditionally, the primary role of any bank, in the days before they came to be about selling dubious products and unfathomable financial instruments.

Throughout the book, sustainability – whether it is environmental or economic or, most often, both, because they are so interrelated – emerges as a critical theme for these businesses. One of the things that makes them bold is their ambition to be around for a long time and to enable the rest of us to stick around for a while too.

So what they do is a function of the way they think and that is a function of who they are. And that takes us inevitably to the individuals themselves.

The bold people: the who

Maybe you have to be crazy...

'The people who are crazy enough to think they can change the world are the ones who do.'

Penned over a decade ago, Apple's now iconic 'Think different' advert captures the very essence of what it is to be bold. It's not about businesses or brands or even simply being different. It's about Individual people having belief in something, a commitment to achieving it and a determination to see it sustain.

This book is about some great brands but more than that, it is about some wonderful people. In reading these stories (in editing this book we tried to ensure that we protected the tone of voice of each interviewee) you get a real sense that these brands are all about people and their passions. Whether it is Brian Binnie and Trevor Beattie sharing a boyhood dream of flying into space or Christopher Bailey and Angela Ahrendts seeing themselves as writers of the next chapter in the book of Burberry.

Sir Ernest Shackleton, one of the greatest Antarctic explorers (and an early customer of Burberry), was probably one of the boldest people who ever lived. He certainly exhibited many of the bold practices. For example, in recruiting for his South Polar expedition he advertised:

> Men wanted for Hazardous Journey. Small wages, bitter cold, long months of complete darkness, constant danger. Safe return doubtful. Honour and recognition in case of success.

Nearly 5,000 people applied for the 30 vacancies on the Endurance and he used some innovative recruitment techniques to find out whether they would fit the expedition culture. For example, he asked tough sailors to sing so he could see if they would boost or sap morale on the long voyage. But more than anything else, Shackleton exhibited bold traits as a leader, which we shall now describe as these traits are shared by many of the people we interviewed for this book.

But you don't have to be a great explorer, founder, entrepreneur or chief executive to be bold. Boldness comes in many shapes and sizes but it shares a common characteristic: *the belief that you can make a difference.*

    http://www.youtube.com/watch?v=vNDEwsIGJKI

Through talking with the people in the bold brands that feature in this book, we identified key characteristics that most often distinguish them, that they regularly display and that have, we believe, helped them to be successful. We've listed these below as specific approaches to business – perhaps even to life – that you can judge yourself against.

And remember, you don't have to be running a business to think and be bold; as Robert Stephens of The Geek Squad says:

> The world is populated mainly by boring businesses but for creative people, that's where the opportunities are to contribute.

So even if you are within a 'boring business', there's an opportunity for you to contribute, to be bold. Maybe it's a project you're working on, a person or team you're working with or an initiative, even an everyday improvement you want to make.

How bold are you?

1   Envisage success – paint a very clear picture in your own mind of your goal. Having a vague idea of 'wanting to be successful' won't do it. Be passionate about your goal even if you don't yet know how or when you will achieve it. If you're going to have a vision, make it inspiring and worth doing. 'Do we want to be about shoes, or do we want to be about something more meaningful?' asked Tony Hsieh of Zappos.

2   Tune in – be tuned in to the world. The clearer your vision is, the more likely it is that you will begin to notice small coincidences that are really steps that will move you in the right direction. See them less as coincidences and more as opportunities to test your resolve and actually do something about your vision. 'I always had faith that as long as I prepared myself, opportunity would find me,' is how Brian Binnie of Virgin Galactic puts it.

3   Commit wholeheartedly – take chances and be prepared to do uncomfortable things. Stop worrying about the outcome and have belief that it will turn out well in the end. Check and change any language of procrastination; giving excuses or reasons not to do it. As Samuel Johnson said, 'Nothing will ever be attempted if all possible objections must first be overcome.' Nike's 'Just do it' says it all. And Richard Reed's story of how they relentlessly pursued funding even though everyone and anyone had turned them down is one of the great examples of this characteristic in the book.

4   Follow your gut – use your instinct and intuition as a guidance system rather than relying too heavily on research. If the answer really lay in the data, someone else would have seen it by now. Notice when you feel excited or enthused by something or when you feel bored or lethargic. The former usually tells you you're on the right track. As Sonu Shivdasani of Six Senses said, 'Our innovations were based on gut feel and gut instinct.'

For case studies on how to use gut instinct in business, see: http://www.amazon.co.uk/See-Feel-Think-Do

5   Be authentic – don't fake it, force it or fudge it. If you don't passionately believe in what you do, nor will anyone else. You need to educate and enthuse others, so find ways to bring your ideas alive and engage others through your own behaviour and communication. Be the brand. As Mahatma Gandhi said, 'Be the change you want to see in the world.' Richard Reed of innocent calls it 'congruency', the coming together of your deeds and your words.

6   Keep it simple – look first to the simple way of doing something or communicating an idea. Complexity confuses, distracts and paralyses people. It saps the original energy. 'Simplicity is everything we do,' observes Moses Devanayagam of AirAsia X.

7   Persist – don't give up despite encountering setbacks. Bold people find a path around or over obstacles and believe there has to be a better way. The more entrenched the industry, the more likely there is one. Refuse to take no for an answer unless there is a genuinely compelling counter-argument which wins your heart and mind. Be tenacious and resilient even when people say that 'you must be mad' because when they do, it usually means you are onto something great. Ray Davis of Umpqua sees resistance as an endorsement: 'Their reaction was validating exactly what we thought was right.'

8   Sweat the detail – pay attention to the small details that make a huge difference. All of the leaders we spoke to pay an enormous attention to detail without ever losing sight of the big picture. It's by the way you deal with the little things that people often judge you. 'You might think they're little (things) but they're very important to me because they're important to the customer,' says Sir Anthony Bamford of JCB.

9   Find like-minded people – journeys are more fun when you are in good company. Travel with people who share your values. Don't be afraid to ask questions that really test people's fit with your culture. Zappos asks interviewees the question, 'On a scale of 1 to 10, how weird are you?'

10 Keep the main thing the main thing – focus on the few key indicators of success and celebrate achievement of them. Don't be distracted by the many small paths along the way. Eric Bohm of WWF tells people: 'This is the end goal. Never lose sight of it. Never get off that end goal.'

And finally, just in case you thought we were offering you 'Ten steps to success'...

11 Hold on to your vision – never forget what started you on the journey in the first place. As you grow, be careful you don't 'grow up' and lose the passion that made you special. As Angela Ahrendts of Burberry puts it: 'My job is to write the most exciting chapters that I can and leave a greater novel than when I arrived.'

Chapter Sixteen
Bold practice survey

We constructed a survey that measures the eight practices and asked each interviewee to complete this along with some of their senior colleagues. We also asked 145 executives from other companies chosen at random from a variety of sectors in the UK and US to complete the same self-assessment on their own brands. Although we are still dealing with small sets of data as we go to print, what we found is that the executives from the bold companies score their organizations higher on these eight practices in every area, whereas the executives from the 'average' companies we surveyed score significantly lower overall, rating certain dimensions as being much weaker. These findings certainly seem to support the practices that we identified through the qualitative research. As we gather more data we shall refine these profiles and our findings further.

Our conclusion is that the quantitative research supports what we found in the interviews, namely that these executives place emphasis on quite different things from many executives in typical companies.

How does your organization compare? You can complete our online survey and by doing so contribute to our continuing research. You will also be able to compile your own company profile. Having completed the survey you can check out the latest profiles on the *BOLD* website.

www.boldthebook.com

Or you can complete the survey in Table 16.1 and plot your scores for each section to find out how you compare with the bold brands and average company profiles as they stand at the time of going to print.

Or best of all, you can download our free *BOLD* practice app from Apple and it will create your profile for you, compare it with the bold brands and other companies in our current database and then suggest tactics you can use to improve your performance, with links to the appropriate chapters to guide you.

http://spacebarinteractive.com/bold/ipad

Please use this survey to assess your own organization. Rate each individual statement as accurately as you can, awarding a 4 or 5 if you feel that your organization is distinctly different or market leading, 3 if it is average and 1 or 2 if there is considerable room for improvement or this is an area where your organization does not currently focus.

TABLE 16.1   Bold practice survey

1) KEEP THE MAIN THING THE MAIN THING	AV =
We have a bold strategy or vision that permeates the company	1 2 3 4 5
We are willing to trade short-term profit to achieve our long-term vision	1 2 3 4 5
We have a clearly defined brand/customer promise	1 2 3 4 5
The strategy, the brand, and our customer experience are inseparable	1 2 3 4 5
We are boldly changing/challenging the traditional thinking in our industry	1 2 3 4 5
2) DEMONSTRATE ZEALOUS LEADERSHIP	**AV =**
There is a unique leadership style in this organization	1 2 3 4 5
Leaders communicate our vision and purpose powerfully and clearly	1 2 3 4 5
Our leaders 'Walk the talk' when it comes to modelling our values	1 2 3 4 5
Our leaders spend significant time with customers and employees talking about our vision	1 2 3 4 5
We tend to rely more on gut instinct and intuition than we do on research and analysis	1 2 3 4 5
3) ENGAGE IN INFECTIOUS COMMUNICATION	**AV =**
We clearly and honestly communicate our brand promise and values to customers	1 2 3 4 5
Our customers are actively involved in helping to create/improve/protect our brand	1 2 3 4 5
We use innovative viral marketing techniques to reach our target customers	1 2 3 4 5
We foster active customer communities that support our brand	1 2 3 4 5
We aim to achieve high levels of customer advocacy which drives referral business	1 2 3 4 5
4) DRAMATIZE THE CUSTOMER EXPERIENCE	**AV =**
We deliver a customer experience that is consistent, intentional, differentiated and valuable	1 2 3 4 5
We place a high priority on protecting and managing our brand	1 2 3 4 5
We seek to bring alive our brand promise for customers in dramatic ways	1 2 3 4 5
Our entire company is focused on delivering a dramatic customer experience	1 2 3 4 5
We have a strong alignment between marketing, operations and HR around the experience	1 2 3 4 5

5) BE IN PURSUIT OF WOW	AV =
We constantly innovate in this organization	1 2 3 4 5
Innovation is driven by a deep understanding of what our target customers value	1 2 3 4 5
Our products, services or people are distinctive and in keeping with our brand	1 2 3 4 5
We apply innovative technology and processes to support the delivery of a competitively superior customer experience	1 2 3 4 5
We demonstrate superior customer service skills and capabilities	1 2 3 4 5
6) CREATE A CULT	AV =
We believe in, and are committed to a 'higher purpose'	1 2 3 4 5
Our internal values are closely aligned with our brand values	1 2 3 4 5
We have a distinctive culture and a brand DNA that permeates our company	1 2 3 4 5
We reward our people and share their stories about delivering our promise to customers	1 2 3 4 5
We have our own unique phrases or language in this organization	1 2 3 4 5
7) DEVELOP RITES AND RITUALS	AV =
Our employee experience is as distinctive as our customer experience	1 2 3 4 5
We hire for attitude and fit with our culture	1 2 3 4 5
Our reward systems reinforce the behaviours we promote around serving customers	1 2 3 4 5
Our people are trained in innovative ways to help them understand our brand promise	1 2 3 4 5
We do not tolerate people for long who fail to demonstrate our values	1 2 3 4 5
8) MEASURE WHAT MATTERS	AV =
We have a clear focus on target customers and what they value	1 2 3 4 5
Our customer measurement systems provide performance data on the complete customer experience, not just satisfaction	1 2 3 4 5
We regularly gather feedback to/from the front line of the organization	1 2 3 4 5
Our executive team focus on employee and customer satisfaction, not just the bottom line	1 2 3 4 5
We understand and measure the upstream indicators that drive economic results	1 2 3 4 5

Now calculate the average scores for each of the eight bold practices and write each in the box provided in the survey. Finally, plot the average (AV) scores for each of the practices in Figure 16.1 and 'join up the dots'.

FIGURE 16.1   My company profile

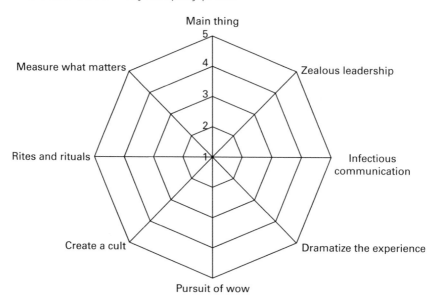

Which are our strongest practices?

1 _____

2 _____

3 _____

Which practices do we need to focus on?

1 _____

2 _____

3 _____

So how do you compare with the bold brands and the comparison companies in our survey? Compare your profile with the ones in Figures 16.2 and 16.3.

FIGURE 16.2   Bold brands

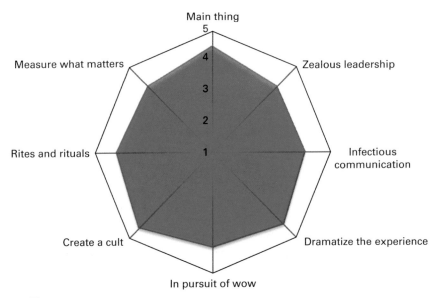

n = 62

FIGURE 16.3   Comparison companies

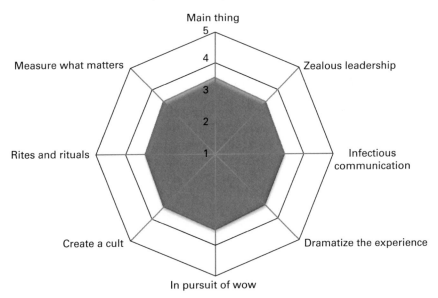

n = 145

The most significant difference is that the bold companies pay much more attention to keeping the main thing the main thing. It is their sense of purpose which drives them. The comparison companies are significantly less focused on dramatizing their customer experience than the bold brands. As a result, their experience is much more generic. This is also reflected in their cultures, which are less distinct than the Bold brands.

Bold action – how do you build a bold brand?

It is evident from the stories in this book that there are many paths to becoming bold, although they share some common features. We do not offer a recipe therefore, because, as we have said before, in our view cookbooks and management books belong on different shelves.

However, having completed the self-assessment and examined your profile you may be asking the question, 'So what do we need to put in place to become bold?' The following model represents a simple visual guide to those things to pay attention to on your journey. In our work with clients we build an implementation roadmap that uses this model as its starting point.

FIGURE 16.4 Bold model image page one

How to Build a Bold Brand

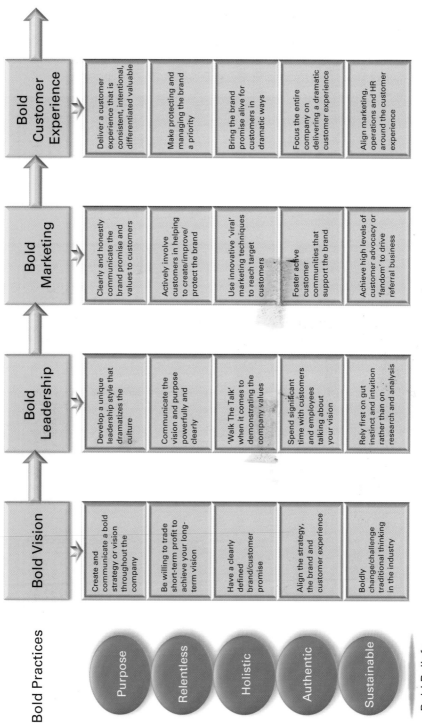

Bold Practices

Bold Vision	Bold Leadership	Bold Marketing	Bold Customer Experience
Create and communicate a bold strategy or vision throughout the company	Develop a unique leadership style that dramatizes the culture	Clearly and honestly communicate the brand promise and values to customers	Deliver a customer experience that is consistent, intentional, differentiated valuable
Be willing to trade short-term profit to achieve your long-term vision	Communicate the vision and purpose powerfully and clearly	Actively involve customers in helping to create/improve/protect the brand	Make protecting and managing the brand a priority
Have a clearly defined brand/customer promise	'Walk The Talk' when it comes to demonstrating the company values	Use innovative 'viral' marketing techniques to reach target customers	Bring the brand promise alive for customers in dramatic ways
Align the strategy, the brand and customer experience	Spend significant time with customers and employees talking about your vision	Foster active customer communities that support the brand	Focus the entire company on delivering a dramatic customer experience
Boldly change/challenge traditional thinking in the industry	Rely first on gut instinct and intuition rather than on research and analysis	Achieve high levels of customer advocacy or 'fandom' to drive referral business	Align marketing, operations and HR around the customer experience

Bold Beliefs

- Purpose
- Relentless
- Holistic
- Authentic
- Sustainable

FIGURE 16.5 Bold model image page two

How to Build a Bold Brand

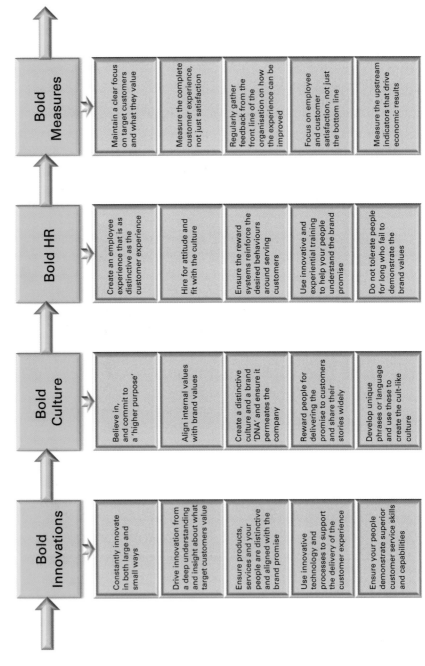

Bold Innovations	Bold Culture	Bold HR	Bold Measures
Constantly innovate in both large and small ways	Believe in, and commit to a 'higher purpose'	Create an employee experience that is as distinctive as the customer experience	Maintain a clear focus on target customers and what they value
Drive innovation from a deep understanding and insight about what target customers value	Align internal values with brand values	Hire for attitude and fit with the culture	Measure the complete customer experience, not just satisfaction
Ensure products, services and your people are distinctive and aligned with the brand promise	Create a distinctive culture and a brand 'DNA' and ensure it permeates the company	Ensure the reward systems reinforce the desired behaviours around serving customers	Regularly gather feedback from the front line of the organisation on how the experience can be improved
Use innovative technology and processes to support the delivery of the customer experience	Reward people for delivering the promise to customers and share their stories widely	Use innovative and experiential training to help your people understand the brand promise	Focus on employee and customer satisfaction, not just the bottom line
Ensure your people demonstrate superior customer service skills and capabilities	Develop unique phrases or language and use these to create the cult-like culture	Do not tolerate people for long who fail to demonstrate the brand values	Measure the upstream indicators that drive economic results

Would you like to get to know more about the bold brands and their leaders?

Bold – the keynote presentation

Bold is an attitude of mind, but it's measured by how you behave. As we emerge from the recession it is becoming evident that those brands that have stayed true to their purpose and focused on differentiation are those that are gaining and sustaining market share. Find out the secrets of their success.

In this high-energy, engaging multimedia presentation we will take you deep into the minds and thinking of the executives within these companies: the difficult (sometimes seemingly reckless) decisions they made in their relentless strive to differentiate, how they made these decisions, how they overcame the challenges and engaged their people in the process. We will identify the key insights underlying these organizations' success – principles that you can take away and apply to your business. You will be inspired to develop new ideas to exceed your customer expectations; and the knowledge to translate these ideas into practical actions that will accelerate your organization's growth.

In designing a keynote presentation to meet the specific needs of your event, we draw upon those stories and examples from our research that are most likely to resonate with your audience and align with the themes of your conference.

To see a video taster, click here:
http://www.boldthebook.com

For more information contact **jd@shaunsmithco.com**

Bold – the webinar

If your time is limited but you wish to get a deeper insight into some of the bold practices and hear some of the stories first hand, you can register for one of our 60-minute Bold webinars. These online presentations, conducted by one of the authors, give you an espresso shot of inspiration delivered right to your desk. Please see our website for dates and details.

Visit http://www.boldthebook.com/
for details and how you can register.

Bold – the Brand Experience Masters programme

Eight practices define the essence of bold. They capture the very heart of what differentiates those that make a difference in their markets from those that merely copy; those that turn bold ideas into bold practice and ultimately into brand experiences that turn employees and customers into fans. In this book, you learned through reading the words of the executives themselves just how they create these experiences. Now we can help you translate that learning into practical steps that can help transform your business performance.

To stand out as a brand, you need to create an experience that is bold, different and valuable. We've designed our programme to be just that.

Led by the two authors of *BOLD*, Shaun Smith and Andy Milligan, Brand Experience Masters is for people who already have a good understanding of the theory and practice of customer experience and brand differentiation but now want to apply advanced thinking to their own situations.

You've read the books, you've attended the conferences, you've followed the blogs and you may already be involved in some kind of brand experience programme within your organization. But perhaps things are moving a little too slowly, you're not getting buy-in from the executive team, there's confusion about where to start, a lack of clarity about where to invest, the enthusiasm's waning, the strategy's uninspiring, or you are just not seeing the results you expected. Or perhaps you haven't even started yet and want to get it right first time. If any of these resonate, this programme is for you.

The Brand Experience Masters programme is new and unique. It brings together not only our experience and expertise of working with leading brands, but more importantly the insights from the bold brand leaders we interviewed. You will learn from the research we conducted with the best exemplars of brand and customer experience innovation in the world. You want to know how Zappos, O2, Virgin, AirAsia X or Six Senses do it? Here's how...

What you'll gain

The workshop takes you deep into each of the eight bold practices and how, together, they form the essence of what it is to create a great brand experience:

- It's not just about creating a vision – it's how you simplify it and turn it into a purpose that will engage people and keep the main thing the main thing.
- It's not just about mapping the touch points and designing an experience – it's about where you choose to over-index and dramatize that experience.
- It's not just about leaders communicating the experience – it's about how you, and your colleagues, *become* the experience.

- It's not just about creating customer loyalty – it's about how you create 'fandom'.

- It's not just about innovating products and services – it's about how you constantly innovate *the experience*.

- It's not just about training your people – it's about changing the whole way you hire, motivate and reward them to create a cult-like culture.

- It's not just about an annual mystery shop or satisfaction survey – it's about how you measure the complete end-to-end experience and the upstream indicators that drive your financial results.

- Above all, it's totally holistic – it's not CRM or any other three-letter quick fix, but about how you create an organization that is authentic and truly lives the brand.

Brand Experience Masters gets you right to the heart of these issues – and gives you the framework and tools for applying the principles to your own brand. We'll take you through the obstacles, the challenges and the pitfalls – and how you anticipate, avoid or overcome them. We will share with you our combined experience of working with leading brands worldwide – some of which are in the book – to create great brand experiences. This workshop is designed to be small on theory and big on application so that you walk away with tangible and valuable outcomes.

When and where

- Highly engaging one-day public programmes: held twice a year, open to all organizations but limited to only 30 senior executives per programme so that networking and sharing of experiences are an important benefit.

- Highly interactive two-day executive workshop: specifically designed for and around the needs of your organization, where we select the examples and case studies most relevant to your sector. You will also complete the bold assessment prior to the workshop so that your team has real data to identify your opportunity areas and then work on these together. For this reason we advise bringing senior people representing the key functions of marketing, operations and HR.

- Innovative venues that stimulate the thinking, indulge the senses, excite the creative juices and are themselves great branded experiences. The venues provide the perfect environment for you to reflect, refresh and renew your personal sense of purpose.

Visit **http://www.boldthebook.com/** for details and how you can register.

For more information contact **jd@shaunsmithco.com**

The *BOLD* authors

Over the last decade, **Shaun Smith** has been a key catalyst in expanding management focus from the tactical issues of customer service to the much wider and strategic issue of customer experience. He has developed some of the latest thinking and practice around this subject, helping organizations worldwide create compelling customer experiences that achieve brand differentiation and long-term customer loyalty.

He has featured a number of times on *Ask the Expert* on CNBC and is co-author of three critically acclaimed business books. His first book with Andy Milligan, *Uncommon Practice: People Who Deliver a Great Brand Experience*, examines those companies that create exceptional customer experiences. His second book, *Managing the Customer Experience: Turning Customers into Advocates*, reveals how leaders can build this kind of competitive advantage for their own organizations. His most recent book, *See, Feel, Think, Do: The Power of Instinct in Business*, also co-authored with Andy Milligan, explores how highly successful business leaders and entrepreneurs use the power of instinct to achieve results.

Shaun is founder of and partner in the customer experience consultancy smith+co, which works with leading brands around the world to design, develop and deliver dramatic customer experiences. He is a Fellow of the Professional Speakers Association, a Member of the International Federation for Professional Speakers, and is rated one of the top business speakers. Visit **http://www.smithcoconsultancy.com/** for more information.

Andy Milligan is a leading international consultant on brand and business culture. He has worked for almost 20 years advising major organizations on strategies for brand building, customer experience and internal culture, as well as running seminars and conferences on brand alignment and employee engagement worldwide. He has worked on a wide range of projects internationally and across a number of market sectors including airlines, financial services, packaged goods, telecommunications, sports and leisure. He has directed major projects in Japan, South Korea, Singapore, the USA and throughout Europe.

Andy appears regularly in the media to comment on brand issues including appearances on CNN, Sky, CNBC and the BBC. He is an acclaimed author on the subject of branding and has published four bestselling books: *Uncommon Practice* and *See, Feel, Think, Do* with Shaun Smith, *Brand it like Beckham*, which analyses how the Beckham brand has become a global phenomenon, and *Don't Mess With the Logo*, co-written with the designer Jon Edge, which has been described as doing 'for brand management what the Haynes workshop manuals do for cars': making it simple, easy to understand and enjoyable!

Andy is a founder of and partner in The Caffeine Partnership, which helps businesses, their brands and people develop and grow.

Visit **www.thecaffeinepartnership.com** for more information.

Acknowledgements

First of all, a huge thank you to the executives, employees and customers of the bold brands who gave us so much of their time.

We thank John Aves of smith+co and João Batista Ferreira for their invaluable assistance with the O2 and Chilli Beans interviews.

For their assistance with the survey distribution we thank our friends at:

Mycustomer.com. See: **http://www.mycustomer.com/**

CustomerThink.com. See: **http://www.customerthink.com/**

GCEM.com. See: **http://gccrm.com/eng/content_e.jsp**

If you haven't seen these portals you should. They are an invaluable source of all the latest and best thinking around customer experience.

Our CEM partners, TOTE-M, in the Netherlands for their help with promotion. See: **http://www.tote-m.com/**

We couldn't have kept track without excellent project management and research support from Rob Smith. Rob did much of the desk research and maintained communications with numerous people in the organizations we feature.

Our thanks go to Janine Dyer for her support and honest (although, at times, brutal) comments on the draft. Janine handles our marketing and designed the *BOLD* website and has a wonderful gift of being able to detect the slightest whiff of BS in our writing.

Ged Equi has a similar gift in being able to turn the *BOLD* concepts into some really engaging *BOLD* designs.

Personal thanks to Liz Gooster for her advice and support.

And finally, thanks to Jon Finch and his colleagues at Kogan Page, our publishers, for their enthusiasm and tremendous support for the book, to Jim Banting for his invaluable help with marketing the book and the team at Spacebar for developing the very cool *BOLD* app. See **www.spacebarinteractive.com**.

It is refreshing to work with people who share many of the characteristics of the bold leaders.

With over 1,000 titles in printed and digital format, **Kogan Page** offers affordable, sound business advice

www.koganpage.com

KoganPage